Preparing the Higher Education Space for Gen Z

Heidi Lee Schnackenberg
State University of New York at Plattsburgh, USA

Christine Johnson
University of Western Kentucky, USA

A volume in the Advances in
Higher Education and Professional
Development (AHEPD) Book Series

IGI Global
DISSEMINATOR OF KNOWLEDGE

Published in the United States of America by
IGI Global
Information Science Reference (an imprint of IGI Global)
701 E. Chocolate Avenue
Hershey PA, USA 17033
Tel: 717-533-8845
Fax: 717-533-8661
E-mail: cust@igi-global.com
Web site: http://www.igi-global.com

Library of Congress Cataloging-in-Publication Data

Names: Schnackenberg, Heidi L, editor. | Johnson, Christine, 1966- editor.
Title: Preparing the Higher Education Space for Gen Z / Heidi Lee Schnackenberg and Christine Johnson, Editors.
Description: Hershey, PA : Information Science Reference, [2019] | Includes bibliographical references.
Identifiers: LCCN 2018035053| ISBN 9781522577638 (hardcover) | ISBN 9781522577645 (ebook)
Subjects: LCSH: Internet in higher education. | Social media in education. | Education, Higher--Effect of technological innovations on. | Generation Z.
Classification: LCC LB2395.7 .P73 2019 | DDC 378.17344678--dc23 LC record available at https://lccn.loc.gov/2018035053

This book is published in the IGI Global book series Advances in Higher Education and Professional Development (AHEPD) (ISSN: 2327-6983; eISSN: 2327-6991)

British Cataloguing in Publication Data
A Cataloguing in Publication record for this book is available from the British Library.

Advances in Higher Education and Professional Development (AHEPD) Book Series

ISSN:2327-6983
EISSN:2327-6991

Editor-in-Chief: Jared Keengwe, University of North Dakota, USA

MISSION

As world economies continue to shift and change in response to global financial situations, job markets have begun to demand a more highly-skilled workforce. In many industries a college degree is the minimum requirement and further educational development is expected to advance. With these current trends in mind, the **Advances in Higher Education & Professional Development (AHEPD) Book Series** provides an outlet for researchers and academics to publish their research in these areas and to distribute these works to practitioners and other researchers.

AHEPD encompasses all research dealing with higher education pedagogy, development, and curriculum design, as well as all areas of professional development, regardless of focus.

COVERAGE

- Adult Education
- Assessment in Higher Education
- Career Training
- Coaching and Mentoring
- Continuing Professional Development
- Governance in Higher Education
- Higher Education Policy
- Pedagogy of Teaching Higher Education
- Vocational Education

The Advances in Higher Education and Professional Development (AHEPD) Book Series (ISSN 2327-6983) is published by IGI Global, 701 E. Chocolate Avenue, Hershey, PA 17033-1240, USA, www.igi-global.com. This series is composed of titles available for purchase individually; each title is edited to be contextually exclusive from any other title within the series. For pricing and ordering information please visit http://www.igi-global.com/book-series/advances-higher-education-professional-development/73681. Postmaster: Send all address changes to above address.

Titles in this Series

For a list of additional titles in this series, please visit:
https://www.igi-global.com/book-series/advances-higher-education-professional-development/73681

Handbook of Research on Challenges and Opportunities in Launching a Technology-Driven International University
Mehdi Khosrow-Pour, D.B.A. (Information Resources Management Association, USA)
Information Science Reference • ©2019 • 420pp • H/C (ISBN: 9781522562559) • US $275.00

Advanced Web Applications and Progressing E-Learning 2.0 Technologies in Higher Education
Jean-Éric Pelet (ESCE International Business School, France)
Information Science Reference • ©2019 • 271pp • H/C (ISBN: 9781522574354) • US $175.00

Higher Education and the Evolution of Management, Applied Sciences, and Engineering...
Carolina F. Machado (University of Minho, Portugal) and J. Paulo Davim (University of Aveiro, Portugal)
Engineering Science Reference • ©2019 • 258pp • H/C (ISBN: 9781522572596) • US $185.00

Handbook of Research on Critical Thinking Strategies in Pre-Service Learning Environments
Gina J. Mariano (Troy University, USA) and Fred J. Figliano (Troy University, USA)
Information Science Reference • ©2019 • 657pp • H/C (ISBN: 9781522578239) • US $265.00

Fostering Multiple Levels of Engagement in Higher Education Environments
Kelley Walters (Northcentral University, USA) and Patricia Henry (Northcentral University, USA)
Information Science Reference • ©2019 • 316pp • H/C (ISBN: 9781522574705) • US $185.00

Study Abroad Opportunities for Community College Students and Strategies for Global...
Gregory F. Malveaux (Montgomery College, USA) and Rosalind Latiner Raby (California State University Northridge, USA)
Information Science Reference • ©2019 • 324pp • H/C (ISBN: 9781522562528) • US $195.00

For an entire list of titles in this series, please visit:
https://www.igi-global.com/book-series/advances-higher-education-professional-development/73681

IGI Global
DISSEMINATOR OF KNOWLEDGE

701 East Chocolate Avenue, Hershey, PA 17033, USA
Tel: 717-533-8845 x100 • Fax: 717-533-8661
E-Mail: cust@igi-global.com • www.igi-global.com

Table of Contents

Detailed Table of Contents

Social media use is a complex topic. The type and use of social media presents a variety of formats and creates a multitude of directions for research. Pearson provides research on personal, professional, and teaching social media use in higher education that shows the use of social media in higher education is growing. While this research provides a foundation, it raises many questions. The purpose of this chapter is to provide an overview of common Learning Management Systems or platforms and social media networks that are often used in college courses. This chapter also provides common ways that social media is used outside of the classroom. The chapter concludes with concerns that are raised regardless of the type of social media use, platform, or network.

Generation Z students are inherently different than previous generations. These students may need adapted forms of instruction in order to match their learning styles. Collaborative learning can be adapted using cloud-computing, which helps students work together online and manage their interactions. These students may benefit from a technological twist to a common instructional strategy and are inclined to use online means of communication to complete coursework. Technology has dominated the educational experiences of these students and they are no strangers to collaborative work through e-learning platforms. Higher education institutions and instructors must develop the format of courses in order to meet the technological learning preferences of Generation Z.

Access to post-secondary education is an essential condition for advancing women's leadership opportunities. This chapter provides an expert commentary on how distance education in Saudi Arabia contributes to the advancement of female leadership opportunities by providing women greater access to education and new opportunities for leadership roles. However, despite the new opportunities that distance education offers to Saudi women, there are pervasive challenges that hinder them from acquiring leadership roles in education. The expert commentary draws on professional experience and research to provide insight into the advantages and disadvantages of distance education to prepare Saudi women to be leaders in higher education. It also offers recommendations on how to better leverage distance education experience for female students and instructors by applying the rules of netiquette in Saudi online learning environments.

In the past decade, social media has become an increasingly prevalent, being the daily form of communication and entertainment for a majority of individuals. Social media and networking sites are not designed to appeal to a specific type of personality and are designed to benefit many. The students of Generation Z respond positively to teaching styles that incorporate technology-based learning, and frequent communication or feedback. Gen Z students with disabilities are entitled to the same opportunities and experiences as their peers without disabilities. This includes being exposed to various forms of social media to discover alternative ways to communicate, interact with the community, find information and access entertainment. While other members of Generation Z possess the capability to pick up a smart phone or computer, create a social media account and figure out the functions independently, students with disabilities may require explicit instruction, strategies and practice with social media usage.

Using the authors' varied experiences in the classroom with Gen Z and the next generation on its way, this chapter investigates an urgent and often unseen issue for students in higher education. With increased pressure to perform, a tension between time and technology, and lasting impacts from the Great Recession, Gen Z students suffer from a growing number of mental health issues. College coursework should challenge students; however, Gen Z often becomes impaired by what is a real and prevalent anxiety. The authors explore the ways Gen Z operates in the classroom, potential causes for this crisis, and solutions to improve Gen Z experiences in our institutions.

Do a quick search in Google Scholar and you will find overwhelming evidence that teachers both are and are not using technology in meaningful ways to enhance student learning. Actually, just do a simple Google search and you will find many news and magazine articles revealing the exact same confusing information. Yet despite all of the Internet traffic, are teachers any better at using technology to enhance student learning now than they were when educational technologies first arrived in schools? And are teacher preparation programs hindering or helping pre-service teachers in this endeavor? As Gen Z enters college and becomes practicing teachers, with their own particular characteristics and digital abilities and needs, it is important that we re-examine these questions and find out how to best serve the newest generation of teachers.

When it comes to Generation Z's participation in higher education, few topics receive as much attention as their use of social media. However, much of the focus rests on marketing to Generation Z through social media. The connectedness of Generation Z is accompanied with assumptions about their technological abilities. Although they are generally comfortable with technology, their tech acumen is likely limited.

Preface

Social media (e.g. Facebook, Snapchat, Twitter, Instagram) has mirrored the type of interactive, virtual, community that has been created in online courses over the years. Boyd and Ellison (2007) define social media, or social networking sites (SNSs) as web-based interfaces where users create profiles within a specific system, delineate other individuals with whom they are willing to virtually associate, and view their and other profiles within the system. Text-based discussion, graphics, photos, video, etc. are all also incorporated to enable users to communicate and share ideas, thoughts, feelings, and experiences. Although similar to online learning environments in many ways, social media is not intended as an academic venue. It is simply a forum for users to form various types of relationships (Gilbert & Karahalios, 2009), and expand the opportunity for individuals to satisfy the human need to connect (Maslow, 1971). While forming social relationships is a part of what makes us fulfilled human beings, it is also one of the core foundational elements to an effective education (Witmer, 2005). Therefore, it would seem logical that using the rapidly increasing venue of social media networks for teaching and learning would be a successful way for individuals to both connect with others and acquire an education. Unfortunately, this approach has met with mixed results.

In their study, Roblyer, McDaniel, Webb, Herman, and Witty (2010) found that students responded positively to the idea using Facebook (FB) for class purposes, while faculty did not. Similarly, Kabilan, Ahmad, and Abidin (2010) ascertained that undergraduate second language learners believed that FB could be a useful environment in which to learn English. More specifically, the "Group" application on Facebook is useful for language learners to gain authentic experience and interaction with each other as well as with native speakers (Blattner & Fiori, 2009). In related research, Yu, Tian, Vogel, and Kwok (2010) concluded that online social networking impacts university student's engagement in student learning processes. Overall, Forkosh-Baruch and Hershkovitz (2012) state that social networking systems promote knowledge sharing and facilitate informal learning.

Conversely, Orphus, and Abitt (2010) found that although participants responded positively to the potential of using Facebook as a study aid, they were also both reticent and worried about issues of privacy and the overall distraction of using a social space for school work. In corresponding research, Madge, Meek, Wellens, and Hooley (2009) determined that undergraduate college students felt that the most important use for Facebook was socializing and not formal teaching purposes. Access to the technological infrastructure that supports social networks and other web 2.0 applications is also a mitigating factor in the use of these technologies for educational purposes (Bosch, 2009). Interestingly, Datnow (2012) found that while social networks may help to bring about change in teacher education practices and initiatives, they can also effectively thwart change. Finally, Aydin (2012) and Tess (2013) both found a lack of research on the use of Facebook as an educational tool, despite there being an established literature base on the use of social networks as a learning environment.

In 2010, the EDUCAUSE Center for Applied Research (ECAR) administered a survey exploring individual's uses of online, interactive, platforms (Smith & Caruso, 2010). The data reflected that social media, which are used by more than two thirds of the respondents in their personal lives, were utilized by less than a third to communicate with peers in online courses. Additionally fewer than eight percent of respondents used social media to communicate with instructors regarding course content or questions. These data seem to imply that students do not like to interact "academically" in virtual social networks. Simard and Schnackenberg (2012) found that some of the reasons for student resistance to the idea of conducting classes in social media networks includes the idea that students do not want faculty arranging, controlling, or manipulating their social spaces (electronic or otherwise).

Fascinatingly, the research cited above was conducted on students in university settings prior to the current generation matriculating into college. The freshman classes now entering higher education were born in the very late 1990's and are classified as "Generation Z," or "Gen Z" for short. One of the defining aspects of this generation is its exposure to technology since birth, and use of the Internet at a very young age (Jenkins, 2017; Prensky, 2001). This generation, more than the one preceding it (Millenials), views participatory technological interfaces as an integral part of their lives. Therefore every experience in which they engage, particularly schooling, is viewed and experienced through that highly technological lens. At no other time in higher education has the nature of teaching and learning experiences been so defined by the technological interactivity of its student population. In an unprecedented way, higher education is likely to change, or need to change, to meet the needs of the incoming groups of students and the ways in which the learn, communicate, and experience information and the world around them.

The current volume explores issues of social media platforms, technological participatory culture, virtual communication, and a variety of other Web 2.0 innovations and their use in higher education. These uses include teaching, learning, communication, administrative uses, family outreach, alumni networking, and a variety of other topics. Most importantly, social media and virtual communication platforms used with Generation Z in the college teaching and learning environment are explored. History, individual experiences, research, findings, challenges and successes are presented and discussed. Finally, strategies for social media best practice with Gen Z in the higher education context are offered.

The target audience for this book is faculty in Higher Education, administrators in Higher Education, Higher Education professional staff, graduate students, researchers, P-12 teachers, P-12 administrators, and school counselors. The various chapters offer something for everyone. A brief description of each follows below:

"Finding Balance: Social Media Use in Higher Education" by Danielle McKain and Julia Bennett Grise sets the stage for the current volume. The authors provide an overview of various learning management systems and social networks that are or can be utilized within the college classroom. The ways in which social networks are used outside of the classroom is also discussed, as well as overall concerns about social media and learning management systems in general.

"The Use of Cloud-Computing to Promote Collaborative Learning in Higher Education" by Melissa S. Martin, Rachel E. Hughes, and Alison Pulliate addresses the technological needs of our latest generation to enroll in college and university, Generation Z. The authors discuss how this generation not only expects but needs to learn in technology-enhanced environments. They purport that cloud-computing is one of the most effective and efficient technologies to utilize with Generation Z.

In "Expert Commentary on New Opportunities and Challenges for Women within Saudi Distance Education Institutions" by Eman Walabe and Rocci Luppicini, the advantages that distance learning offers to Generation Z women from Saudi Arabia is described. Not only does tele-learning provide Saudi women with educational opportunities that they may not have access to otherwise, this learning modality may also help them prepare for leadership opportunities when they arise.

"Social Media and Student with Disabilities: Challenges and Opportunities" by Caiomhe Doran and Heidi L. Schnackenberg outlines the lack of social media education available to and provided for students with disabilities. While their Generation Z peers are fluent in the world of online social interactions, Generation Z students with disabilities are often segregated from this world because they are not taught how to navigate within it. The authors champion the need for students with disabilities to be educated in the ways of social media and interact in this digital world in the same ways as their Generation Z counterparts.

"What's Seen and Unseen: The Gen Z Experience in the Classroom" by Claudia Marie Bertolone-Smith and Ana Maria Spagna discusses the growing concern over mental health issues seen in some Generation Z college and university students. The authors investigate the causes of these issues, and offer potential solutions that may help Generation Z better navigate the higher education experience.

"Are We Part of the Problem? Teacher Preparation Programs, Educational Technology, and the Mis-Education of Future Teachers" by Heidi L. Schnackenberg addresses the multi-layered issue of educational technology in teacher education programs. With Generation Z as the present student population in colleges and universities, it is imperative that instructors meet their educational needs and expectations with regard to learning with technology. Not only is this imperative in all college curricula, but it is particularly important in teacher preparation programs. The coursework in these programs should not only model best teaching practices with technology, but also teach the pre-service teachers enrolled in them to use technology for teaching and learning purposes. The chapter examines whether or not this is occurring and offers ways in which teacher preparation programs can better meet the needs of Generation Z.

In "Connecting with Generation Z Through Social Media," Brian Bourke characterizes Generation Z as a generation of Digital Natives. Particular to this set of Digital Natives however, is the electronic connectivity and interactivity into which they were born. Generation Z has always known Smart Phones and data plans, they expect the interactivity of Web 2.0 with it's real-time video capability and communities of learners and knowledge creators. Understandably, Generation Z expects more technologically from their university experience than did their predecessors. This chapter offers strategies to instructors in higher education on ways to connect with students using social media.

"Using Social Media in the Classroom: Preparing Faculty for Change" by Victoria Reynolds describes the use of non-traditional, digital strategies, in a college course in Communication Sciences and Disorders. The chapter illustrates both the challenges and successes of engaging Generation Z digitally, and how teaching and learning is affected when meeting the learning needs of today's university students.

Finally, "Texting With Students: Facilitating Learning in Higher Education" by A.S. CohenMiller, illustrates the novel, perhaps even controversial, idea of texting with students as a part of the teaching and learning process. In this chapter, the author describes the strategies, methods, benefits, and challenges of texting with students as part of a course expectation. Embedded in 21st-century learning, this chapter offers a fascinating look at what might be the quintessential intersection of learning in higher education and the most common form of communication for Generation Z.

Overall, this volume informs readers and expands their horizons about specific challenges, issues, strategies, and solutions that are associated with using participatory social media and virtual communication in higher education, and its particular implications for Generation Z. The book includes a variety of emerging evidence-based professional practice for professional staff and faculty in higher education who are currently teaching or working with Generation Z in the academy. It is hoped that this work is of value to instructors, administrators, professional staff, and graduate students. Perhaps most importantly, the current publication is both critical and timely given that Generation Z is the current population of college and university students and they are, more than any other generation, true Digital Natives.

REFERENCES

Aydin, S. (2012). A review of research on Facebook as an educational environment. *Educational Technology Research and Development*, *60*(6), 1093–1106. doi:10.100711423-012-9260-7

Blattner, G., & Fiori, M. (2009). Facebook in the language classroom: Promises and possibilities. *International Journal of Instructional Technology and Distance Learning*, *6*(1), 17–28.

Bosch, T. (2009). Using online social networking for teaching and learning: Facebook use at the University of Cape Town. *Communicatio: South African Journal for Communication Theory and Research*, *35*(2), 185–200.

Boyd, D. M., & Ellison, N. B. (2007). Social network sites: Definition, history, and scholarship. *Journal of Computer-Mediated Communication*, *13*(1), 11. doi:10.1111/j.1083-6101.2007.00393.x

Datnow, A. (2012). Teacher agency in educational reform: Lessons from social networks research. *American Journal of Education*, *119*(1), 193–201. doi:10.1086/667708

Forkosh-Baruch, A., & Hershkovitz, A. (2012). A case study of Israeli higher education institutes sharing scholarly information with the community via social networks. *The Internet and Higher Education*, *15*(1), 58–68. doi:10.1016/j.iheduc.2011.08.003

Gilbert, E., & Karahalios, K. (2009). Predicting tie strength with social media. In *Proceedings of the International Conference on Human Factors in Computing Systems* (pp. 211-220).

Jenkins, R. (2017). Who is Generation Z? This timeline reveals it all. *Inc.* Retrieved from https://www.inc.com/ryan-jenkins/complete-guide-to-who-is-generation-z.html

Kabilan, M. K., Ahmad, N. A., & Abidin, M. J. Z. (2010). Facebook: An online environment for learning of English in institutions of higher education. *The Internet and Higher Education*, *13*(4), 179–187. doi:10.1016/j.iheduc.2010.07.003

Madge, C., Meek, J., Wellens, J., & Hooley, T. (2009). Facebook, social integration and informal learning at university: 'It is more for socializing and talking to friends about work than for actually doing work.' *Learning, Media and Technology*, *34*(2), 141–155. doi:10.1080/17439880902923606

Maslow, A. (1971). *The farther reaches of human nature*. New York, NY: The Viking Press.

Orphus, J. D., & Abbitt, J. T. (2009). Exploring the potential perceptions of social networking systems in university courses. *MERLOT Journal of Online Learning and Teaching*, *5*(4). Retrieved from http://jolt.merlot.org/vol5no4/ophus_1209.htm

Prensky, M. (2001). Digital Natives Digital Immigrants. *On the Horizon*, *9*(5), 1–6. doi:10.1108/10748120110424816

Roblyer, M. D., McDaniel, M., Webb, M., Herman, J., & Witty, J. V. (2010). Findings on Facebook in higher education: A comparison of college faculty and student uses and perceptions of social networking sites. *The Internet and Higher Education*, *13*(3), 134–140. doi:10.1016/j.iheduc.2010.03.002

Simard, D. A., & Schnackenberg, H. L. (2012). Student and faculty preferences toward the use of social networks for academic purposes. In Q. Lin (Ed.), *Advancement in Online Education: Exploring the Best Practices* (Vol. 1). New York, NY: Nova Science Publishers.

Smith, S.D. & Caruso, J.B. (2010, October). *The ECAR Study of Undergraduate Students and Information Technology*. Boulder, CO: EDUCAUSE Center for Applied Research.

Witmer, M. M. (2005). The fourth R in education – relationships. *The Clearing House: A Journal of Educational Strategies, Issues and Ideas*, *78*(5), 224–228. doi:10.3200/TCHS.78.5.224-228

Yu, A. Y., Tian, S. W., Vogel, D., & Kwok, R. C.-W. (2010). Can learning be virtually boosted? An investigation of online social networking impacts. *Computers & Education*, *55*(4), 1494–1503. doi:10.1016/j.compedu.2010.06.015

Chapter 1
Finding Balance:
Social Media Use in Higher Education

Danielle McKain
Beaver Area School District, USA

Julia Bennett Grise
Beaver Area School District, USA

ABSTRACT

Social media use is a complex topic. The type and use of social media presents a variety of formats and creates a multitude of directions for research. Pearson provides research on personal, professional, and teaching social media use in higher education that shows the use of social media in higher education is growing. While this research provides a foundation, it raises many questions. The purpose of this chapter is to provide an overview of common Learning Management Systems or platforms and social media networks that are often used in college courses. This chapter also provides common ways that social media is used outside of the classroom. The chapter concludes with concerns that are raised regardless of the type of social media use, platform, or network.

DOI: 10.4018/978-1-5225-7763-8.ch001

INTRODUCTION

Social media is prevalent independent of education, race/ethnicity, or health care access (Chou et al., 2009). Cell phones, in the past, were not allowed to be used in many schools; now they are an integral part of teaching and learning. For Generation Z, technology and social media play a role in nearly everything they do, including higher education. Social media use is expected in higher education, but research is needed on effective social media practices (Rowan-Kenyon et al., 2016). While there are many resources for using social media in the classroom, the issue is two-fold. Future employers look for not only strong technology skills, but also effective personal communication skills (Greenhow & Robelia, 2009). Research is showing that these two skills are difficult to maintain simultaneously (Yildirim, 2014).

The National Education Association in the United States recently released Preparing 21st Century Students for a Global Society: An Educator's Guide to the "Four Cs". The four Cs are (1) Critical Thinking and Problem Solving, (2) Communication, (3) Collaboration, and (4) Creativity and Innovation. The Educator's Guide to the "Four Cs" emphasizes the need to prepare young people for citizenship and the global workforce, and the ability to work with people of various backgrounds. Communication skills such as clearly expressing thoughts, effectively expressing opinions, providing logical and consistent instructions, and motivating others, are valuable and important for communication in the workplace today (An Educator's Guide to the Four Cs, n.d.).

Many platforms for social media promote communication and collaborative learning. Using the world wide web, content and applications are often continuously altered and expanded by participants in a collaborative way rather than created and published by individuals (Kaplan & Haenlein, 2010). The interaction created by social media supports social learning theories, but there is a lack of research to distinguish between face-to-face collaboration and social media collaboration. Vygotsky's Sociocultural theory of cognitive development was based on the importance of social interactions for cognitive development, but did not consider social media interactions (Slavin, 2018). More recently, Siemens (2005) refers to connectivism theory as a way to explain how social learning takes place through social media use. Learners acquire information through connecting to others knowledge and educators provide students with ways to make connections (Chen & Bryer, 2012).

Social media also serves as a bridge to connect formal and informal learning. Banks et al. (2007) found that the impact of formal learning decreases after high school. Informal learning becomes more important after high school as adults learn through interactions. Yet, the difference between interacting in person versus interacting via social media requires more research. In 2006, Hew and Brush identified the following typical barriers for integrating technology: resources, institution, subject culture, attitudes and beliefs, knowledge and skills, and assessment. Furthermore, they suggested the following strategies to overcome these barriers: having a shared vision and technology integration plan, overcoming the scarcity of resources, changing attitudes and beliefs, conducting professional development, and reconsidering assessments. Social media use is common in informal environments and could be beneficial in formal environments, but research on formal academic use is limited; in addition, it is difficult to implement social network use in formal learning environments due to privacy and security restrictions (Chen & Bryer, 2012).

"Social learning is based on the premise that our understanding of content is socially constructed through conversations about that content and through grounded interactions, especially with others, around problems or actions" (Brown & Adler, 2008, p. 18). Technology is changing faster than ever and there is a growing global demand for continuous learning and the creation of new ideas and skills; furthermore, the internet has the ability to expand and support social learning in various ways (Brown & Adler, 2008).

Keeping up with the current definition of social media along with deciding which platform to use in higher education can be overwhelming for educators. Although aligning curriculum to educational standards and ensuring that students meet each standard is primary in all areas of education, the resources used to assist students with meeting these goals is up to interpretation; therefore, using technology and a variety of social medias in the classroom can be implemented if educators choose to do so. The existing research on social media provides educators with an assortment of websites, applications, and platforms that can potentially be used in the higher education classroom. Although technology is ever-changing, the information presented in this chapter, found in recent literature and shared from practitioner experience, provide readers with a place to start when deciding whether or not to use social media in higher education settings. Additionally, research studies on social media have found common issues and concerns that reoccur regardless of social media platform, application, or website.

The purpose of this chapter is to discuss the existing research on digital participation through the use of social media in higher education settings. Additionally, this chapter will present concerns of digital participation in higher education. Although using social media in the classroom is debatable, educators can benefit from existing research on specially designed technology and social media use that can be used for educational purposes. The objectives of this chapter include:

1. **Social Media Progression:** Providing a description of how complex the term social media is based on the type, aspect, and use.
2. **Different Uses Social Media:** Explaining the differences between personal social media use, professional social media use, and teaching use of social media.
3. **Social Media in the Classroom:** Describing a variety of social media websites and applications.
4. **Social Media Outside the Classroom:** Providing an overview of non-academic uses for social media including student recruitment, communication, and research.
5. **General Social Media Concerns:** Providing an overview of cell phone addiction, privacy, and health concerns that could result from excessive use of mobile devices and/or social media.
6. **Limitations of Current Research and Future Recommendations:** Explaining what research currently lacks in terms of social media in the higher education classroom and providing researchers with suggestions of how to contribute to the literature on social media and higher education.

BACKGROUND: SOCIAL MEDIA PROGRESSION

Social media can be defined in a variety of ways and is often categorized by use and type. Pearson explains that social media is a hazy term due to the fact that it is non-centralized, user created, user controlled, flexible, democratic, and transparent (Moran, Seaman, & Tinti-Kane, 2011). Further emphasizing that content becomes conversation transforming outgoing information into exchanging information leading to individual, industry, societal, and global change. The Education Council of New Zealand describes Social Media as web-based and mobile-based technologies used to facilitate interactive communication between organizations, communities, and individuals (What is Social Media, n.d.). Furthermore, they explain that some of the most common types of social media platforms include collaboration, networking, image-sharing, blogging, and video-sharing.

Golding, Raeymaeckers, and Sousa (2017) consider four aspects of social media: the uncertainty of the term, the scale and speed of the development, the impact on social behavior and sociability, and the financial scale of these technologies. The uncertainty of the term is seen in the various attempts to classify types of social media. Kaplan and Haenlein (2010) present the following six types of social media: collaborative projects, blogs and microblogs, content communities, social networking sites, virtual game worlds, and virtual social worlds. Meanwhile, Schlagwein and Hu (2017) identify the following five different social media use types: broadcast, dialogue, collaboration, knowledge management, and sociability. These examples demonstrate how complex it is just to classify the types of social media. This is further compounded by how these types are used.

Different Uses of Social Media

The British publishing and assessment company, Pearson, began studying social media use in higher education in 2010 when they used a sample of 900 Pearson customers. Over time, the study expanded to over 8,000 higher education faculty. As social media use has changed and expanded, platforms have come and gone and been debated. Faculty use of social media has evolved from simply watching, reading, or listening to interacting and collaborating. The studies strive to make sense of not just how social media is being used or not used, but why.

Pearson produced reports of their social media use in higher education studies in 2011, 2012, and 2013. Each year, overall social media use increased and barriers decreased. The goal of the studies was to reveal how higher education faculty used social media and the value that they saw in using social media for instructional purposes. The three categories for use were: personal, professional (for higher education, but not teaching), and teaching. Teaching included traditional, blended, and fully online courses. Those surveyed included both full-time and part-time faculty, tenured, non-tenured, and adjunct. To allow comparison of results, the wording and presentation of the questions were consistent for the three consecutive years. The social networks, however, did vary from year to year.

Based on the original 2010 data, surveyed faculty response themes emerged concerning social media use in higher education. Faculty viewed social media as a way to extend the classroom, talk to students in the language they were using, break up class, review, and reinforce content; however, social media was not viewed as the primary means of teaching. The social networks presented for the survey were: YouTube, Facebook, Skype, LinkedIn, Twitter, SlideShare, Flickr, MySpace, and Google Wave. As for instructional use, approximately 45% indicated that they had used online videos or podcasts for class, while approximately 10% or less used comments on blogs, wikis, videos, or podcasts (Tinti-Kane, Seaman, & Levy, 2010).

In 2011, the survey included Facebook, Twitter, Myspace, LinkedIn, SlideShare, Flickr, blogs, wikis, video, and podcasts. At that time, 81% of faculty surveyed agreed or strongly agreed that social networks take more time than they are worth, yet 60% indicated that they used social media professionally at least once per month.

YouTube and online videos were viewed as the most valuable resources for class, followed by podcasts and wikis. Approximately half of the faculty viewed Facebook and Twitter as having a negative value for class. As for the overall value of social media for teaching, 70% agreed that video, podcasts, blogs, and wikis were valuable tools, and 58% agreed that social media can be valuable for collaborative learning (Moran, Seaman, & Tinti-Kane, 2011).

In 2012, Pearson released blogs, wikis, podcasts, and Facebook, how today's higher education faculty use social media followed by *Social Media for Teaching and Learning* in 2013. The surveys revealed that higher education faculty were much more likely to use social media in their personal lives than academically. Although overall higher education faculty were very aware of social media, they were not as likely to use it for instructional purposes. Facebook was by far the most commonly used social media for higher education, followed by podcasts, LinkedIn, blogs, wikis, and lastly Twitter. Social media use and age revealed a negative correlation, as use declined with age. Video resources showed to be popular among higher education faculty, while many sought out internet video sources, publishers' videos were also commonly used. The main concerns about social media use were privacy and integrity of student submissions. There was also a concern for separating personal and professional accounts and a decline in concern for the time required for social media use.

Social media use consistently increased from 2012 to 2013 in all three categories: personal, professional, and teaching monthly use. Personal social media use increased from 64% to 70%. Professional use increased from 45% to 55% and using social media in teaching increased from 34% to 41%. Social media use continues to grow and transform. Despite the complexity of the various types, uses, and definitions of social media, the ability to share information is consistent. This chapter will use the Oxford dictionary definition for social media: websites and applications that enable users to create and share content or to participate in social networking. Furthermore, the different categories of social media use will be defined based on the Pearson reports of personal, professional, and teaching.

Personal Social Media Use

The first component, personal social media use, asked faculty specifically about their own personal social media use outside of professional or class use. More specifically, this component represented faculty use versus knowledge of social media. The 2013 results found 16.1% did not use social media, 13.6% rarely used social media, and 70.3% used social media at least monthly. Furthermore, when broken down by age, faculty 35 years and younger tended to use social media more. The study also found there was a relationship between social media use and discipline. Humanities and Arts had the highest rate of social media use while Natural Sciences had the lowest rate of social media use. Approximately one-third of faculty expressed that they used social media on a daily basis for personal use, with almost all of them using Facebook.

Professional Social Media Use

The second component, professional social media use found nearly 55% of faculty used social media at least once per month in 2013 (Seaman & Tinti-Kane, 2013). Social media use that supported faculty's professional careers for any aspect other than teaching was considered professional social media use. The same correlation with age was found with professional use as was found with personal use, the older the faculty, the less they used social media. As for the relationship with discipline, it was found that Humanities and Arts, Social Sciences, and Applied Sciences had higher rates than those in the Natural Sciences, Mathematics, and Computer Science. In comparing 2011 results to 2012, LinkedIn professional use increased by 6%, while Facebook use decreased by 11%.

The 2013 report included virtual communities. Pearson defined a virtual community as: "A community of people sharing common interests, experiences, ideas, and feelings over the Internet or other online collaborative networks" (Seaman & Tinti-Kane, 2013, p. 27). Virtual communities take on different forms and may leverage social media, forums, and blogs. Examples include a LinkedIn or Google Group, Message Board, Chat Room, or User Group. When asked if they participated in virtual communities, more faculty reported participation for professional interests (50%) than personal interests (40%). LinkedIn was reported as the most used social media site for professional purposes. When analyzing virtual communities in relation to online courses, it was found that those who teach online courses are more likely to use social media and participate in virtual communities, both professionally and personally.

Teaching/Educational Social Media Use

The third component, teaching use of social media found almost 41% of faculty used social media for teaching within their courses at least once per month in 2013 (Seaman & Tinti-Kane, 2013). Again, similar results were found based on age. Younger faculty were more likely to use social media in teaching. Similarly, it was found again that Humanities and Arts, Social Sciences, and Applied Sciences faculty had higher rates than those in the Natural Sciences, Mathematics, and Computer Science. Blogs and wikis were the most used format for teaching. Facebook and LinkedIn use was much lower compared to personal and professional use. The use of social media in teaching leads to many more questions, as use could simply be directing students to refer to something, or it can be more involved by asking students to post or respond.

A major component of the 2013 survey was how social media was used for assignments. This component was broken down by platform (blogs & wikis, podcasts, Twitter, LinkedIn, and Facebook) and type of assignment (create, add comments, and read, watch, listen). The results showed that faculty were most likely to ask students to individually create a blog or wiki. Twitter, LinkedIn, and Facebook were not commonly used for assignments in any form. These results were almost identical when comparing group assignments to individual assignments (Seaman & Tinti-Kane, 2013).

Videos as Social Media

Higher education faculty video use was found to be very common, with nearly 88% of faculty using videos for class. Again, similar to social media use, it was found that Humanities and Arts, Social Sciences, and Applied Sciences had the highest rate of video use. The most common method for video selection was searching online, yet over half of faculty acknowledged use of publisher's videos and over one-third had created their own video. Some faculty indicated selecting videos based on reviews and ratings, but more commonly, they used recommendations from other faculty members. Video viewing was common in class, while 79% made assignments to view videos outside of class. In addition, 25% assigned students to create videos of their own, with video creation being most common in Humanities and Arts (Moran, Seaman & Tinti-Kane, 2012).

Concerns for Social Media Use in Teaching (vs. General Social Media Concerns)

Concerns for social media use included (presented in order of highest concern): integrity of student submissions, concerns about privacy, separate course and personal accounts, grading and assessment, inability to measure effectiveness, lack of integration with Learning Management System (LMS), too much time to learn or use, and lack of support (Moran, Seaman, & Tinti-Kane, 2012). Although faculty reported these as important concerns, the percentage of concern for each decreased from the previous year. Similar to other findings there was a correlation with level of concern and faculty age. The older faculty members had higher levels of concern.

Simard and Schnackenberg (2006) provide research that acknowledges the value of virtual learning but point out the challenge of bringing interface literacy and online pedagogy together. Furthermore, they point out that classrooms have changed and so must teaching and learning; therefore, synchronous and asynchronous discussion must be carefully implemented. Virtual learning can promote student involvement, collaboration, and interaction.

The 2013 *Social Media in Higher Education* survey revealed that social media use in higher education continued to increase, but there were still concerns. When responding to the statement "the interactive nature of online and mobile technologies can create better learning environments," 13.3% of faculty strongly agreed, 45.9% somewhat agreed, 33.1% somewhat disagreed, and 7.7% strongly disagreed. When asked about "The impact of digital communication has had on your communication with students", 78.9% responded that it increased, 16.6% responded no impact, and 4.4% responded that it had decreased. Over half of faculty members felt that mobile technologies are more distracting than helpful to students for academic work. This is a recurring concern in the Pearson series of research. When presented with the statement, "Online and Mobile Technologies Are More Distracting Than Helpful to Students for Academic Work," 14.8% Strongly agreed, 41.2% somewhat agreed, 34.7% somewhat disagreed, 9.2% strongly disagreed (Seaman & Tinti-Kane, 2013).

Simard and Schnackenberg (2006) explain that university faculty must create engaging learning environments due to the constant growth of online learning and propose that online course facilitation is the new classroom management. Faculty agreed that social media and technology promote digital communication, but with this comes expectations for feedback outside of class and office hours. This was found to extend the day for faculty and was reported as causing stress. Almost half of faculty in this study reported that digital communication had increased their level of stress and over 66% reported longer work hours as a result of digital communication (Seaman & Tinti-Kane, 2013).

Privacy was again revealed as one of the top concerns with social media use for faculty. Thus, Pearson analyzed privacy in more detail. When presented with the following: risks to the personal privacy of faculty, risks to the personal privacy of students, others outside of class should not be able to view class-related content, others outside of class should not be able to view class discussions, and others outside of class should not be able to participate in class discussions, faculty were asked if they strongly agree, somewhat agree, somewhat disagree, or strongly disagree with the statements (Seaman & Tinti-Kane, 2013). Over 80% of the faculty strongly agreed or somewhat agreed with the five statements. The highest level of concern was having non-class members view or participate in class discussions (over 66% strongly agreed). Faculty was then asked to rate each as very important or important. Risks to the personal privacy of faculty was rated the highest as very important (70%). Many of the concerns for social media use in teaching could be addressed through private accounts. Although multiple concerns exist regarding social media us in the classroom, the next section of the chapter will present educational platforms and social media websites that students can use in the classroom.

Educational Platforms and Social Media in the Classroom

The abundance of social media options makes it difficult to decide how to implement use. This section of the chapter will provide examples of social media options that can be used in the classroom and accessed by students through educational platforms or Learning Management Systems. This section will also discuss popular social networks and media sites or applications used around the world. Having students access the particular applications or websites through an approved educational location may help the transition to a social media-based environment while promoting the use of mobile devices inside and outside of the classroom.

According to Hutt (2017), in January 2017 the most popular social networks around the globe were: Facebook, Twitter, Instagram, LinkedIn, QZone, V Kontakte, and Odnoklassniki. A few of these along with other social networks or media are briefly explained in this section.

Facebook

Facebook, a free social media website, founded by Mark Zuckerberg and four other Harvard students, began in 2004. Facebook originated in the United States; however, it is now a global social media and networking site and the most popular social network in the world (Hutt, 2017). Facebook is a way to connect with people, groups, and businesses. It allows users to post a status of written information, video links, or pictures. When users are in a "closed group" only members of that group can view the information posted. Facebook can be used in higher education by instructors and students using the closed group option. Course information and assignments can be posted while group discussions can take place using Facebook. News stations, businesses, and other colleges and universities distribute knowledge to the public using Facebook; this makes it possible for students to gather information and share it directly within a classroom group for others to view.

Facebook is a social media example that students and faculty members may already use personally; therefore, determining creative ways to integrate Facebook into higher education courses will promote the use of using social media for teaching/ educational purposes.

Twitter

Another popular global social networking site, Twitter, allows users to post messages, limited to 280 characters. The main use of Twitter is to remain updated about local, global, and international news; however, users can post messages about anything. Embedded within a Twitter message or "tweet" can be a hashtag. If a user hashtags, using the (#) symbol before a word, any person can search the hashtag to read every tweet associated with it. Using a specific hashtag that students can use in a particular class can be helpful.

Many studies have been conducted to determine the appropriate use and benefits of using Twitter in higher education. It has been found that students tend to be more willing to use Twitter on a regular basis and potentially use it in the classroom, as opposed to instructors (Jacquemin, Smelser, & Bernot, 2014); however, a two-year study that consisted of nursing, psychology, and geography students that incorporated Twitter to promote in class discussions and student questioning in larger class sizes found that this social media site improved student perceptions about feeling a sense of belonging and community in their class (Ross, Banow, & Yu, 2015). Twitter can be used in the classroom for discussion purposes, asking or answering questions, and sharing relevant content information and news. Additionally, instructors can share or advertise their students' work and teaching strategies by tweeting images, videos, or brief messages. Additionally, using a specific hashtag with multiple classes can promote collaboration with students who take the same course at a different time or location, and promote communication and collaboration between students in completely different classes. This may emphasize the importance of cross-curricular communication.

These examples will promote the use of social media for teaching and educational purposes; however, Twitter can also be used by faculty members outside of the classroom for professional use. Instructors can use their school Twitter account to connect with professional organizations, other colleagues, and professors and researchers across the globe. This will allow instructors to build their own professional network related to their field, research interests, and teaching agenda.

Instagram

Instagram operates similarly to Twitter but is more commonly used as only a photo or video-sharing platform. Each post can be seen by a users' followers or can be searched by others if the post contains a specific hashtag. Instagram can be used in higher education classrooms by sharing images that promote class discussion, short videos to break up class lecture, or provide images or videos with links or hashtags as the caption that link students to outside articles or media (Al-Bahrani & Patel, 2015). Al-Bahrani & Patel (2015) suggest that Instagram, Twitter, and Facebook can be incorporated into a higher education economics class in two ways: (1) voluntary non-graded assignments or (2) mandatory graded assignments (p. 64). The way in which an instructor incorporates social media into the classroom depends on the content and course design; however, it can promote collaboration, class discussion, and can be an easier and more direct way to communicate with students. As mentioned previously, Instagram, similar to Facebook and Twitter can promote the use of social media in the classroom for teaching/educational and professional use.

YouTube

Mentioned previously in the Different Uses of Social Media section, was the fact that faculty member video use was very common. YouTube is one of the most popular video sharing websites that faculty members could use. YouTube, founded in 2005, is a website that allows users to create an account and upload videos. Without an account, visitors to the website can search and view videos. Instructors can find videos on YouTube that relate to course content and assign students to view the videos either inside or outside of the classroom by accessing the links through the assigned LMS. Class discussions can be sparked through viewing YouTube videos, students can create their own educational videos and upload them to YouTube, or YouTube videos can be used by students as a way to learn or review content material.

Kahoot

Kahoot! launched in 2013 and is a free game-based learning platform designed to make learning fun, inclusive and engaging in all contexts, and can be used by learners who have a mobile device with internet connection. Kahoot! is advertised as being flexible, simple, diverse, and engaging. An account or login is not required; participants can join using a provided pin from an instructor. Kahoot! games can be used to introduce new concepts, take surveys or for a class review. The games can be played individually or as teams to build collaboration. Currently, Kahoot! can be played in real-time with players in over 180 countries. Over 50 million people use Kahoot every month and by early 2017, they had over 1 billion cumulative participating players (What is Kahoot!, 2017).

Instructors can create new Kahoots as a quiz, jumble, discussion, or survey. Videos, images, and diagrams can be added and Kahoot! can be assigned for students to complete on their own time. Although instructors can create their own Kahoots, there are hundreds of premade Kahoots available for use. The Kahoot! site provides a getting started guide, templates, tips and tricks, and video tutorials for first-time users. Instructors and students, of any age, can use Kahoot! as a way to collaborate, communicate, or compete.

VoiceThread

VoiceThread, a learning tool, aims to fill the gap of social presence in online learning. Students and teachers can upload pictures, videos, presentations, or documents into an online collection that mirrors a slideshow. After the media is added, instructors and students can record comments, ask questions, critique ideas, and engage in conversation. VoiceThread allows students to create their work, communicate their work with instructors and peers, and think critically about course content. Participants watching a VoiceThread can write a comment or draw directly on the image or slide in a presentation. A variety of recent research studies show that VoiceThread, as multi-sensory interaction, has a positive impact on learning (VoiceThread, n.d.).

Kahoot! and VoiceThread are social media examples that should primarily be used for teaching or educational use. It is rare that students will have a personal account for either of these; therefore, exploring and experimenting with these two websites prior to having students use them is important for faculty members to recognize. Appropriate use may need to be modeled for classes.

QQ and QZone

QQ and QZone are an instant messaging and social networking website based in China. These social networking options are available in China while other networking sites, such as Facebook and YouTube, are blocked in mainland China. QQ is available in Chinese, English, French, Japanese, Korean, and Spanish while QZone is only available in Chinese.

V Kontakte and Odnoklassniki

V Kontakte, also known as VK, is a social networking website based out of Russia. It is available in over 80 languages but is primarily used by Russian-speaking persons. Odnoklassniki, founded in 2006, is also used by those in the Russian Federation and Soviet Republics and is available in 14 different languages.

Using these social networking sites, similar to Facebook or Twitter, in higher education classrooms around the globe is a way to integrate social media into the classroom. Although more social media and networking sites continue to be created, the ones mentioned in this section have been found to be the most commonly used or those used by the authors of this chapter. In addition to instructors and students using social media to access and create course content, communicate, and collaborate, social media is used by colleges and universities for additional purposed.

Social Media Outside of the Classroom

Although social media can be used by instructors and students for classroom purposes, social media is also present outside of the classroom. Colleges and universities have been using social media accounts on Facebook, Twitter, and Instagram for other reasons: student recruitment, communication, and research. These are examples of how social media is used for personal and professional reasons.

Student Recruitment

Social networks such as Twitter, Facebook, and Instagram are being used by colleges and universities to advertise their academics, sports teams, research projects, awards, etc., as a student recruitment technique. Students who follow specific school accounts or those who stay up-to-date with college and university news or sports, are more likely to view their advertisements via social media. Figure 1 provides an image of five different universities who have Twitter accounts.

Robert Morris University's Twitter page provides a link to take a virtual tour of their campus along with hashtags related to the school while the Technical University of Munich's page provides a link to their Facebook and Instagram accounts and a YouTube video about the university. Instead of viewing traditional commercials or billboards, social media sites that students use on a regular basis are becoming the new form of advertisement in hopes of recruiting students.

Figure 1. Screenshot of five different college or university Twitter accounts

Communication

Aside from using Twitter, Facebook, and Instagram for recruitment purposes, school accounts are used to communicate with the local community and student population. School extracurricular and sporting events, club activities, conferences, crisis or emergency situations, and delays or closures due to weather are only a few examples of important information that can be communicated through social media. Any student who follows their college or university, or searches for specific hashtags, can receive instant alerts about their school. Using social media to remain informed about everyday happenings can be extremely helpful to students. It is vital that students receive immediate notifications if and when an emergency situation occurs; this can be done using school social media accounts.

Research

Another way that colleges and universities are using social media is to inform followers about research projects, conferences, and achievements. Certain universities are known for their research, while others strive to be named a research institute; using social media accounts to share upcoming and innovative research with colleagues, students, and competitors is done easily through a school account. By sharing innovative research and current projects, colleges and universities can find research partners or potential companies or businesses interested in funding such projects.

General Social Media Concerns

While there are a variety of social network options to enhance college courses, there are many concerns that accompany their use. In addition to the faculty concerns from the Pearson reports, the long-term effects of social media use are unknown, and possible concerns include addiction, privacy, and health. Cell phone addiction is a growing concern for children and adults. Privacy continues to be a concern and the impact of social media on health is a critical and timely issue.

Addiction

Research on cell phone addiction is becoming more available and there are now ways to diagnose addiction. Bhise, Ghatule, and Ghatule (2014) used a 10-item questionnaire to conduct a study on mobile addiction among students. The study found that more than 75% of students have mobile addiction. They go on to compare cell phones to cigarettes, classifying it as one of the biggest non-drug addiction of the 21st century. Addiction is clear when an obsession disrupts other things in life such as relationships, school or work (Bhise et al., 2014).

There are five risk factors for Mobile Addiction described by Bhise et al. (2014):

1. **Anxiety Disorders:** Those who suffer from anxiety may use mobile phones to distract them from fear or worry. Obsessive-compulsive disorder may contribute to excessive SMS/MMS checking and compulsive mobile use.
2. **Depression:** Those who suffer from depression may use mobile phones to distract them from feelings of depression. Too much time online can make these feelings worse and further contribute to stress, isolation, and loneliness.
3. **Lack of Social Support:** Those who lack social support may use social networking as a way to establish new relationships and relate to others.

4. **Less Social Activity:** Those who are less mobile or socially active than before due to disability, parenting, or other circumstances that limit leaving home, may turn to mobile use.
5. **Stress:** Those who turn to mobile use to relieve stress. This is usually counterproductive as more time dedicated to mobile use can increase stress.

Yildirim (2014) offers a 20-item questionnaire to determine if one suffers from Nomophobia, the fear of not being able to use your cell phone. His study showed those who score high on the questionnaire may avoid personal interactions and suffer from social anxiety and depression. He further explains that if a person is too dependent on their smartphone, they are decreasing their ability to pay attention. This is a concern for communication in the global workforce.

A study published in the Journal of Media Education found that college students check their digital devices for non-class related content an average of 11.43 times per class (McCoy, 2016). This means that students spend approximately 20% of class time using mobile devices for things that do not related to class. When students were asked if they use their mobile device 10 times or more for non-learning reasons during class, 34% reported yes. Specific reasons for non-class related mobile use included to stay connected and boredom. The consequences for using mobile devices for non-class related things included not paying attention and missing instruction. Thus, 53% of students reported that it would be helpful to have policies that limit non-class related use of mobile devices.

The current studies on cell phone addiction do not distinguish between personal, professional, and teaching or educational use. More research is needed to establish when a student is using social media for things unrelated to class. A student who is actively using social media for class collaboration would increase class communication, but a student who is using social media for personal accounts would decrease class communication. Personal social media use could interfere with intended class collaboration use. Regardless of the type of use, social media can increase virtual interaction, but possibly interfere with or take away from face to face communication.

Privacy

The Pearson reports consistently revealed that higher education faculty were concerned about students' privacy through social media use. Additionally, higher education faculty stated a concern in the lack of integrity in student submissions (Moran, Seaman, & Tinti-Kane, 2012). Parents of adolescents are encouraged to monitor potential problems with bullying, depression, sexting, and inappropriate content (O'Keeffe & Clarke-Pearson, 2011). As young adults transition to higher education, they bring a lot of social media experience.

Another privacy concern is course content. Social media could reveal and expose course content to future students. While many of the platforms only grant access to those with a code or log-in, there is potential for easier access and shared information. When considering privacy as a concern, it is reasonable to consider the category of use as personal, professional, or educational use and the platform that is used. More steps can be taken to separate personal from professional accounts.

Health

Acharya, Acharya, and Waghrey (2013) studied the effects of cell phone use on health among college students. Headaches, irritability, and anger were found as symptoms of cell phone addiction. Mental problems included lack of concentration, poor academic performance, insomnia, and anxiety. Additionally, physical problems included body aches, eye strain, and digital thumb. For a 2013 study through Ottawa Public Health, researchers collected data from 750 teens in grades 7 through 12 concerning social media habits, mental health, and psychological well-being, and mental health support.

The results revealed that teens who use social media for more than two hours per day are more likely to struggle with mental health, psychological distress and suicidal thoughts (Sampasa-Kanyinga & Lewis, 2015).

A study linked Facebook to depressive symptoms due to social comparison. Steers, Wickham and Acitelli (2014) found in a study of 180 people there was a link between time spent on Facebook and depressive symptoms regardless of gender. Another study found an association between online social networking and depression in high school students (Pantic et al., 2012). Pantic et al., (2012) found online social networking was related to depression after interviewing 160 high school students using an anonymous, structured questionnaire and back depression inventory. Another study through the University of Pittsburgh found that young adults who spend more than two hours per day on social media are 2.7 more likely to be depressed. Adults ages 19-32 were surveyed about social media use and depression. Of the 1,787 participants, those who had the highest use of social media had significantly increased odds of depression (Lin et al., 2016).

A study by Twenge, Joiner, Rogers, and Martin (2017) found links to increased new media (means of mass communication using digital technologies such as the Internet) screen time among U.S. adolescents and depressive symptoms, suicide related outcomes, and suicide rates after 2010. In two nationally representative surveys of a total of 506,820 U.S. adolescents in grades 8 through 12, found that adolescents who spent more time on new media were more likely to report mental health issues than those who spent more time on non-screen activities. When compared to national statistics on suicide deaths for ages 13 to 18, from 2010 to 2015, adolescents' depressive symptoms, suicide-related outcomes, and suicide rates all increased. The study concluded that adolescents have spent more time on new media screen activities since 2010 and that may account for the increase in depression and suicide.

A report by the Royal Society for Public Health in the United Kingdom presented the findings of a survey presented to almost 1,500 people between the ages of 14 and 24 concerning how Facebook, Instagram, YouTube, Twitter, and Snapchat made them feel (Young Health Movement, n.d.). The survey consisted of 14 questions about each social media platform. To measure the impact of social media on overall wellbeing, the questions asked participants about their feelings of anxiety, depression, and loneliness, as well as the impact on body image, sleep, bullying, and level of FOMO (fear of missing out), while using or after using each social media platform. All of the social media platforms were associated with poor sleep and tiredness. The results also revealed that Instagram, Snapchat, Facebook, and Twitter all resulted in a worse wellbeing. YouTube was the only platform that slightly improved well-being. Recommendations were to set reminders or trackers to limit social media use, focus on what brings joy, positive content, keep in mind others are not posting their real lives, spend more time posting, liking, and messaging versus simply looking at social media content, and ask why you are looking at social media content.

As with addiction and privacy, when considering health as a concern, current research does not distinguish between personal, professional, or teaching use. Time spent on social media should be further researched to include how the time is spent (personal, professional, or teaching). Perhaps academic social media use would take away from the social pressure that these studies revealed.

Limitations of Current Research

The following research studies provide valuable information, but many lack specific details and direction. Based on the idea that mobile learning has grown informally through individual use more than formal use in education, Hao et al. (2017), analyzed mobile learning as an innovation in higher education. Their comparative study focused on how students in the United States, China, and Turkey perceive mobile learning as an innovation based on relative advantage, compatibility, complexity, trialability, and observability. The survey results showed that students were ready to use mobile learning and many already use a form informally. The survey also revealed student concern for support and infrastructure, but lacks recommendations.

Gikas and Grant (2013) interviewed student focus groups across the United States concerning their perspectives on learning with cellphones, smartphones, and social media. They found that mobile devices and the use of social media allowed interaction and provided opportunities for collaboration. Students shared a fear of technology not working, difficulty typing and concern for distractibility.

A 2005 study found students who used laptops learned more collaboratively, did more project-based learning (PBL), and were more likely to engage in problem-solving (Burns & Polman, 2006). Collaboration was found to be the most popular mobile learning environment in a meta-analysis study that compared collaboration, situated learning, peer-assessment, multidimensional, and PBL to analyze students' critical thinking using mobile technology in the learning environment (Ismail, Harun, Salleh, & Zakaria, 2016).

Casey's (2013) action research study found that when students created an online identity, communicated with peers, reviewed, and assessed through social media platforms, they were active and valued the learning process. A 2015 study compared the use of social networking sites between medical students and medical educators. The results were consistent with Pearson's studies finding that social media use continues to grow in higher education, but with barriers. Educators in the study tended to use social media to post videos, articles, and comments and students indicated a preference in posting quizzes and revision files (Bialy & Jalali, 2015).

The research presented provides a lot of valuable information, yet it is difficult to make specific recommendations and keep up with constantly changing social media. Teens today use completely different social media platforms that were not even mentioned in the Pearson surveys. The most preferred social networks for teenagers in the United States has changed drastically in the past five years. According to Statista (2018), in 2012, Facebook was the most preferred social media among American teenagers (42%). By 2017, Facebook was one of the least favorite among teenagers (9%). Snapchat was one of the least preferred in 2015 (11%) but in 2016 and 2017, was the most preferred among teens, with 47% of teenagers listing it as their most preferred social network. As teens transition into college and social media fads come and go, educators strive to make connections and adapt. Current research is also lacking practical examples or guides on how to incorporate or transition to a social media environment for higher education faculty members.

SOLUTIONS AND RECOMMENDATIONS

Social media use in higher education raises many questions. In addition to the concerns discussed in this chapter, there are many other things to consider. Higher education faculty must be familiar with the social media platform they wish to implement. Additionally, the level and goal of the collaboration must be considered, as well as, the value of formal versus informal learning. There are many aspects of social media in the classroom that can be viewed as advantageous. Social media is part of our everyday lives and creates easy access to information that can be viewed instantly. Research shows that technology is changing the way we learn and that students prefer mobile learning (Benson, 2011). Arokiasamy (2017) notes the flexibility, portability, affordability, and popularity of mobile devices such as iPads, tablets, e-readers, and smartphones as primary reasons for educators to implement their use. Furthermore, he adds that integrating mobile devices into instruction can support digital learners and promote meaningful learning. There are countless ways to use social media in higher education. Providing higher education faculty with research and information on social media can be the first step to allow them to make informed decisions on social media use in their courses. Current research and concerns must be acknowledged to help faculty make informed decisions concerning the use of social media in higher education courses.

Mentioned previously was that students may check their mobile devices, for non-class related information, on average 11.43 times per class (McCoy, 2016). Students stated that this was a result of boredom. The study conducted by Jacquemin et al. (2014) found that using Twitter in the classroom improved the feeling of belonging in the classroom. Noting this, using social media in the classroom will allow students to use their devices during instruction, for educational purposes, which can promote a sense of belonging while potentially diminishing the feeling of boredom or need to use their phone for non-class related purposes.

Battling student phone addiction and personal use in class can raise concerns and may prevent higher education instructors from promoting mobile device and social media in the classroom; however, if a device and social media policy is created, acceptable use is modeled by instructors, and implementation is properly planned and implemented it can change the dynamic of the classroom while allowing students to build the skills for the Four Cs.

FUTURE RESEARCH DIRECTIONS

Most current research on social media use in higher education does not differentiate between personal, professional, and educational use. Future research could be based on personal, professional, and educational use of social media and cell phone addiction and health. Future research could also include social media use in formal and informal learning, social media communication and collaboration, social media use based on discipline, social media use outside of the classroom, and the impact of social media communication on face to face communication.

Many of the studies presented in this chapter could be used as a foundation for further research. Based on the comparative study by Hao et al. (2017), future studies should focus on what form of mobile learning students are most prepared to use and what concerns they have for support and infrastructure.

A follow up to Gikas and Grant's 2013 focus groups could compare social media versus face-to-face interaction and collaboration and ways to handle technology not working and distractibility. Furthermore, a follow up to Casey's (2013) action research study could investigate if students are more active learners when communicating through social media.

Lastly, research currently lacks a "How to Guide" for social media implementation to provide faculty members with practical examples of implementation for multiple age levels and subject areas. Providing a "How to Guide" could provide institutes and instructors with policy suggestions, different types of social media platforms and uses, and suggestions of how to properly implement social media use for teaching and educational purposes. These research suggestions will not only contribute to the literature, but also provide up-to-date references for those hoping to use social media in higher education.

CONCLUSION

Benson (2011) from the Association for the Advancement of Computing in Education explains that social media is changing the way we think and process information. It can be overwhelming for educators to keep up with current social media use and decide which platforms to use. Educational goals should be the first priority. Social media use in higher education could provide benefits through collaboration, communication, and technology skills. As social media use continues to increase, educators must find the most appropriate and effective ways to incorporate social media use into courses. It is nearly impossible to keep up with all of the platforms and predict what social media will be used in the years ahead. Social media choices are constantly changing and the apps that are most used one year can completely change the next. Although the applications presented in much of the research may be used more or less today than when they were studied, the results are valuable in that there are many common issues and concerns regardless of which social media applications are used.

REFERENCES

Acharya, J. P., Acharya, I., & Waghrey, D. (2013). A study on some psychological health effects of cell-phone usage amongst college going students. *International Journal of Medical Research & Health Sciences, 2*(3), 388. doi:10.5958/j.2319-5886.2.3.068

Al-Bahrani, A., & Patel, D. (2015). Incorporating Twitter, Instagram, and Facebook in economics classrooms. *The Journal of Economic Education, 46*(1), 56-67. from http://reddog.rmu.edu:2061/eds/pdfviewer/pdfviewer?vid=3&sid=650d2878-c8d1-4897-8cd7-b53af0f42def@sessionmgr4008

An Educator's Guide to the "Four Cs". (n.d.). *NEA*. Retrieved from http://www.nea.org/tools/52217.htm

Arokiasamy, A. R. (2017). A systematic review approach of mobile technology adoption in higher education. *Economics, Management and Sustainability, 2*(2), 48-55. Retrieved from https://zenodo.org/record/1145854/files/05_Anantha_01.pdf

Banks, J., Au, K., Ball, A. F., Bell, P., Gordon, E., Gutiérrez, K., ... & Valdes, G. (2007). Learning in and out of school in diverse environments. Retrieved from http://life-slc.org/docs/Banks_etal-LIFE-Diversity-Report.pdf

Benson, S. (2011). Social media and the classroom. *AACE Review*. Retrieved from https://www.aace.org/social-media-and-the-classroom/

Bhise, A., Ghatule, A., & Ghatule, A. (2014). Study of mobile addiction among students. *Indian Journal of Research in Management, Business and Social Sciences, 21*(1A), 17-21. Retrieved from http://www.ijrmbss.com/assets/pdf/Vol2Iss1a/5.pdf

Bialy, S.E. & Jalali, A. (2015). Go where the students are: A comparison of the use of social networking sites between medical students and medical educators. *JMIR Medical Education, 1*(2). Retrieved from http://mededu.jmir.org/2015/2/e7/

Brown, J. S., & Adler, R. P. (2008). Minds on fire: open education, the long tail, and learning 2.0. *Educause Review,* 16-32. Retrieved from http://www.oss.net/dynamaster/file_archive/080618/bdb5129a636e9ffbe734351363466c23/Minds%20on%20Fire.%20Open%20Education,%20the%20Long%20Tail,%20and%20Learning%202. 0%20-%20Brown,%20Adler%20(2008).pdf

Burns, K., & Polman, J. (2006). The impact of ubiquitous computing in the internet age: How middle school teachers integrated wireless laptops in the initial stages of implementation. *Journal of Technology and Teacher Education, 14*(2), 363-385. Retrieved from https://www.learntechlib.org/p/5777/

Casey, G. (2013). Social media in the classroom: A simple yet complex hybrid environment for students. *Journal of Educational Multimedia and Hypermedia, 22*(1), 5-24. Retrieved from https://www.learntechlib.org/p/41333/

Chen, B., & Bryer, T. (2012). Investigating instructional strategies for using social media in formal and informal learning. *The International Review of Research in Open and Distributed Learning, 13*(1). Retrieved from http://www.irrodl.org/index.php/irrodl/article/view/1027/2073?utm_campaign=elearningindustry.com&utm_source=/10-tips-to-effectively-use-social-media-in-formal-learning&utm_medium=link

Chou, W. S., Hunt, Y. M., Beckjord, E. B., Moser, R. P., & Hesse, B. W. (2009). Social media use in the United States: Implications for health communication. *Journal of Medical Internet Research, 11*(4), e48. doi:10.2196/jmir.1249 PMID:19945947

Gikas, J., & Grant, M. M. (2013). Mobile computing devices in higher education: Student perspectives on learning with cellphones, smartphones & social media. *The Internet and Higher Education, 19*, 18–26. doi:10.1016/j.iheduc.2013.06.002

Golding, P., Raeymaeckers, K., & Sousa, H. (2017). Social media – New challenges and approaches for communications research. *European Journal of Communication, 32*(1), 3–5. doi:10.1177/0267323116682801

Greenhow, C., & Robelia, B. (2009). Informal learning and identity formation in online social networks. *Learning, Media and Technology, 34*(2), 119–140. doi:10.1080/17439880902923580

Hao, S., Cui, M., Dennen, V. P., Türel, Y. K., & Mei, L. (2017). Analysis of mobile learning as an innovation in higher education: A comparative study of three countries. *International Journal of Mobile Learning and Organization, 11*(4), 314. Retrieved from http://www.inderscience.com/info/inarticle.php?artid=87080 doi:10.1504/IJMLO.2017.087080

Hew, K. F., & Brush, T. (2006). Integrating technology into K-12 teaching and learning: current knowledge gaps and recommendations for future research. *Educational Technology Research and Development, 55*(3), 223-252. Retrieved from https://www.researchgate.net/publication/225668789_Integrating_technology_into_K-12_teaching_and_learning_Current_knowledge_gaps_and_recommendations_for_future_research

Hutt, R. (2017). The world's most popular social networks, mapped. *World Economic Forum*. Retrieved from https://www.weforum.org/agenda/2017/03/most-popular-social-networks-mapped/

Ismail, N. S., Harun, J., Salleh, S. M., & Zakaria, M. A. (2016). Supporting students' critical thinking with a mobile learning environment: A meta-analysis. In *INTED2016 Proceedings*. Retrieved from https://www.researchgate.net/publication/312940527_SUPPORTING_STUDENTS'_CRITICAL_THINKING_WITH_A_MOBILE_LEARNING_ENVIRONMENT_A_META-ANALYSIS

Jacquemin, S. J., Smelser, L. K., & Bernot, M. J. (2014). Twitter in the higher education classroom: A student and faculty assessment of use and perception. *Journal of College Science Teaching, 43*(6), 22-27. Retrieved from http://reddog.rmu.edu:2061/eds/pdfviewer/pdfviewer?vid=10&sid=df38a0c7-71a8-446d-a62a-587a3d7c43c6%40sessionmgr4010

Kaplan, A. M., & Haenlein, M. (2010). Users of the world, unite! The challenges and opportunities of Social Media. *Business Horizons, 53*(1), 59–68. Retrieved from http://michaelhaenlein.eu/Publications/Kaplan,%20Andreas%20-%20Users%20of%20the%20wor ld,%20unite.pdf doi:10.1016/j.bushor.2009.09.003

Lin, L. Y., Sidani, J. E., Shensa, A., Radovic, A., Miller, E., & Colditz, J. …Primack, B. A. (2016). Association between social media use and depression among U.S. young adults. *Depression and Anxiety, 33*(4), 323-331. Retrieved from https://www.ncbi.nlm.nih.gov/pmc/articles/PMC4853817/pdf/nihms749957.pdf

McCoy, B. (2016). Digital distractions in the classroom phase II: Student classroom use of digital devices for non-class related purposes. *Journal of Media Education* (7) 5-32. Retrieved on 20 January 2018 from https://digitalcommons.unl.edu/cgi/viewcontent.cgi?referer=https://www.google.com/&httpsredir=1&article=1091&context=journalismfacpub

Moran, M., Seaman, J., & Tinti-Kane, H. (2011). Teaching, learning, and sharing: How today's higher education faculty use social media. Pearson. Retrieved from https://files.eric.ed.gov/fulltext/ED535130.pdf

Moran, M., Seaman, J., & Tinti-Kane, H. (2012). *Blogs, wikis, podcasts And Facebook. Pearson Learning Solutions: how today's higher education faculty use social media*. Pearson. Retrieved from https://www.onlinelearningsurvey.com/reports/blogswikispodcasts.pdf

O'Keeffe, G. S., & Clarke-Pearson, K. (2011). The impact of social media on children, adolescents, and families. *American Academy of Pediatrics, 127*(4). Retrieved from http://research3.fit.edu/sealevelriselibrary/documents/doc_mgr/1006/O'Keeffe_and_Pearson._2011._The_Impact_of_Social_Media_on_Children,_Adolescents,_and_Families.pdf

Pantic, I., Damjanovic, A., Todorovic, J., Topalovic, D., Bojovic-Jovic, D., Ristic, S., & Pantic, S. (2012). Association between online social networking and depression in high school students: Behavioral physiology viewpoint. *Psychiatria Danubina, 24*(1), 90–93. Retrieved on 20 January 2018 from http://www.hdbp.org/psychiatria_danubina/pdf/dnb_vol24_no1/dnb_vol24_no1_90.pdf PMID:22447092

Ross, H. M., Banow, R., & Yu, S. (2015). The use of Twitter in large lecture courses: Do the students see a benefit? *Contemporary Educational Technology, 6*(2), 126-139. Retrieved from http://reddog.rmu.edu:2061/eds/pdfviewer/pdfviewer?vid=11&sid=df38a0c7-71a8-446d-a62a-587a3d7c43c6%40sessionmgr4010

Rowan-Kenyon, H. T., Alemán, A. M., Gin, K., Blakeley, B., Gismondi, A., & Lewis, J. … Knight, S. (2016). Social media in higher education. *ASHE Higher Education Report, 42*(5), 7-128. Retrieved from http://onlinelibrary.wiley.com/doi/10.1002/aehe.20088/epdf

Sampasa-Kanyinga, H., & Lewis, R. F. (2015). Frequent use of social networking sites is associated with poor psychological functioning among children and adolescents. *Cyberpsychology, Behavior, and Social Networking, 18*(7), 380–385. doi:10.1089/cyber.2015.0055 PMID:26167836

Schlagwein, D., & Hu, M. (2017). How and why organizations use social media: Five use types and their relation to absorptive capacity. *Journal of Information Technology, 32*(2), 194–209. doi:10.1057/jit.2016.7

Seaman, J., & Tinti-Kane, H. (2013). *Social media for teaching and learning*. Pearson. Retrieved from http://www.pearsonlearningsolutions.com/assets/downloads/reports/social-media-for-teaching-and-learning-2013-report.pdf#view=FitH,0

Siemens, G. (2005). Connectivism: A learning theory for the digital age. *International Journal of Instructional Technology and Distance Learning (ITDL)*. Retrieved from http://www.itdl.org/journal/jan_05/article01.htm

Simard, D. A., & Schnackenberg, H. L. (2006). Online Course Creation and Facilitation: The New Classroom Management. Department of Special Education SUNY Plattsburgh, New York. Retrieved from http://citeseerx.ist.psu.edu/viewdoc/download?doi=10.1.1.627.422&rep=rep1&type=pdf

Slavin, R. E. (2018). *Educational Psychology: theory and practice*. NY, NY: Pearson.

Statista. (2018). *Most popular social networks of teenagers in the United States from fall 2012 to fall 2017*. Retrieved from https://www.statista.com/statistics/250172/social-network-usage-of-us-teens-and-young-adults/

Steers, M. N., Wickham, R. E., & Acitelli, L. K. (2014). Seeing everyone else's highlight reels: How Facebook usage is linked to depressive symptoms. *Journal of Social and Clinical Psychology*, *33*(8), 701–731. doi:10.1521/jscp.2014.33.8.701

Tinti-Kane, H., Seaman, J., & Levy, J. (2010). *Social media in higher education: The survey*. Pearson. Retrieved from https://www.babson.edu/Academics/Documents/babson-survey-research-group/social-media-in-hi gher-education.pdf

Twenge, J. M., Joiner, T. E., Rogers, M. L., & Martin, G. N. (2017). Increases in depressive symptoms, suicide-related outcomes, and suicide rates among U.S. adolescents after 2010 and links to increased new media screen time. *Clinical Psychological Science*, *6*(1), 3–17. doi:10.1177/2167702617723376

VoiceThread. (n.d.). VoiceThread fills the social presence gap found in online learning interactions. Retrieved from https://voicethread.com/products/highered/

What is Kahoot! (2017). Kahoot. Retrieved from https://kahoot.com/what-is-kahoot/

What is Social Media. (n.d.). Educational Council of New Zealand. Retrieved from https://www.teachersandsocialmedia.co.nz/what-social-media

Yildirim, C. (2014). Exploring the dimensions of nomophobia: Developing and validating a questionnaire using mixed methods research. Retrieved from https://lib.dr.iastate.edu/cgi/viewcontent.cgi?article=5012&context=etd

Young Health Movement. (n.d.). Retrieved from http://www.yhm.org.uk/

ADDITIONAL READING

Basu, B. (2017). Analyzing the perception of social networking sites as a learning tool among university students: Case study of a business school in India. *World Academy of Science, Engineering and Technology International Journal of Educational and Pedagogical Sciences,11*(7), 1683-1689. Retrieved from https://waset.org/publications/10007520/analyzing-the-perception-of-social-networking-sites-as-a-learning-tool-among-university-students-case-study-of-a-business-school-in-india

Bhutia, Y., & Tariang, A. (2016). Mobile phone addiction among college going students in Shillong. *International Journal of Education and Psychological Research, 5*(2), 29–35. Retrieved from http://ijepr.org/doc/V5_Is2_June16/ij6.pdf

Duke, B., Harper, G., & Johnston, M. (2013). Connectivism as a digital age learning theory. *HETL Review,* 4-13. Retrieved from https://www.hetl.org/wp-content/uploads/2013/09/HETLReview2013SpecialIssueArticle1.pdf

Kaplan, A., & Haenlein, M. (2014). Collaborative projects (social media application): About Wikipedia, the free encyclopedia. *Business Horizons, 57*(5), 617–626. doi:10.1016/j.bushor.2014.05.004

Kaplan, A. M., & Haenlein, M. (2012). Social media: Back to the roots and back to the future. *Journal of Systems and Information Technology*, 14(2), 101-104. Retrieved from http://www.michaelhaenlein.eu/Publications/Kaplan,%20Andreas%20-%20Back%20to%20the%20roots%20and%20back%20to%20the%20future.pdf

Misra, S., Cheng, L., Genevie, J., & Yuan, M. (2014). The iPhone effect. *Environment and Behavior, 48*(2), 275-298. Retrieved from https://www.researchgate.net/publication/270730343_The_iPhone_Effect_The_Quality_of_In-Person_Social_Interactions_in_the_Presence_of_Mobile_Devices

Pearson Student Mobile Device Survey 2013. National Report: College Students. (2013). Retrieved from https://www.pearsoned.com/wp-content/uploads/Pearson-Student-Mobile-Device-Survey-2013-National-Report-on-College-Students-public-release.pdf

Pearson Student Mobile Device Survey 2015. National Report: College Students. (2015). Retrieved from https://www.pearsoned.com/wp-content/uploads/2015-Pearson-Student-Mobile-Device-Survey-College.pdf

Przybylski, A. K., & Weinstein, N. (2012). Can you connect with me now? How the presence of mobile communication technology influences face-to-face conversation quality. *Journal of Social and Personal Relationships*, *30*(3), 237–246. doi:10.1177/0265407512453827

KEY TERMS AND DEFINITIONS

Connectivism Theory: Learning theory for the digital age that explains how complex and constantly changing the social digital world is.

Constructivism Learning: Learning through experience, one develops their own understanding and knowledge.

Formal Learning: Structured learning with planned objectives.

Informal Learning: Learning through participation (unorganized, unstructured).

Learning Management System (LMS): A system for educational courses to be delivered, documented, and overseen.

Personal Social Media Use: Social media use unrelated to higher education.

Professional Social Media Use: Social media use for higher education, but not teaching or class.

Problem-Based Learning (PBL): Given a challenging situation, or complex problem, students are given extended time to investigate and work.

Social Learning: Learning from one another through social situations that can include observing, imitating, or modeling.

Teaching Social Media Use: Social media use specifically for teaching or class.

Chapter 2
The Use of Cloud-Computing to Promote Collaborative Learning in Higher Education

Melissa S. Martin
University of South Carolina – Aiken, USA

Rachel E. Hugues
State University of New York at Plattsburgh, USA

Alison Puliatte
State University of New York at Plattsburgh, USA

ABSTRACT

Generation Z students are inherently different than previous generations. These students may need adapted forms of instruction in order to match their learning styles. Collaborative learning can be adapted using cloud-computing, which helps students work together online and manage their interactions. These students may benefit from a technological twist to a common instructional strategy and are inclined to use online means of communication to complete coursework. Technology has dominated the educational experiences of these students and they are no strangers to collaborative work through e-learning platforms. Higher education institutions and instructors must develop the format of courses in order to meet the technological learning preferences of Generation Z.

DOI: 10.4018/978-1-5225-7763-8.ch002

INTRODUCTION

The students of Generation Z have started to graduate from high school and enter higher education. Because the students in this generation are inherently different than previous generations, it is important for university and college-level faculty to understand the key differences among students. Importantly, it is critical we learn the characteristics of these students in order to better meet their needs and provide appropriate, meaningful instruction, and opportunities for them to grow as learners.

Many college instructors embed collaborative learning throughout their courses because this instructional strategy supports positive academic outcomes (Umbach & Wawrzynski, 2005). However, is working together face-to-face the best way to provide access to course content for our Generation Z students? One way to incorporate their learning styles may be to implement cloud computing, which is a social networking system that fosters interactions online, during collaborative learning both inside and outside the face-to-face classroom. This chapter will outline the characteristics of Generation Z and describe how cloud-computing may be a beneficial resource to support collaborative learning for this connected generation.

CHARACTERISTICS OF GENERATION Z STUDENTS

With the arrival of Generation Z students on college campuses, it is important for faculty and staff to glean information about this vastly different generation. A major difference between this generation and the preceding generations is the use of technology, but that is not the only way in which these students are different than their predecessors. According to Seemiller and Grace (2016), this is the "most racially diverse generation" (p. 6) that the world has shaped into solution-oriented students who rely on technology. Because of their life experiences (e.g., September 11th and subsequent war on terrorism), these students provide a different perspective and seem to have different goals than the most recent students to graduate from college (e.g., the millennials). Seemiller & Grace (2016) conducted a nationwide study to learn more about this generation. Results indicate that this generation views themselves as responsible (69% of respondents), loyal (85%), and determined (74%). The authors of this study believe their experiences in the world have shaped these views and made them more self-sufficient.

Technology seems to be a major difference for Generation Zers, as they were born and raised in a "highly technological era" (Seemiller & Grace, 2016, p. 6). In fact, these students were born with technology that many of us did not have access to until much later in life. Smartphones and social media are commonplace and used throughout much, if not all, of their lives. In fact, these students are often referred to as "digital natives" (Brotheim, 2014; Turner, 2015; Seemiller & Grace, 2016) and they "identify themselves and their lives in digital terms" (Zorn, 2017, p. 61).

Because of this unending access to technology, Generation Zers are well-versed in how to find information. They have grown up knowing and using Google and other search engines to essentially have an abundance of knowledge at their fingertips (Zorn, 2017). Therefore, unlike previous students, Generation Zers likely do not need training related to technology skills when entering college. Oftentimes, they seem to arrive on campus knowing far more than the instructors about technological opportunities and advancements.

Not surprisingly, Generation Zers spend more time than other generations online and using media. According to Turner (2015), results from a study comparing online usage from 2004 to 2009 indicated that students spend over an additional hour more using media per day than previous generations of students. Almost a decade later, we venture that students in 2019 likely use media for an even greater amount of time than in 2009. This generation also prefers to use social media and other online platforms to communicate. Unlike previous generations, Generation Zers almost exclusively use technology to communicate with family members, friends, and peers. According to Brotheim (2014), these students receive about 100 text messages daily. Although this seems like an extensive amount of online interaction, it appears students in this generation value and prefer this method of communication.

Generation Zers also seem to value communicating online during coursework. Seemiller and Grace (2016) noted that these students prefer working remotely with their peers. Because they are often fluent technologically, it seems these students work well with others online (as opposed to traditional face-to-face). Moreover, they may prefer this option. It seems Generation Zers are somewhat less social in face-to-face interactions. The large amount of online interactions does not necessarily indicate these students have adequate social skills in classrooms or working face-to-face with peers on out-of-class work or projects. In fact, Turner (2015) noted that students in Generation Z may actually lack social skills because of the use of technology. Therefore, the decreased face-to-face interactions may be, in fact, also hindering their social skills development. Moreover, Igel and Urquahart (2012) noted that students in this generation are often not "team players" because of their limited meaningful interactions with people not online. In other words, students may find it difficult to work with others. Brotheim (2014) echoed these sentiments and indicated that Generation Zers not only lack social skills, they may also have difficulty empathizing and understanding others' points of views or opinions.

It is also important to note that Generation Z students do not dislike face-to-face interactions all together. These students actually prefer to meet in person to outline and plan before working independently online (Seemiller & Grace, 2016). Therefore, they still crave some interaction before working alone. Since collaborative learning is an integral part of many college classrooms, college-level faculty must find a balance between Generation Z students' desire to work minimally face-to-face with peers and their preference to work independently in order to meet the needs of their students.

COLLABORATIVE LEARNING IN COLLEGE

Collaborative learning has been researched for decades. This instructional strategy was first implemented in K-12 schools (Summers, Beretvas, Svinicki, & Gorin, 2005), and it was later utilized in post-secondary education. Chickering and Gamson (1987) outlined the principles of effective undergraduate education, and among these principles included the implementation of activities that build cooperation among students. These researchers noted the "team" mentality helps students develop content knowledge (i.e., learning).

Although the research related to collaborative learning in college developed later, much research exists supporting its use with students enrolled in post-secondary education. Ventimiglia (1993) noted that the use of collaborative learning made the content of courses "more meaningful and useful" (p. 6) because students could build their own knowledge. This allows the learner to have ownership over his/her coursework (Ventimiglia, 1993). Additionally, Umbach and Wawrzynski (2005) noted that "collaborative learning techniques were positively related with levels of academic challenges and student-faculty interactions" (p. 165). Thus, this learning strategy promotes rigor and engagement (Umbach & Wawrzynski, 2005).

Many college courses incorporate some type of collaborative learning throughout the semester. Although this instructional strategy is common, the terminology used to describe it differs. Collaborative and cooperative learning are often used synonymously in literature and conversations. However, there are distinctions between the two strategies.

Collaborative learning is the "umbrella term" often used to describe students working together with each other and possibly the instructor (Goodsell, Maher, Tinto, Smith, & MacGregor, 1992; Davidson & Major, 2014). This strategy provides an opportunity for students to learn together, which is beneficial because many scholars believe learning is a social experience (Goodsell et al., 1992). Davidson and Major

(2014) outlined the stages of the collaborative process including engagement, exploration, transformation, presentation, and reflection. These five stages help outline this strategy – the essence is working together for *one* goal. During this process, however, students may only be held accountable in terms of team success or failure, not individual success or failure. In college, for example, students may be asked to create an interactive presentation about how to teach students with autism. One student may be asked to research strategies, while another may be responsible for the actual presentation (e.g., PowerPoint). A third group member may need to find activities to demonstrate the ways to teach students with autism, and the final groupmate may need to develop an assessment for participants. The only accountability these students have would be the team success. Ultimately, in collaborative learning, they are all responsible for the one culminating project.

Collaborative learning differs from cooperative learning in terms of this accountability. *Cooperative learning* is an instructional strategy that requires students to work together, but not necessarily on the exact same project (Davidson & Major, 2014). Two commonly used cooperative learning tasks include think-pair-share and jigsaw (Davidson & Major, 2014). These strategies assign a specific student to think and learn independently before coming back together in a group to share. For example, if students were assigned to learn about ways in which to teach students with autism using cooperative learning, one student could research the characteristics of students with autism, while another could research math strategies. A third student could investigate reading strategies, and a fourth could learn about social skills training. Then, after learning on their own, students could come together to share (either formally or informally) about the topics they were assigned to research. Because of this accountability, Jones and Jones (2008) noted that this type of learning "is one of the most effective ways for students to maximize their own learning and the academic accomplishments of their classmates" (p. 63).

GENERATION Z AND COLLABORATIVE LEARNING

Because of the proven positive impact of both collaborative and cooperative learning, these two strategies are commonly used in the college classroom. But, how do these strategies impact Generation Z students? Do faculty members need to modify or adapt the way in which they implement these strategies for this connected generation?

Generation Z students prefer to work independently and online, yet they do not nix group work altogether. Hope (2016) indicated that students from this generation do not mind group work if it stems from work they completed independently beforehand. Based on this, we can assume Generation Z students may benefit (and possibly enjoy) cooperative learning in which they are responsible for researching information and then meeting with their group to share. This accountability is vital as it requires all group members to contribute in order to help learn content and skills.

Although we may need to help facilitate social interactions, Generation Z students typically do not need help with technology. Among the connected generation, these students may know far more than college-level faculty about the technological options and advancements. We propose using this strength (tech) to help compensate for a possible challenge (social skills). Therefore, we posit the use of cloud-computing may give Generation Zers the opportunity to communicate and work together on their terms.

CLOUD-COMPUTING IN HIGHER EDUCATION

Cloud-computing has become a technological phenomenon that makes accessing computing services and sharing or retrieving data over the internet synchronous (Denton, 2012). According to the National Institute of Standards and Technology (NIST), cloud-computing is defined as a computer social networking system that conveniently configures information into a shared database (networks, servers, storage, applications and services) in order to foster efficient interactions amongst its users (Ashtari & Eydgahi, 2017). This agent for effortless and seamless network gratification is particularly alluring for those who make up Generation Z. For those who are classified as Generation Z, cloud computing has become a tremendous factor that influences their experiences with cooperative learning efforts. As the members of this generation enter higher educational settings, the use of e-learning systems has become the new norm.

Online social platforms, such as Google Apps for Education (GAFE), serve as tools for 21st century learners because they create a hybrid option for education and online communication (Brown & Hocutt, 2015). GAFE is an accumulation of free cloud-based Google Apps that store all user information to a Google Drive system. Within the Google Drive functions (e.g., Google Docs, Sheets, Slide, and Hangouts), users have access to various apps in order to communicate, create, and collaborate (Brown & Hocutt, 2015). This Google app platform allows its users to engage in interactive content and maximize productivity when participating in "global knowledge building" (Awuah, 2015, p.13). In the eyes of Generation Zers, this is the epitome of efficiency considering 41% of their time is spent apart from a classroom on computers, phones, and other connecting devices (Seemiller & Grace, 2016).

Institutions of higher education are transitioning towards initiating cloud-based technologies, such as GAFE, to satisfy the tech savvy students of Generation Z who are accustomed to a lifestyle of instant gratification. In fact, it was reported that in 2012, 43% of higher education organizations began or continued to utilize a cloud-computing platform to enhance the academic experiences of its students (Ashtari & Eydgahi, 2017). This transition involves using services such as GAFE to connect the personal learning environments (PLEs) of the students to any virtual learning environments (VLEs) and face-to-face interactions in learning (Round, 2011). Higher education establishments now find it customary to provide e-learning platforms for its students, and have even invested in other supplementary learning management systems (LMS) to utilize cloud-computing methods and broaden content accessibility. Some of the common LMS that institutions are known to use for courses and other means of communication include Blackboard Learn, Canvas, Desire2Learn, Moodle, and Sakai (Linder, Bruenjes, & Smith, 2017).

GENERATION Z PREFERENCES FOR CLOUD-COMPUTING

Cloud-based communication follows a constructivist approach to collaborative and cooperative learning and aids students to facilitate group dialogue, activate prior knowledge, control the difficulty level, and combine their metacognitive skills (Denton, 2012). Generation Zers are highly motivated by solving problems in a realistic and authentic way. They also tend to focus on logic-based and experiential learning to dictate how they interpret information. Both of these approaches follow an organizational foundation, which explains why these particular students find the cloud-computing fitting for their just-in-time ideas (Seemiller & Grace, 2016). They can attend class or access the online materials offered by instructors, and use the information saved on the cloud-computing platforms to learn and share any extended research or answer clarifying questions with peers (Seemiller and Grace, 2016). This supports their get-it-when-you-want-it preferences because Generation Z students want to structure their learning toward an intrapersonal approach, while still having the flexibility to embed social learning aspects into instruction (Seemiller & Grace, 2016). They are comfortable with learning independently because of their self-reliant mindset and feel the need to set their own pace (Seemiller & Grace, 2016).

Collaborative learning, which is a broader strategy in which students work with each other and possibly the instructor, is frequently used in higher education. But, this strategy is less regulated and students have less accountability as the achievement is rated based on a team success or failure – not individual. Because of the desire to work independently by many Generation Zers, college-level faculty may need to adapt group projects that lack individual structure. Moreover, we may need to facilitate effective face-to-face group interactions in order to help these students develop appropriate social skills. We can no longer assume they know how to work collaboratively together. Instead, we may need to be very planful and thoughtful when preparing and implementing group activities and projects. This may include having a structured time in class to meet with their peers. Or, perhaps, groups may need more support during the planning process to divide the work in order to work independently later during the project timeline. This approach also may be beneficial because, as Seemiller and Grace (2016) noted, these students actually prefer to meet in person to outline and plan before working independently online.

Students prefer the option to utilize web-based collaboration largely because of its convenience and the ability to retrieve stored data from personal devices at any time (Ashtari & Eydgahi, 2017). This is ideal for students who have grown accustomed to the use of multimedia to support their various learning styles, and compliments their proficiency with technology (Round, 2011). These students are also attracted to the idea that their work is continuously saved to a cloud storage database, and there is not a need to back-up data (Ashtari & Eydgahi, 2017). The cloud relieves the fear that work will be lost in tech abyss, which then diminishes any of the computer anxiety that apprehensive students experience. Along with the collaborative aspects to cloud-computing, it also has a self-serving element in that students can generate online portfolios and personal documents that can be shared globally in a matter of a few clicks (Ashtari & Eydgahi, 2017).

Members of Generation Z have a high level of computer self-efficacy and expect to be granted information in an immediate fashion, along with being granted access to each other (Ashtari & Eydgahi, 2017). The GAFE apps allow for diverse conversations amongst peers and instructors, hold people accountable for contributions made because of the detailed log of saved activity on a document, provide the opportunity for student-centered instant feedback, make drafting and peer editing a synchronous and asynchronous process, and give students an autonomous option to control how they conduct a collaborative assignment (Brown & Hocutt, 2015).

The use of cloud-based communication is desirable for the students of Generation Z because of their quick decision-making tendencies, giving them the feeling of transparency and empowerment (Seemiller & Grace, 2016). The trend of online forums for cloud-based interactions allow students to create a thread or submission for any relevant topic and have their peers comment and share their insight. The online platforms and GAFE apps that offer discussion boards saved to the cloud are similar to the popular social media discussion boards that students use recreationally. The most well-known of these online forum platforms is Reddit (Seemiller & Grace, 2016). Higher education institutions have incorporated GAFE apps and other online communication tools for fostering virtual communities, making the learning experience for students relevant to pop culture and masking the reluctance for cooperative work.

Most students, even members of other generations, have a less than thrilled response to group assignments. Typically, the students of Generation Z tend to rely on combining individual work instead of verbally collaborating or participating in extended meeting times for these types of assignments. Even though a group project was assigned, students will break up the objective into smaller tasks and divide them out amongst each other. After each individual's tasks are put together, roles are assigned for the editing and finalizing process. In doing this, students are still able to practice their autonomy and leadership tendencies (Seemiller & Grace, 2016). Generation Zers have redefined the meaning of a group project by use of the cloud-computing database and have essentially removed the traditional components of interacting from the equation.

CLOUD-COMPUTING DRAWBACKS FOR EDUCATION

There are some limitations to this instantaneous cooperative working style. The access to communication through technology over these cloud-computing platforms does limit the chance for in-person meetings, despite the value that students place on this. This leaves Generation Zers with insufficient opportunities to practice authentic in-person communication skills, resulting in inferior interpersonal skills compared to previous generations (Seemiller & Grace, 2016). This is especially true when examining how the students of Generation Z interpret leadership. Students of Generation Z respond well to an organized command chain, and their proactive mentality creates individual leadership confidence. In fact, 60% of Generation Z students consider themselves as being better equipped in terms of leadership qualities (Seemiller & Grace, 2016). If every student assigned to a group project views themselves as the prime leader, the cooperative aspect suffers because of delegative controversy. When looking at the higher order thinking capabilities of students, the instant access to research and online information makes the investigative process simplified. With that being said, the critical thinking skills of Generation Z may be compromised because there is less of a need to spend time analyzing information and developing rationales (Seemiller & Grace, 2016).

HIGHER EDUCATION PROFESSIONALS USING CLOUD-COMPUTING

The students of Generation Z have set a new wave of expectations for higher education in that they want to learn on their own time and in the way they see best fit (Seemiller & Grace, 2016). Students want to have access to the resources to make educational gains, as well as have the ability to reinforce this learning through socially cooperative opportunities with their peers. In a way, institutions and instructors are forced to make these accommodations and adjust to student preferences because that is their most conducive learning approach (Seemiller & Grace, 2016). Educators use the cloud-computing platforms and other LMS to manage courses and monitor the academic achievements of the students within them (Linder, Bruenjes, & Smith, 2017). There are tools embedded in the systems that allow for professors to organize the content, track the students, assess student performances, monitor learner growth, and actually monitor the collaborative interactions (Linder, Bruenjes, & Smith, 2017).

Research suggests that students who take courses that encourage "dialogic interactivity involving interaction with content resources (e.g., with quizzes, simulations, games, interactive tutorials, etc.) and with people (e.g., with peer learners and teachers in forums, online role plays, wikis, blogs, etc.)" have more effective and sustainable learning outcomes (Linder, Bruenjes, Smith, 2017, p. 28). The combination of these synchronous and asynchronous tools allows students to satisfy their needs for real time cooperative activity, while still engaging in higher order thinking provoked by peers and instructors (Linder, Bruenjes, & Smith, 2017). In order for students to practice these skills, teachers can use specific strategies to integrate cloud-computing in their instruction that are external from the classroom. Some higher education institutions offer a modified option for incorporating cloud-computing platforms and the traditional classroom design for learning. Known as a hybrid classroom, students are able to have that initial face-to-face interaction that they feel is necessary to make meaning of assignments, form connections, delegate roles, and establish the expectations for further communication (Linder, Bruenjes, & Smith, 2017). It is important to note that Generation Z students are not fully inclined to replace all face-to-face interactions with virtual ones. Rather, they value real life experiences to read expressions and emotions, before moving on to more convenient methods of interactions (Seemiller & Grace, 2016). In fact, 83% of Generation Zers still find face-to-face interactions to be valuable (Seemiller & Grace, 2016).

Professors have learned that students do not absorb the course content if it is simply posted on these online cloud-based platforms. Students not only need to have exposure, but also need to actually interact with the material, and engage in a cooperative approach to understanding (Linder, Bruenjes, & Smith, 2017). This is where the collaborative features of the GAFE apps and the other LMS systems come into effect. Cloud-computing and creating an online inquiry community can be done through group projects, peer assessments, student constructed presentations, simultaneous class discussions, collaborative reflections, shared writing, learning illustrations, class inventories, cooperative rubric construction, and informative publishing (Denton, 2012). By using cloud-computing platforms to complete these collaborative assignments, the construction and feedback process becomes fluid. For example, students may be asked to assess a writing project for one of their peers and fill out a rubric. Instead of each student bringing a hard copy of their papers to class, they have the convenient option of sharing the work with their peers over the cloud drive. The teacher can then share an online version of the rubric. When conducting the assessment, students can open the shared documents and simultaneously add their comments. The entire process is an efficient and reliable method of sharing documents which can all be done in or out of the classroom.

Teachers and higher education institutions are drawn to cloud-computing platforms because of its economic benefits (Ashtari & Eydgahi, 2017). Technological outlets and computer usage for learning are anticipated by the student body, and cloud-based systems provide a low-cost avenue for collaborative learning. Universities and colleges have adopted the cloud because it allows for resources and equipment to be sustainable for extended periods of time and solves the issue of limited storage in the typical computer hardware systems (Behrend, Wiebe, London, & Johnson, 2011). In addition, college classes are typically lecture based and professors rely on presentation slides using the cloud. When these lecture notes are saved to the cloud, they become available at any location with internet accessibility and can easily be shared with students or colleagues (Aaron & Roche, 2011). Higher education institutions can now satisfy the needs of more students because of the flexibility factor when students go to complete coursework. For example, student and faculty commuters are able to access the materials needed for a class anywhere they have access to the Internet, which saves money in travel costs. This alone increases the appeal for students and attitudes of satisfaction within an institution (Behrend, Wiebe, London, & Johnson, 2011).

CONCLUSION

The use of cloud-computing in higher education for Generation Zers may transform the way students approach collaborative work. The online platforms for GAFE and other e-learning platforms embed this technological means for communication and satisfy the learning needs for Generation Zers. Higher education institutions are supporting positive educational outcomes of these tech savvy students by incorporating cloud computing resources that provide instant access to information and support collaborative work through online interactions.

REFERENCES

Aaron, L. S., & Roche, C. M. (2011). Teaching learning, and collaborating in the cloud: Applications of cloud computing for educators in post-secondary institutions. *Journal of Educational Technology Systems*, *40*(2), 95–111. doi:10.2190/ET.40.2.b

Ashtari, S., & Eydgahi, A. (2016). Student perceptions of cloud applications effectiveness in higher education. *Journal of Computational Science*, *23*, 173–180. doi:10.1016/j.jocs.2016.12.007

Awuah, L. J. (2015). Supporting 21st-century teaching and learning: The role of google apps for education (GAFE). *Journal of Instructional Research, 4*, 12-22.

Behrend, T. S., Wiebe, E. N., London, J. E., & Johnson, E. C. (2011). Cloud computing adoption and usage in community colleges. *Behaviour & Information Technology*, *30*(2), 231–240. doi:10.1080/0144929X.2010.489118

Brotheim, H. (2014). Introducing generation Z. *American Jails*, 15-20.

Brown, M. E., & Hocutt, D. L. (2015). Learning to use, useful for learning: A usability study of Google apps for education. *Journal of Usability Studies*, *10*(4), 160–181.

Chickering, A. W., & Gamson, Z. F. (1987). Seven principles for good practice in undergraduate education. *AAHE Bulletin*, *3*, 2–6.

Davidson, N., & Major, C. H. (2014). Boundary crossing: Cooperative learning, collaborative learning, and problem-based learning. *Journal on Excellence in College Teaching*, *25*(3&4), 7–55.

Denton, D. (2012). Enhancing instruction through constructivism, cooperative learning, and cloud computing. *TechTrends*, *56*(4), 34–41. doi:10.100711528-012-0585-1

Goodsell, A.S., Maher, M.R., Tinto, V., Smith, B.L., & MacGregor, J. (1992). *Collaborative learning: A sourcebook for higher education*. National Center on Postsecondary Teaching, Learning, and Assessment.

Hope, J. (2016). Get your campus ready for Generation Z. *Dean & Provost: Practical Advice and Strategies for Academic Leaders*, *17*(8), 5–7. doi:10.1002/dap.30177

Igel, C., & Urquahart, V. (2012). Generation Z, meet cooperative learning. *Middle School Journal*, *43*(4), 16–21. doi:10.1080/00940771.2012.11461816

Jones, K.A. & Jones, J.L. (2008). Making cooperative learning work in the college classroom: An application of the 'five pillars' of cooperative learning to post-secondary instruction. *The Journal of Effective Teaching, 8*(2), 61-76.

Liao, H. (2014). Examining the role of collaborative learning in a public speaking course. *College Teaching, 62*(2), 47–54. doi:10.1080/87567555.2013.855891

Linder, K. E., Bruenjes, L. S., & Smith, S. A. (2017). Hybrid platforms, tools, and resources. *New Directions for Teaching and Learning, 2017*(149), 27–36. doi:10.1002/tl.20224

Round, K. (2011). E-Learning 2.0: Cloud computing and the online learner. *Journal of Applied Learning Technology, 1*(4), 24–27.

Seemiller, C., & Grace, M. (2016). *Generation Z goes to college*. San Francisco, CA: Jossey-Bass.

Summers, J. J., Bertetvas, S. N., Svinicki, M. D., & Gorin, J. S. (2005). Evaluating collaborative learning and community. *Journal of Experimental Education, 73*(3), 165–188. doi:10.3200/JEXE.73.3.165-188

Turner, A. (2015). Generation Z: Technology and social interest. *Journal of Individual Psychology, 71*(2), 103–113. doi:10.1353/jip.2015.0021

Umbach, P. D., & Wawrzynski, M. R. (2005). Faculty do matter: The role of college faculty in student learning and engagement. *Research in Higher Education, 46*(2), 153–184. doi:10.100711162-004-1598-1

Ventimiglia, L.M. (1993). Cooperative learning at the college level. *The NEA Higher Education Journal*, 5-30.

Zorn, R. L. (2017). Coming in 2017: A new generation of graduate students – the Z generation. *College and University, 92*(1), 61–63.

Chapter 3
Expert Commentary on New Opportunities and Challenges for Women Within Saudi Distance Education Institutions

Eman Walabe
University of Ottawa, Canada

Rocci Luppicini
University of Ottawa, Canada

ABSTRACT

Access to post-secondary education is an essential condition for advancing women's leadership opportunities. This chapter provides an expert commentary on how distance education in Saudi Arabia contributes to the advancement of female leadership opportunities by providing women greater access to education and new opportunities for leadership roles. However, despite the new opportunities that distance education offers to Saudi women, there are pervasive challenges that hinder them from acquiring leadership roles in education. The expert commentary draws on professional experience and research to provide insight into the advantages and disadvantages of distance education to prepare Saudi women to be leaders in higher education. It also offers recommendations on how to better leverage distance education experience for female students and instructors by applying the rules of netiquette in Saudi online learning environments.

DOI: 10.4018/978-1-5225-7763-8.ch003

INTRODUCTION

I believe the future of Saudi higher education, and especially the successful implementation of e-learning, will be driven by women faculty, despite the difficulties they face. The women faculty I worked with showed great determination and a commitment to change which was not always present with the male faculty. (Bates, 2009)

This chapter assumes that a holistic picture of women in leadership requires a systemic understanding of women in leadership, as well as the underlying drivers that shape it. One key driver that this chapter focuses on is Distance Education and the greater access to learning and opportunities for future leadership roles it provides to women in Saudi Arabia. Tony Bates, a Canadian consultant who runs many e-learning workshops and provides e-learning training across Saudi Arabia, was one of the first international experts to recognize the potential of e-learning to leverage leadership opportunities for woman within Saudi society. Indeed, leadership opportunities are expanding, as Hanan Al-Ahmadi observes that "Saudi women are slowly but definitely assuming high positions that include deputy minister, university president, Shura Council consultants, board members of Chambers of commerce and many other new and exciting positions in both the public and private sectors" (2011, p. 150). Within the education sector, the highest leadership position ever held by a Saudi woman is deputy minister of education, first held by Norah al Faiz in 2009 (House, 2012).

Gender equality in terms of women's leadership not unique to Saudi Arabia; rather, it is a global concern. However, despite strides in recent years, as Carli and Eagly (2017) note, "Gender equality remains a distant goal, with men currently possessing considerably more power and authority than women in organizations and governments. Patriarchy, although weakened, still prevails" (245). For example, academic women tend to occupy lower level positions worldwide (Airini et al., 2011), while men still hold more powerful positions within Higher Education as well as in other areas (David, 2017). This issue was explored by Davidson and Burke (2004), who invited authors from twenty-one countries, including both developed and developing countries, to discuss the status of women in management in each of their countries in general topics such as women in education and their country's legislation supporting women's advancement. The main finding was that women were not holding senior management positions at a comparable rate with their male counterparts (Davidson & Burke, 2004). Seven years later, Davidson and Burke (2011) decided to update their first book and requested some of the authors who participated previously in that book to update their chapters in presenting the current status of women at management and expressing the changes that has occurred within the previous six or seven years. Additionally, they invited new authors to represent new countries and cultures. The main finding was that in general women have made advancements at lower-management positions; however, they are still marginalized within senior management positions (Davidson & Burke, 2011).

Gender equality is a particularly complex challenge to women's leadership in Arabic societies where culturally-entrenched gender roles create formidable barriers for women seeking leadership roles in society. Research has indicated that the unique Arab culture constitute a different set of challenges for women "(Hodges, 2017). Arab societies are still considered to be highly masculine with significant gender-role variances (Omair, 2008). There are a variety of reasons why Saudi women have received unequal opportunities compared to Saudi men within traditional Saudi society, including social, economic, and cultural aspects (Saleh & Luppicini, 2017). Family obligations, geography, limited female mobility, gender segregation, and cultural norms create Higher Education access challenges for Saudi women

However, within contemporary Saudi society, one major reason for optimism concerning leadership opportunities for women stems from the advancement of information communication technologies (ICT's) and the rise of online social networks. The importance of ICT's to women's leadership is particularly salient in countries like Saudi Arabia where women have historically experienced restricted mobility compared to male family members who have power and authority over female family members (Luppicini & Saleh, 2017). In a recent survey research study completed by 248 divorced Saudi women, Luppicini and Saleh (2017) found that online social networks played an important role in helping divorced Saudi women navigate social, psychological, economic, and legal challenges faced in society.

In an effort to leverage future opportunities for women in leadership, online learning within Distance Education institutions is an attractive option for female students who may otherwise not have the chance to be educated. Not only does it help address women's restricted mobility and provide greater access to post-secondary education, it also opens the door for more engagement of female instructors to educate students in Saudi Arabia. Therefore, the purpose of this chapter is to explore how Distance Education in Saudi Arabia advances female leadership opportunities by providing women with education and greater access to leadership roles. That leads to the research question: "What are the current opportunities and challenges for women within Saudi Distance Education institutions?"

BACKGROUND

The history of education in Saudi Arabia starts shortly after King Abdulaziz unified the kingdom, when he established the Directorate of Education and created government schools in 1925 (Rugh, 2002). In 1953, the Ministry of Education was established to supervise boys' schools (AlMunajjed, 2009). It was only in 1960 when the Kingdom of Saudi Arabia opened schools for girls and established the General Presidency of Girls' Education (Rugh, 2002). Girls' schools at all levels—elementary, intermediate, high school and university—were under the supervision of the Department of Religious Guidance until 2002, while boys' education was supervised by the Ministry of Education (Hamdan, 2005). This was to guarantee that girls' education did not go beyond its main purpose (Hamdan, 2005), which was considered to be teaching her "to perform her duty in life, be an ideal and successful housewife and a good mother, ready to do jobs suitable to her nature such as teaching, nursing and medical treatment" (Al-Rasheed, 2013, p. 90). In 2002, the supervision of girls' education was finally included under the Ministry of Education with boys as a result of requests from both the general public and the government (Hamdan, 2005). However, the educational system in Saudi Arabia remains gender-segregated at all levels with the exception of a few colleges (Zuhur, 2011; Alwasal & Solaiman, 2012).

Despite pervasive constraints for females within Saudi Higher Education, the enrollment of Saudi women in universities has experienced an astonishing 512% growth rate between 1990 and 2014, compared to men's enrollment growth rate of 339.2% (Jamjoom & Kelly, 2013). Currently, women represent 50% of the Saudi population, 60% of students in Saudi universities and 25% of recipients of overseas scholarships (Thompson, 2015). These accomplishments, along with King Abdullah's 2013 initiative in nominating thirty women to be the first female cohort in the Saudi parliament, provide "inspiration to women in general and to young women in particular to aspire to leadership positions" (Hamdan et al., 2016, p. 37).

During the early 2000s, Higher Education in the Kingdom of Saudi Arabia introduced a new way of learning that utilizes technology to teach online (Aljabre, 2012). Since that time, Saudi universities have been using technology and the Internet in teaching and learning to eliminate economic and geographic boundaries (Alsaqqaf, 2015). Online learning, along with Distance Education using online means, has been viewed by Saudi educators as a method of increasing the accessibility to Higher Education (Hamdan, 2014). It offers access to many Saudi students who desire to pursue their Higher Education despite constraints such as having a full-time job or living in a remote area, which previously made them unable to attend face-to-face classes (Hamdan, 2014). Thus, the Ministry of Education in Saudi Arabia has begun to recognize the need of implementing online technologies and to offer opportunities for the growing number of students graduating from high school (Hamdan, 2015).

THE EMERGENCE OF DISTANCE EDUCATION IN SAUDI ARABIA

It is also important to consider how the demographics of Saudi Arabia affect their education needs. Most of the population in Saudi Arabia is relatively young, with those aged 20 and under forming 50 percent of the nation's 27 million people (Quraishi, 2012; Alrashidi, 2014). Researchers estimate that the percentage of Saudi youth will grow by a third every eight years (AlMegren & Yassin, 2013). Because of this high rate of growth in the Saudi population, many high school graduates are unable to find places in conventional Saudi universities (Hamdan, 2014). In 2011, the total number of high school graduates was 360,000 students; however, the Saudi Ministry of Education had limited the universities' capacities to only 306,000 students (Ghamdi et al., 2011). Similarly, in 2013, the total number of high school graduates was 380,000 and only 360,000 students were accepted; therefore, about 20,000 students did not have the opportunity to pursue higher education (Alturki, 2014). Online education offered the opportunity of expanding the total number of students who can be enrolled in Saudi universities without the need to increase the physical capacity of the universities and associated facilities (Hamdan, 2014). Another important factor to consider is that the technology adoption rate in Saudi Arabia is also one of the highest in the world (Alshahrani & Ally, 2017). For example, according to the Saudi Ministry of Communications and Information Technology, the total number of mobile broadband subscriptions continues to increase and reached around 35.2 million households by the end of Q2 2015, with a penetration rate of 113% (Alshahrani & Ally, 2017).

THE CURRENT OPPORTUNITIES AND CHALLENGES FOR SAUDI WOMEN IN DISTANCE EDUCATION

In the past, Saudi women were required to get permission from fathers, brothers, husbands or guardians to fulfill daily needs. This included "permission to go to school, obtain a passport, attend university, work, get married, be admitted to hospital, obtain an official government identity card, and buy property or a car, as well as permission to travel abroad" (Thompson, 2015, p. 19). Recently, in May 2017, the Saudi government relaxed the male guardianship rule to only being required to provide their female relatives with permission to travel and get married (Aldubais, 2017). However, this still creates an obstacle for Saudi women to access Higher Education, as they are not always able to obtain permission to travel to the university (AlMunajjed, 2009). To cope with these cultural and religious rules, Distance Education opened the door for female students to pursue their education and created more employment opportunities for female instructors working in Saudi Higher Education.

Female students often do not attend universities due to factors such as early marriage, motherhood and family obligations, or mobility restrictions (Al Alhareth et al., 2013; Al-Asmari & Khan, 2014). As it offers a way to overcome some of these constraints, online learning or distance learning in Saudi Arabia has gained a lot of popularity in recent years, particularly amongst the young married women who otherwise find it a challenge to pursue their education (Yamin, 2013). Middle-aged Saudi women (who carry home and family responsibilities) also find that Distance Education provides an opportunity to become educated (Alrashidi, 2014). As one female student put it according to Hamdan (2014):

I believe that culture is influencing online education because it is not simple for us girls to travel abroad for higher education in our society. Therefore, I think that it motivates the female to turn to studying online due to our limited options. (Hamdan, 2014, p. 325)

In addition, Distance Education breaks traditional face-to-face social gender barriers and can provide anonymity, which helps female students in Saudi Arabia. Through the virtual learning environment, they can seek knowledge from either male or female instructors with no cultural limitations. According to Chester and Gwynne (1998), anonymous online environments can increase student participation, especially for students who are constrained by race, age, and gender. That is, Distance Education enhances effective communication between female students and male instructors; this would not be possible in a face-to-face learning environment because of religious and cultural constraints. For instance, a female student noted the effect of technology on communication with male instructors, saying that "as female students, technology did not only allow us to learn and benefit from good male teachers, it has also helped us to easily communicate with our teachers, and exchange information and experiences with each other as a learning community" (Al-Shehri, 2017, p. 41).

It does not only benefit female students to have a platform that allows them to interact effectively with their male instructors in the virtual learning environment; female instructors also benefit from the online environment. For example, in the Saudi Electronic University, male and female instructors can conduct synchronous virtual meetings together from all the branches of the university around the Kingdom. In that way, female instructors will not miss any of the important information discussed in the male instructors' section and will also be able to make their own contributions in these meetings. It should be noted, however, that cultural norms prohibit female instructors from teaching male students, even when using the same tools that male instructors use to teach female students.

Up until recently, very few researchers have addressed the advantages that female instructors can receive from online learning (Asiri et al., 2012; Al-Asmari & Khan, 2014). Studies have indicated that there is a significant shortage of female instructors in Saudi universities, which results in these e-courses being taught by male instructors (Al-Khalifa, 2010; Asiri et al., 2012; Al-Asmari & Khan, 2014). Furthermore, there are specific modifications that must be applied in the utilization of technology for male instructors so that the course does not violate cultural values while ensuring the quality of education the female students receive (Quraishi, 2012). An example of this kind of modification includes setting up a two-way audio connection but only one-way video connection, so that the female students can see the male instructor, but he cannot see them.

Despite the considerable shortage of female lecturers in Saudi universities, however, they have nevertheless shown their initiative towards online learning. Badrul Khan, an American consultant who runs various e-learning workshops in 2010 at Saudi universities noticed the Saudi female instructors' initiatives toward online learning, saying that "the girls who participated in workshops are very serious and they take it very seriously" (Khan, 2010). In the subsequent years, some actions have been taken to try to help advance female instructors. For example, in 2015, the Open Education Consortium (OEC) entered into a partnership with the National Center for e-Learning and Distance Education (NCeL) in Saudi Arabia to provide a year-long, comprehensive eLearning Pioneers Program particularly for Saudi female instructors (Daly & Young, 2016). One of the motivations in forming the partnership between OEC and NCeL is because "cultural and religious restrictions on females can make online learning an attractive option for them" (Daly & Young, 2016). The program is focused on sharing the principles of online learning in the United States and providing mentoring and internships to prepare Saudi female faculty and university leaders with skills in online and blending learning (Daly & Young, 2016). Mary Lou Forward, executive director of Open Education Consortium, describes the program in this way:

The impetus to bring Saudi Arabian female teachers to the U.S. to learn our teaching strategies is strong. For the first time in history, we can give woman teachers the opportunity and the edge that they need to lead education practices in Saudi Arabia. The OEC is proud to bring together some of the top U.S. institutions of education in the world to provide these renowned, top-tier programs to this well-skilled set of faculty members and teachers. (Tam, 2015)

By providing a strong foundation in e-learning tools and techniques, pedagogy, and learning theory, the goal is for participants to be able to use these new skills and strategies to better educate the Saudi population of girls and women (Tam, 2015).

In the eLearning Pioneers Program, 25 female faculty members and 25 female administrators were nominated from 13 universities across the Kingdom of Saudi Arabia (Tam, 2015). The program's training was in four phases. In the first phase, the participants were trained in Riyadh for three months to gain the Online Learning Consortium (OLC) teaching certificate (Tam, 2015). In the second phase, they participated in placements at American universities beginning July 20th, 2015 for a period of two weeks (Tam, 2015). The placements were provided by the College of the Canyons, the University of New Hampshire, the University of Massachusetts, Tufts University, and the University of California, Irvine (Tam, 2015). In these American institutions, the female participants met 154 faculty and administrators, participated in student panels, visited academic technology centers, and had 220 hours of training, meetings, tours, and discussions about pedagogies and techniques for online teaching (Daly & Young, 2016). After they returned to Saudi Arabia, they began the third phase of the program by attending 178 hours of online workshops, webinars and MOOCs focusing on online and blended learning, including techniques and strategies to enhance the interaction between the students and the instructors in an online environment (Daly & Young, 2016). In the last phase of the program, the participants attended international online conferences in the United States and Germany (Daly & Young, 2016), including Online Educe (Berlin, Germany), EADTU (Hagen, Germany), and Online Learning Consortium (Orlando, Florida) (Daly & Young, 2016). At the end of the program, one of participants reflected on her experience by saying that "the program has provided me with great opportunities to understand e-learning context in US, KSA and Europe" (Daly & Young, 2016). Indeed, the eLearning Pioneers Program has equipped female faculty and university leaders with the best practices in using technology for teaching and learning (Abdul-Alim, 2015).

Despite the important advancements in the number of female students participating in online courses as well as the increasing number of female instructors being given the tools they need to succeed, online learning does have some drawbacks. In her study, Hamdan (2014) highlights some of the challenges of online learning faced by Saudi female students. For example, female students in Hamdan's (2014) study indicated that online learning has a negative effect on them because it reduces the frequency of face-to-face interactions with their instructors and peers. Some other female students also agreed that online communication has the disadvantage of sometimes sending a different message than that which is intended (Hamdan, 2014). In addition, some of the female students indicated that it is occasionally impossible or extremely time-consuming to log onto the Internet (Hamdan, 2014). While these and similar challenges may be shared by both male and female students who experience online-only education, these issues nevertheless have a greater effect on women in Saudi universities as women are more likely to rely exclusively on e-learning.

Censorship is also a concern in Distance Education and e-learning, particularly in counties like Saudi Arabia where there are well entrenched regulations in place governing Internet content rules and restrictions. Most Middle Eastern countries commonly practice some form of censorship to control the Internet access (Luppicini, 2010; Mirza & Al-Abdulkareem, 2011). It has been demonstrated that the Saudi centralized server is destructive to learning because it restricts access to online resources related to controversial issues, such as those of a political, sexual or religious nature, even though these websites discuss these issues within an educational context (Hamdan, 2015). This is problematic since, as Hamdan (2015: 203) has stated, "thinking should not be restricted or censored, regardless of the subject." Therefore, while it is known that centralization helps to standardize the practical procedures of Saudi Arabia's e-learning programs, it also may restrict the students from accessing many useful web resources (Hamdan, 2015).

Another problem facing e-learning is the digital divide issue, which refers to the accessibility of the Internet and the digital literacy gap in Saudi Arabia. As Luppicini (2010) indicated, there is a gap between regions and people who have access to the Internet and to those who do not. Even though the growth of the information and communication technology (ICT) in Saudi Arabia has been steady and continuing (AlShaya & Oyaid, 2017), many small cities and villages are still do not have proper Internet connections (Alghamdi et al., 2011). That may create a digital divide between women who live in the villages and small cities compared to women who live in major cities. Also, there is digital technology divide that reveals a gap between individuals who have the skills or interest required to use the technology and those who do not, regardless of their access to it (Luppicini, 2010).

For instance, young people in Saudi Arabia demonstrate a particular interest in using technologies and mobile devices compare to the older generation (AlShaya & Oyaid, 2017). Therefore, older students or teachers were not as disposed to use the technologies for an online learning context as were their younger counterparts (Al-Shehri, 2017, p. 42). This also may result in creating a gap between young Saudi women who are competent and willing to use the technology for learning in comparison with older women who are not.

There are also accessibility issues that can hinder women who have disabilities from pursing higher education online learning. It has been recognized that "the application of assistive technologies in special education contexts is a challenging area of educational technoethics" (Luppicini, 2010, p. 169). Jane Seale (2014) has stated that designing and developing accessible online learning is an important and necessary part of teaching and assisting disabled learners. Examples of disabilities that may create a barrier toward online learning accessibility are vision loss, hearing impairment and cognitive impairment (Gay, 2014). This may create an obstacle that gets in the way of women's learning, particularly in countries like Saudi Arabia where Distance Education is still in its infancy. However, as learning should be accessible by everyone, it is essential that Saudi universities design online learning content that is accessible by all learners regardless of their disabilities. Accommodating the needs of those disabled leaners will create and deliver better online learning opportunities.

POSITIONING GEN Z SAUDI WOMEN FOR SUCCESS IN HIGHER EDUCATION

Building on researcher findings related to current opportunities and challenges for Saudi women in Distance Education, Gen Z Saudi women benefit from distance learning in similar and unique ways that are important to highlight. While Distance Education has opened the door for female students to pursue their education and created more employment opportunities for female instructors working in Saudi Higher Education, Gen Z Saudi women will have the greatest potential opportunity to leverage their careers in Higher Education compared to older women. The main reason connects to the limited period of time individuals have to work and advance their careers before they reach retirement age. Within Higher Education, it can take decades for full-time regular teaching staff to reach the rank and status of Professor, Program Director, Department Chair, or Dean (and many never do). Because of increased access to Higher Education through Distance Education and more potential time left in their careers for professional advancement, Gen Z Saudi women are in a unique position to maximize career opportunities within Higher Education. Moreover, Gen Z graduates from Distance Education programs are also in a unique position to have access to the larger professional job market beyond the academic walls and adequate time to nurture their careers.

FUTURE OUTLOOK

One key driver this chapter focuses on is Distance Education and the greater access to learning and opportunities it provides to women in Saudi Arabia for future leadership roles. The authors of this chapter expect that online educational will continue to be an important factor in the topic of women in leadership because access to education acts as either a powerful enabler or inhibitor of women's leadership opportunities. This is particularly salient with regards to work in education. As Bates (2009) indicated, the future for Saudi female instructors in the context of online learning is promising. They have shown their continuous interest in building up the required skills and knowledge of distance learning in order to better educate Saudi girls. Their initiatives toward online learning have been demonstrated particularly in their participation in the eLearning Pioneers Program.

Due to the fact that online learning has only recently emerged in Saudi Arabia, there has not been extensive research into the ethical concerns that are particular to the online learning context (Musbahtiti, Saady & Muhammad, 2013; Muhammad et al., 2013; Muhammad et al., 2014; Muhammad et al., 2016). Therefore, there is a need to explore this area further in future studies. For example, rules of netiquette, which refers to the dos and don'ts of online communication (Buelens et al., 2007), could be applied to the Saudi online learning context to better leverage the education experience for female students and professors. Gearhart (2001) indicated that with the increased utilization of information technology in Distance Education, the level of unethical behaviours did increase. These unethical behaviours were the result of "psychological distance"; namely, acts that are carried out online feel less personal because the individual performing it could not be seen or heard (Gearhart, 2001). Unethical behaviours that can impact e-learning included hacking, infringing on intellectual property rights, plagiarism and cheating (Gearhart, 2014).

Early research has also indicated that the quality of online communication may increase when the participants understand and follow the network etiquette rules or netiquette (Shea, 1994; Scheuermann & Taylor, 1997). Netiquette can help with determining what is proper communication through technology and "is an instance of norms and expectations about behaviour" (Traxler, 2008, p. 528). It is easy to unintentionally give or take offence in online communication based on the way a message is worded (Stewart, 2016). Thus, social norms governing email, chat, and conferencing are examples of netiquette (Traxler, 2008). First, email netiquette includes conventions for the use of emoticons and smileys, abbreviations, and unrestrained attitude toward grammar and spelling; second, instant messaging and chat netiquette contains expectations about inappropriate ringing, and a greater use of abbreviations; third, forums and conferencing often apply published codes of behavior precluding, for instance, spam and flaming (Traxler, 2008). These are examples of netiquette that should be considered in order to enhance the quality of online communication for Saudi female students and instructors.

CONCLUSION

Over the last 40 years, Saudi women have achieved significant advancements in the educational sector as both students and instructors. Despite being late to join the Saudi educational system, the cultural and religious constraints and the unequal educational opportunities compared to Saudi men, Saudi women have shown notable initiative towards education in general and online learning in particular. Indeed, Distance Education has made a significant contribution in preparing Saudi females for leadership roles, which, if properly cultivated, could greatly enhance the quality of life and status of women within Saudi society.

REFERENCES

Abdul-Alim, J. (2015). Saudi Arabian women receive online learning techniques from U.S. *Diverse Education*. Retrieved from http://diverseeducation.com/article/76935/

AbdulHafeez. M., Asadullah, S., Rosydi, M., & Farooq, A. (2013, March). Inculcating ethical values in the students through e-learning platform. In *2013 5th International Conference on Information and Communication Technology for the Muslim World (ICT4M)* (pp. 1-6). IEEE.

Airini, S., Conner, L., McPherson, K., Midson, B., & Wilson, C. (2011). Learning to be leaders in higher education: What helps or hinders women's advancement as leaders in universities. *Educational Management Administration & Leadership*, *39*(1), 44–62. doi:10.1177/1741143210383896

Al-Ahmadi, H. (2011). Challenges facing women leaders in Saudi Arabia. *Human Resource Development International*, *14*(2), 149–166. doi:10.1080/13678868.2011.558311

Al Alhareth, Y., McBride, N., Prior, M., Leigh, M., & Flick, C. (2013). Saudi women and e-learning. *Paper presented at the Pixel International Conference: The Future of Education*, Florence, Italy, June 13–14. Retrieved from http://conference.pixel-online.net/foe2013/common/download/Paper_pdf/142-ELE15-FP-Alhareth-FOE2013.pdf

Al-Asmari, A. & Khan, S. (2014). E-learning in Saudi Arabia: Past, present and future. *Near and Middle Eastern Journal of Research in Education, 2*(1), 2-11.

Al-Khalifa, H. (2010). E-learning and ICT integration in colleges and universities in Saudi Arabia. Retrieved from http://elearnmag.acm.org/featured.cfm?aid=1735849

Al-Munajjed, M. (2009). *Women's education in Saudi Arabia: The way forward.* Retrieved from http://arabdevelopmentportal.com/sites/default/files/publication/211.womens_education_in_saudi_arabia_the_way_forward.pdf

Al-Rasheed, M. (2013). *A most masculine state: Gender, politics and religion in Saudi Arabia.* Cambridge: Cambridge University Press. doi:10.1017/CBO9781139015363

Al-Shehri, S. (2017). Technology-enhanced language instruction: are we in the loop? In K. Alshahrani & M. Ally (Eds.), *Transforming education in the Gulf region: Emerging learning technologies and innovative pedagogy for the 21st century* (pp. 36–50). New York: Routledge.

Aldubais, F. (2017, May 5). تمكين المرأة السعودية من الخدمات دون موافقة ولي الأمر. Retrieved from https://www.okaz.com.sa/article/1544591/

AlGhamdi, R., Drew, S., & AbuGabah, A. (2011). Designing government strategies to facilitate diffusion of online commerce: A focus on KSA. *Journal of Information & System Management*, *1*(3), 97–106.

Aljabre, A. (2012). An exploration of distance learning in Saudi Arabian universities: Current practices and future possibilities. *International Journal of Instructional Technology and Distance Learning*, *2*(9), 21–28.

AlMegren, A., & Yassin, S. Z. (2013). Learning object repositories in e-learning: Challenges for learners in Saudi Arabia. *European Journal of Open. Distance and E-Learning*, *16*(1), 115–130.

Alrashidi, A. (2014). E-learning in Saudi Arabia: A review of the literature. *British Journal of Education, Society &. Behavioral Science*, *4*(5), 656–672.

Alsaqqaf, A. (2015). Toward open educational resources: Opportunities and challenges. In N. Sultan & H. J. Al-Lail (Eds.), *Creative learning and MOOCs: Harnessing the technology for a 21st century education* (pp. 110–127). Newcastle upon Tyne: Cambridge Scholars Publishing.

Alshahrani, K., & Ally, M. (2017). MOOC in the Arab world: A case study. In K. Alshahrani & M. Ally (Eds.), *Transforming education in the Gulf region: Emerging learning technologies and innovative pedagogy for the 21st century* (pp. 178–187). New York: Routledge.

AlShaya, H., & Oyaid, A. (2017). Mobile learning in Gulf Cooperation Council countries: theory and practice. In K. Alshahrani & M. Ally (Eds.), *Transforming education in the Gulf region: Emerging learning technologies and innovative pedagogy for the 21st century* (pp. 83–97). New York: Routledge.

Alturki, U. (2014). The development of online distance education in Saudi Arabia. *Elearnmag*. Retrieved from http://elearnmag.acm.org/archive.cfm?aid=2673861

Alwasal, S., & Alhadlaq, S. (2012). Preparing Middle Eastern students for the future: Saudi Arabia as a case study. In J. Groccia, M. Alsudairi, & W. Buskist (Eds.), *Handbook of college and university teaching: A global perspective* (pp. 77–90). Thousand Oaks, CA: SAGE Publications, Inc. doi:10.4135/9781412996891.n6

Asiri, M., Mahmud, R. B., Abu Bakar, K., & Mohd Ayub, A. F. B. (2012). Factors influencing the use of learning management system in Saudi Arabian higher education: A theoretical framework. *Higher Education Studies*, *2*(2), 125–137. doi:10.5539/hes.v2n2p125

Bates, T. (2009). *A personal view of e-learning in Saudi Arabia*. Retrieved from http://www.tonybates.ca/2009/11/05/a-personal-view-of-e-learning-in-saudi-arabia/

Buelens, H., Totte, N., Deketelaere, A., & Dierickx, K. (2007). Electronic discussion forums in medical ethics education: The impact of didactic guidelines and netiquette. *Medical Education*, *41*(7), 711–717. doi:10.1111/j.1365-2923.2007.02793.x PMID:17614893

Carli, L., & Eagly, A. (2017). Leadership and gender. In J. Antonakis & D. David (Eds.), *The nature of leadership* (pp. 244–271). Sage publications, Inc.

Chester, Andrea & Gwynne, Gillian. (1998). Online teaching: Encouraging collaboration through anonymity. *Journal of Computer-Mediated Communication, 4*(2).

Daly, U., & Young, L. (2016). *Saudi eLearning pioneers transform teaching and learning through open education consortium collaboration*. Retrieved from https://conference.oeconsortium.org/2016/presentation/saudi-elearning-pioneers-transform-teaching-and-learning-through-open-education-consortium-collaboration/

David, M. (2017). Women and gender equality in higher education? In H. Eggins (Ed.), *The changing role of women in higher education: Academic and leadership issues* (pp. 209–225). Switzerland: Springer International Publishing. doi:10.1007/978-3-319-42436-1_11

Davidson, M., & Burke, R. (2004). Women in management worldwide: Facts, figures and analysis–An overview. In M. Davidson & R. Burke (Eds.), *Women in management worldwide: Facts, figures and analysis* (pp. 1–18). Aldershot: Ashgate.

Davidson, M., & Burke, R. (2011). Women in management worldwide: Progress and prospects–An overview. In M. Davidson & R. Burke (Eds.), *Women in management worldwide: Progress and prospects* (pp. 1–20). New York: Routledge.

Gay, G. (2014). *Accessibility in e-learning: What you need to know*. Retrieved from https://www.uwo.ca/tsc/resources/pdf/accessibility-in-e-learning.pdf

Gearhart, D. (2001). Ethics in distance education: Developing ethical policies. *Online Journal of Distance Learning Administration, 4*(1), 1–4.

Gearhart, D. (2014). Ethics for eLearning: Two sides of the ethical coin. In R. Luppicini (Ed.), *Evolving issues surrounding technoethics and society in the digital age* (pp. 232–244). Hershey, PA: IGI Global. doi:10.4018/978-1-4666-6122-6.ch015

Ghamdi, A., Barakati, S., Adal, K., Jumaiah, S., & Soman, A. (2011). *Students outside the walls of higher education*. Retrieved from http://www.okaz.com.sa/new/Issues/20110702/Con20110702430523.htm

Hamdan, A. (2005). Women and education in Saudi Arabia: Challenges and achievements. *International Education Journal, 6*(1), 42–64.

Hamdan, A. (2014). The reciprocal and correlative relationship between learning culture and online education: A case from Saudi Arabia. *International Review of Research in Open and Distance Learning*, *15*(1), 309–336. doi:10.19173/irrodl.v15i1.1408

Hamdan, A. (2015). The interaction between online learning and educational culture: A Saudi Arabian experience. In N. Sultan & H. J. Al-Lail (Eds.), *Creative learning and MOOCs: Harnessing the technology for a 21st century education* (pp. 197–204). Newcastle upon Tyne, UK: Cambridge Scholars Publishing.

Hamdan, A., Alexander, N., & Al-Hattami, A. (2016). Saudi female students' perceptions of leadership: *An overview. Advancing Women in Leadership*, *36*(1), 36–48.

Hodges, J. (2017). Cracking the walls of leadership: Women in Saudi Arabia. *Gender in Management*, *32*(1), 34–46. doi:10.1108/GM-11-2015-0106

House, K. (2012). *On Saudi Arabia: Its people, past, religion, fault lines--and future*. New York: Alfred A. Knopf.

Jamjoom, F., & Kelly, P. (2013). Higher education for women in the Kingdom of Saudi Arabia. In L. Smith & A. Abouammoh (Eds.), *Higher Education in Saudi Arabia Achievements, Challenges and Opportunities* (pp. 117–125). Dordrecht: Springer. doi:10.1007/978-94-007-6321-0_11

Khan, B. (2010, March 20). *Girls' education in Saudi Arabia and the Middle East with e-learning* [YouTube video]. Retrieved from https://www.youtube.com/watch?v=A-HtbStHQoY

Luppicini, R. (2010). Educational and professional technoethics. In R. Luppicini (Ed.), *Technoethics and the Evolving Knowledge Society: Ethical Issues in Technological Design, Research, Development, and Innovation* (pp. 163–179). Hershey, PA: IGI Global. doi:10.4018/978-1-60566-952-6

Luppicini, R., & Saleh, R. (2017). The role of online social networks for divorced Saudi women in the face of social, psychological, economic, and legal challenges. *Technology in Society*, *51*, 142–152. doi:10.1016/j.techsoc.2017.07.008

Mirza, A., & Al-Abdulkareem, M. (2011). Models of e-learning adopted in the Middle East. *Applied Computing and Informatics*, *9*(2), 83–93. doi:10.1016/j.aci.2011.05.001

Muhammad, A., Ghalib, M. F. M. D., Ahmad, F., Naveed, Q. N., & Shah, A. (2016). A study to investigate state of ethical development in e-learning. *J. Adv. Comput. Sci. Appl*, *7*(4), 284–290.

Muhammad, A. H., Wahsheh, H. A., Shah, A., & Ahmad, F. (2014, November). Ethical perspective of learning management system a model to support moral character of online learner. In *The 5th International Conference on Information and Communication Technology for The Muslim World (ICT4M)* (pp. 1-6). IEEE.

Musbahtiti, K., Saady, M. R., & Muhammad, A. (2013). Comprehensive e-learning system based on Islamic principles. In *2013 5th International Conference on Information and Communication Technology for the Muslim World (ICT4M)* (pp. 1-5). IEEE.

Omair, K. (2008). Women in management in the Arab context. *Education, Business and Society*, *1*(2), 107–123. doi:10.1108/17537980810890293

Quraishi, A. (2012). More Saudi universities boarding e-learning bandwagon. *Arab News*. Retrieved from http://www.arabnews.com/more-saudi-universities-boarding-e-learning-bandwagon

Rugh, W. (2002). Education in Saudi Arabia: Choices and constraints. *Middle East Policy*, *9*(2), 40–55. doi:10.1111/1475-4967.00056

Saleh, R., & Luppicini, R. (2017). Exploring the challenges of divorce on Saudi women. *Journal of Family History*, *2*(42), 1–15.

Scheuermann, L., & Taylor, G. (1997). Netiquette. *Internet Research*, *7*(4), 269–273. doi:10.1108/10662249710187268

Seale, J. (2014). *E-learning and disability in higher education: Accessibility theory and practice*. London, New York: Routledge.

Shea, V. (1994). *Netiquette*. San Francisco, CA: Albion Books.

Stewart, Georgina. (2016). Reviewing and ethics in the online academy. *Educational philosophy, 48*(5), 437-442.

Tam, K. (2015). *Saudi Arabia prepares female faculty members for online education* [Press Release]. Retrieved from https://www.prnewswire.com/news-releases/saudi-arabia-prepares-female-faculty-members-for-online-education-300115711.html

Thompson, M. (2015). Saudi women leaders: Challenges and opportunities. *Journal of Arabian Studies*, *5*(1), 15–36. doi:10.1080/21534764.2015.1050880

Traxler, J. (2008). Mobile learning in a social, ethical, and legal environment. In T. Hansson (Ed.), *Handbook of research on digital information technologies: Innovations, methods, and ethical issues* (pp. 520–532). Hershey, PA: IGI Global. doi:10.4018/978-1-59904-970-0.ch033

Yamin, M. (2013). A socio-cultural overview of e-learning in Saudi Arabia. *International Journal of Emerging Technology and Advanced Engineering*, *3*(12), 57–59.

Zuhur, S. (2011). *Saudi Arabia*. Santa Barbara, CA: ABC-CLIO.

Chapter 4
Social Media and Student With Disabilities:
Challenges and Opportunities

Caoimhe Doran
State University of New York at Plattsburgh, USA

Heidi Lee Schnackenberg
State University of New York at Plattsburgh, USA

ABSTRACT

In the past decade, social media has become an increasingly prevalent, being the daily form of communication and entertainment for a majority of individuals. Social media and networking sites are not designed to appeal to a specific type of personality and are designed to benefit many. The students of Generation Z respond positively to teaching styles that incorporate technology-based learning, and frequent communication or feedback. Gen Z students with disabilities are entitled to the same opportunities and experiences as their peers without disabilities. This includes being exposed to various forms of social media to discover alternative ways to communicate, interact with the community, find information and access entertainment. While other members of Generation Z possess the capability to pick up a smart phone or computer, create a social media account and figure out the functions independently, students with disabilities may require explicit instruction, strategies and practice with social media usage.

DOI: 10.4018/978-1-5225-7763-8.ch004

INTRODUCTION

There is an estimated 77% of the United States population engaged in one or more forms of social media use (Statista, 2018). Social media is the broad term used to describe "forms of electronic communication (such as websites for social networking and microblogging) through which users create online communities to share information, ideas, personal messages, and other content" (Merriam-Webster, 2004). The influence of social media and networking can be observed across many settings in our society, both private and public. From sending a private text message to a friend or contacting a colleague through a professional email to sharing a post with the public eye via Twitter or Instagram. Social media can provide multiple opportunities, such as building relationships, sharing expertise, increasing visibility of content, educating oneself and staying connected to others at all times (Friedman, 2014). In the past decade, social media has become an increasingly prevalent, daily form of communication and entertainment for a majority of individuals. Giving people the ability to interact quickly and easily with each other, no matter the distance between them.

Unsurprisingly, social media usage and knowledge differs by generation. "Generation Z" is often known or referred to as the first group of "social natives" (Hill Holiday Media, 2018, p. 3). Generation Z is composed of individuals born from the mid-1990s to early 2010s, who have grown up being exposed to the rise of technology, the internet and social media. According to Darla Rothman (2016), "This generation is tech-savvy and prefers to communicate using social media over direct contact with people. They are the first generation born into an integrated and globally connected world, where the Internet has always been available" (p. 2). Recent studies have shown that over 90% of Gen Z members use a least one social media platform (Hill Holiday Media, 2018, p. 4).

In addition to technology, "social natives" have been around to experience an economic recession and the effects of global warming. Generation Z witnessed communities rebuilding themselves after natural disasters, such as Hurricane Katrina and Hurricane Sandy. As well as experiencing the national changes that followed the 9/11 attack and the Iraq and Afghanistan Wars, Generation Z has also been present to experience the election of the United States's first African-American president and the largest number of women and minorities holding political positions. As a group, they are often characterized as extreme multi-taskers, always looking for the next (mostly electronic) interaction or source of information. They are individuals whose brains are wired to prefer visual imagery over auditory instruction. In terms of learning and the workplace, Gen Z can produce effective results in a shorter period of time compared to older peers (Rothman, 2016, p. 2-5). Perhaps most telling though, is the common description of Gen Z as the babies who held their parents' smartphones and figured out the functions before they became toddlers.

While Generation Z is clearly a technologically adept group, greatly skilled in a variety of tools and applications, there are still individuals in this generation from under-represented groups who are not afforded the same social media access or opportunities as their peers. Individuals with disabilities or special needs are often neglected in terms of acceptance and inclusion. According to Anderson and Perrin (2017):

The amount of time people spend online and their comfort level with technology also varies by disability status. Disabled Americans are less likely than those who don't have a disability to report using the internet on a daily basis (50% vs. 79%). They are also less likely to say that having a high level of confidence in their ability to use the internet and other communication devices to keep up with information describes them "very well." (39% vs. 65%)

This can further be observed based on the lack of social media skills being taught within students with disabilities least restrictive environments (LRE). Students with disabilities may be in need of additional support to learn how to properly develop and implement necessary technology skills. As well, being taught how social networking skills can benefit their disability and the medium can be used to their advantage. As social media and networking embeds itself even more deeply in our society, the need to prepare all students, especially those with disabilities, for a technologically advanced world should be recognized by schools and educators.

BACKGROUND

As Generation Z progresses through their academic careers, educators will need to adapt and modify previous teaching methods to ensure engagement and participation from digitally driven students. Social natives are known for being a generation of visual, multi-taskers. Desai and Lele (2017) categorize the multitasking tendencies as being a superficial or divided form of attention due to their continuous practice of looking back and forth simultaneously between media sources (Desai and Lele, 2017, p. 807). These students learn differently compared to the Generation Y or Millennials who came before them. According to research conducted by Puiu (2017), "The economic, social and technological context of one person influences his/her behavior and way of thinking or making decisions. Regarding the education, this is more based on technology than before for Gen Z" (Puiu, 2017, p. 63). The students of Generation Z respond positively to teaching styles that incorporate technology-based learning, and frequent communication or feedback. Puiu recommends using Youtube over text to create lessons with images, video and audio which will appeal to tech-savvy learners (Puiu, 2017, p. 64). In terms of frequent communication and feedback, the exposure to technology at a young age resulted in a generation who seeks instant gratification. Based on Turner's research (2015), "Generation Z lives in a wired environment and is near their communication devices at all times, which allows them to feel instantly gratified, or hurt, or utterly unimportant, or dismayed by the content or the context of communication— all of these immediately" (Turner, 2015, p.110). The experiences of instant gratification have lead members of Gen Z to expect similar amounts of attention and response during face to face communication. This has made the concept of waiting for a response or feedback from others a potentially difficult process to endure. Educators should be aware of this when responding to student's questions, assignments, and academic progress. Frequent communication should be explicit and include a combination of positive and negative feedback to provide opportunities for future improvements. Singh (2014) describes how Generation Z has access to more resources, programs and mentors than previous generations. Social natives understand the skills necessary to look for information via a website or use online training and courses to benefit their personal goals, as well as staying connected with peers, mentors and personal relationships by reading blogs or direct messaging programs (Singh, 2014, pp. 61-62). The desire to connect with others can be observed in the types of communication used heavily by Generation Z. According to Loveland (2017), text messaging is the prefered form of communication over electronic mail since it is quicker and more personal. This stems from Gen Z preferring conversational methods of communication. The members of Gen Z want to be spoken to, not spoken at, in order to create relationships (Loveland, 2017, pp. 36-37). Gen Z commonly interacts with internet websites such as Netflix, Twitter, Instagram, and Spotify which produce personalized profiles for members based on recent searches, previous engagement and survey results. Schwieger and Ladwig (2018) found that, "Gen Zers desired more personalized micro-experiences and felt like "anything is possible" (Schwieger & Ladwig, 2018, p. 46). The "anything is possible" attitude adopted by Gen Z could be a direct result of the endless access to opportunities being made easily available through the internet. This attitude combined with the individuals of Generation Z has shown trends in producing results intended to serve a higher purpose or give back to the larger community. According to Cater (2018):

Generation Z has indicated a desire to be involved with transformational rather than transactional activities in their world. In other words, they would rather have a career than engenders transformation in the culture than a career that simply provides them with financial prosperity. Likewise, Generation Z has received realistic rather than idealistic parenting in a post- 9/11 world. They have learned that collective security at times is more pressing than individual rights and privileges, and they have learned that terrorism and volatility are ever present. Such experiences have further demonstrated the need for addressing root causes of issues and a need for transformational impact. (Carter, 2018, p. 2)

The ability to find information independently at any time, has created a generation of personalized, connected, self-sufficient learners. Members of Gen Z have been raised feeling connected to not only technology, but social and economic issues present in our society. The individuals who decide to use their resources to help others view the advantages they have been granted and want to use them to help or influence others.

There are a variety of ways Generation Z can use their "tech-savvy" abilities to influence others. Social media has created a society that makes sharing your personal story, message or ideas with a larger community easier than ever. This simplistic process provides the opportunity for individuals to work together, despite geographic distance or communication barriers. According to Kaplan and Haenlein (2010), "The main idea underlying collaborative projects is that the joint effort of many actors leads to a better outcome than any actor could achieve individually" (Kaplan and Haenlein, 2010, p. 62). Joint efforts through social media allows a larger pool of people to contribute different opinions, areas of knowledge, background information and important questions to a project which shares a common goal. The more people involved leads to an increase in voices being heard and a larger amount of people to share or expand the message with. Social media has made it possible for companies or people all around the world to collaborate together. As well as increasing collaboration efforts, social media helps individuals to develop and maintain relationships. According to data collected by Holiday Hill Media (2018), "50% of Gen Z report that social media blends together with other ways in which they interact with friends and find content" (Holiday Hill Media, 2018, p. 5). This can be seen in the different ways introverts and extroverts interact within their community. Not everyone may feel comfortable when approaching an individual on the street or in a store, however that specific individual may react positively to sending an message or commenting on an online post. A study conducted by Wang and colleagues (2018) examined the various benefits extroverts and introverts could experience from making connections through social networking sites. In terms of introverts their research found, "Introverts evaluated Social Networking Sites (SNSs) to be more appealing than traditional communication methods, expressed willingness to spend more time on SNSs, and were more likely to form online relationships" (Wang, Lv and Zhang, 2018, p. 1598). In comparison:

Extroverts' offline sociability could be transferred to SNSs, such that highly extroverted individuals would benefit more from SNSs than would introverts. In line with the social enhancement theory, findings from studies have revealed that, compared to introverts, extroverts have more Facebook friends, are more likely to use social media, have a more positive attitude toward SNSs, belong to more SNS groups, and exchange everyday information through SNSs. (Wang, Lv and Zhang, 2018, pp. 1598-1599)

Social media and networking sites are not designed to appeal to a specific type of personality and are designed to benefit many. This can be observed in features that allow individuals to customize their profile or account. Which further provides the individual the opportunity to interact with others who share similar interests or dislikes, creating a more connected world. Using social media to build relationships can be seen across a variety of settings and ages, including school-aged children. According to the research conducted by DeLay and colleagues (2016), when combining social media with social-emotional learning interventions in the classroom:

By improving social skills, students may form closer relationships with other students. We know that students are more likely to be influenced by close peer relationship partners than by casual peer affiliates and by peers who are more prosocial. Thus, the aim of the relationship building intervention to improve social relationships seems to have created a more socially skilled group of students, allowing for a greater likelihood of peer influence over improved academic performance. (DeLay et al., 2016, p. 911)

In terms of maintaining relationships, which may or may not have been formed through social media, Kim and Drumwright (2016) found, "Individuals can utilize social media to bridge and bond with their weak ties, people with whom they do not interact on a regular basis, and to deepen relationships with their strong ties, the people with whom they have close relationships" (Kim and Drumwright, 2016, p. 970). Social media has provided people the opportunity to interact with each other at any time with fewer limits. The concept of creating connections through social media can be expanded beyond personal connections to observe how businesses or organizations interact with current and potential consumers. Park and Lee's (2013) research found:

With the friending functions of social networking sites, relationships between an organization and its publics have become closer to interpersonal relationships. This phenomenon underscores the importance of understanding how to manage relationships with publics, which has been one of the predominant topics in public relations over the past few decades. (Park and Lee, 2013, p. 266)

It is essential for businesses and organizations to understand the wants or needs of the consumer when interacting via social media. Businesses can use social media to connect with the public about new improvements to their service, handling potential issues, advertising available products, and providing an overall satisfactory experience. This trend can be seen by the growing number of companies who have begun using direct messaging customer service to address concerns or complaints about products. Social media has changed the way people spend money and can help customers connect with other customers. Schlee and Harich (2013) found:

While in the past, marketers used to control the channels of communication to consumers, social media have enabled today's consumers to communicate with one another and post reviews of the products and services that they have used. Thus, consumers now have the power to build and damage brands through the comments they post online. (Schlee and Harich, 2013, p. 209)

Through the use of social media, consumers can read or inquire about another person's experience with a product or service before making a purchase. This process of reviewing companies can either benefit or harm the business when influencing a customer's decision. This is due to the tendency to be drawn towards products or services with higher, more positive ratings. The possibility of receiving negative publicity on social media may push potential customers away.

One population within GenZ that have particular needs with respect to social media is individuals with disabilities. There are similar and additional benefits afforded the larger population that can be granted through social media to individuals with disabilities, particularly school-aged people. While students with and without disabilities are becoming more aware of texting and other forms of online communication, there appears to be a lack of proper instruction on how to use social networking properly. Social media is considered to be a form of augmentative and alternative form of communication. Studies with disabilities who experience communication or language deficits can benefit from learning about the opportunities offered by social media. According to Hemsley and colleagues:

Using social network sites could support people who use AAC to (a) become more persistent in engagement online, (b) become more visible and influential online, (c) grow the audience that they want to reach online, and (d) know how to find online connections that work for them, including locating employment and social opportunities. (Hemsley, Balandin, Palmer and Dann, 2017, p. 14)

With all of the benefits offered by social media, it is essential to inform individuals of how to properly operate applications and social networking sites. The research conducted by Aldridge, Jeffrey, Taylor and Barringer-Brown (2017) found, "... students with special needs text just like their abled peers and that girls typically text more than boys" (Aldridge, Jeffrey, Taylor and Barringer-Brown, 2017 p. 35), leading to further research on how students with disabilities use social networking language. In modern societies, learning how to effectively use social networking as a form of communication is becoming a necessary skill. The recent appearance of text message language, such as LOL being used as a substitute for laugh out loud, may not always be clear to students with disabilities. The inability to interpret and comprehend text messaging language could be leaving a population of individuals isolated from their peers and society (Aldridge, Jeffrey, Taylor and Barringer-Brown, 2017 p. 36). Teaching students with disabilities how to communicate using social media and networking can benefit not only their communication skills, but enhance writing skills as well. According to Wollak and Koppenhaver (2011):

Writing is particularly important for students with disabilities because it enhances communication, increases independence, and makes a unique contribution to literacy learning. Students with disabilities who can write clearly have enormous access to the world through the Internet. (p. 1)

By using writing skills to help further develop social networking abilities, students are given the opportunity to build on two important skills at once. Wollak and Koppenhaver (2011) stated that in order to successfully communicate in modern society, "students must be able to navigate, comprehend, analyze, synthesize, and construct digital texts and multimedia on the World Wide Web" (p. 5). Social media is one of the main sources for communicating and interpreting information in our society. This includes receiving health and wellness information through social networking communities. Individuals with disabilities should not be limited in the amount of information that can be gathered in terms of their physical or mental health. Additionally, while learning how to collect information through social media, individuals with disabilities can explore their own classification further and communicate with others who understand or support them. According to Chiu and Juang (2013):

Past research has investigated Facebook use for patient support groups of diabetes mellitus and breast cancer, and revealed that the similarities in background and health situation of group members would lead to common health goals. Patient groups of children with disabilities should deserve equal opportunities, rights, and access to health communication on Facebook. (Chiu and Juang, 2013, p. 384)

One of the main purposes of social media is to bring people and communities closer together. Teaching students with disabilities how to use social media as a way to communicate can help connect them to other individuals who share similar experiences to them. Using social media to connect and gather information can be considered a tool to promote lifelong learning outside of the classroom. Our students with disabilities are not going to be students forever, meaning research skills needs to be developed to access information in an independent way. According to Kind and Evans (2015) social media can promote lifelong learning because, "Engagement with social media can parallel engagement in the learning process to the extent that online social networking fosters feedback and collaboration. It can also provide a forum and format for reflection, through online blogging and other prompted discussions and journaling" (Kind and Evans, 2015, p. 126). Students with disabilities need to be taught how and where to access essential information on social media to guide their own learning.

In addition to accessing information and building communication skills, teaching students with disabilities how to effectively use social media can correlate with developing social-emotional learning skills. According to research conducted by Probst (2017), "We can begin to see a parallel of concepts and pedagogy which emphasizes similar outcomes for both media literacy education and social and emotional learning including empathy, impulse control, relationship-building, ethical responsibility, organizational skills, and issues with perception" (Probst, 2017, p. 48). Using social media to develop social and emotional learning (SEL) skills places the concepts, pedagogy and outcomes into an online setting where students can practice what is being implemented in the classroom. Alongside, social-emotional learning it is necessary for students with and without disabilities to be informed taught, and practice avoiding the possible dangers that exist when using the internet and social media. Educators should be aware of the possible forms of victimism individuals with disabilities could be exposed to through social media usage. Lough and Fisher (2016) found that for individuals with intellectual or developmental disabilities, "Whilst everyone faces the risks posed by the Internet, individuals with IDD may be especially vulnerable to online victimisation, particularly if they have reduced IQ, difficulties interpreting social communication and understanding social nuances, elevated levels of trust, and feelings of social isolation and loneliness in their daily lives" (Lough and Fisher, 2016, p. 1021). Individuals with disabilities should be made aware of these dangers and taught strategies for how to avoid them. Other than individuals with intellectual or developmental disabilities, there individuals with special needs classifications that can have specific benefits for their needs from social media and assistive technology exposure. Based upon the research of Kelly and Smith (2008), comparing the social media use of students with visual impairments and other disabilities:

Students with visual impairments may not engage in computer chats or telephone conversations with peers because they do not have the social or technological skills they need to participate actively in these forums. Teachers of students with visual impairments can now intertwine the teaching of social skills and assistive technology to address deficits in these areas. (Kelly and Smith, 2008, p. 537)

Students with disabilities are being excluded from the benefits of online communication because the necessary skills are not being focused on enough in the classroom or research studies. By combining the instruction of technology and social skills, students with disabilities can be provided with additional ways to make connections and communicate with others rather than by using strictly face-to-face interactions.

MAIN FOCUS

Students with disabilities are entitled to the same opportunities and experiences as their peers without disabilities. This includes being exposed to various forms of social media to discover alternative ways to communicate, interact with the community, find information and access entertainment. While other members of Generation Z possess the capability to pick up a smart phone or computer, create a social media account and figure out the functions independently, students with disabilities may require explicit instruction, strategies and practice with social media usage. The purpose and opportunities social media can provide should be included in a school curriculum to ensure students with disabilities are being granted equitable access to the same information and communications that are available to their peers.

Common Sense Education (2018) outlines a useful digital citizenship curriculum that can be broken down into six categories. They include: media balance and wellbeing, privacy and security, digital footprint and identity, relationships and communication, cyberbullying, digital drama and hate speech, and news and media literacy (Common Sense Education, 2018). Within this framework, students with disabilities can be taught strategies for how to balance their time between the real world and online community. These same students can also be made aware of what information is appropriate or inappropriate to share online. As well, the concept of digital permanence, i.e. once you have put something on the internet it will be out there forever, is also important to emphasize and discuss. Perhaps most importantly, students with disabilities should be informed of the characteristics of online cyberbullies and how to avoid negative interactions. This is particularly critical for students who experience deficits in social interaction skills. Informing students with disabilities of all of these aspects of social media is essential for maintaining safety and inclusion online. By denying students with disabilities access to this information, there is an entire population of individuals being excluded from the online community.

While social media can be an excellent tool for a variety of positive purposes, there are also significant online dangers that students with disabilities need to be made aware of and learn how to navigate. Not everyone on the internet is using social media for the right or socially moral reasons. By not including social media curriculum in schools, students with disabilities are being blindly exposed to a complex information and communication system with potentially dangerous individuals and experiences. Students with disabilities should be taught the red flags of online predators in order to avoid getting involved in threatening situations. According to Stevens (2015), there are five topics that should be discussed with children to ensure safety online. They are: stranger danger, oversharing personal information, hidden information in pictures, staying in power of information and cyberbullying (Stevens, 2015). Students with disabilities need to be taught that not everyone on the internet is their friend, and that there are individuals who are strangers looking to harm them. Oversharing information and appropriate online postings go hand in hand and require explanation to make students aware of what information is dangerous to post online (for instance, where you live or go to school). This includes the photos that individuals upload to their online profiles and what potentially dangerous information could be interpreted or discovered through them. Since the information we post online is essentially available forever, students should be taught the possible consequences of what they decide to post and how those decisions can gain power or affect other aspects of your life. By teaching students with disabilities how to use social media safely and effectively, a community of safer, more prepared and technologically aware individuals will be created and granted a large possibility of opportunities.

ISSUES, CONTROVERSIES AND PROBLEMS

Often times individuals with disabilities are excluded from society, not by their deficits but from the other members of the community without disabilities. The equal right to an education for students with disabilities was decided in 1972 by PARC v. Pennsylvania and Mills v. D.C. Board of Education. However, it was not until 1975, when the Education for All Handicapped Children Act (EAHCA) was created and school districts became mandated to educate all students with and without disabilities. In the past 43 years, the way students with and without disabilities learn and implement their knowledge has changed immensely. There have already been great efforts to include the benefits, strategies and advancement of technology usage in the classroom (Hoffman et al., 2018; Ahmed, 2018; Coyne et al., 2017). However, there needs to be more change and progress for social media and networking to be embraced within that category (Casey, 2013; Ellahi, 2018; Reinhardt et al., 2011), especially for students with disabilities (Miller, 2017; Ranaldo, 2013; Exceptional Parent, 2016). When students with disabilities are not explicitly taught or educated about technology and social media, this community of individuals is once again being denied the chance to access equal opportunities. Individuals with disabilities are being denied the access to expand their knowledge, find information, sources of communication, and make connections to a larger community. All of the benefits found through social media usage have the ability provide the individual with better quality of life in the 21st century. The online master's in special education program guide (2018) states:

Some experts believe that social media is an effective method for improving the socialization skills of students from all ranges of the autism spectrum...helpful in learning to use appropriate language and communication skills while online. Because many everyday activities take place online, it can be argued that this is an essential skill for special education students to have exposure to while in supervised and in school.

Without proper social media instruction, students with disabilities could be unable to learn new strategies to improve already existing writing and reading skills. This limits the ability to practice using said skills and strategies through real life implementation. By not having access to the strategies made available through social media blogs and profiles, students with disabilities could possibly suffer from a lack of understanding about how to gather new information about an endless number of topics. Such as researching their disability, legal rights or gathering additional information about specific topics of interest. Additionally, students with disabilities are not being properly exposed to a variety of methods for communicating and connecting with the online community. This denies them the opportunity to connect or socialize with others who share similar interests to create new relationships. It also prevents students with disabilities from being able to share information about what makes them passionate or motivated. By not showing students with disabilities how to use social media, the community cannot ensure proper exposure to a variety of resources. This results in a decreased percentage of individuals with disabilities using social media based on necessary information and benefits not being taught.

As the members of Generation Z become more involved in higher education and the workforce, social media and technology expertise are being converted from a unique set of skills to expected knowledge. An individual with a disability may not be able to comprehend or pick up on the social media usage as quickly or independently, leaving them in a position of being less qualified or unable to complete a task. In terms of using social media within higher education Rodriguez (2011) found:

The strength of social media applications is that they offer an assortment of tools that learners can mix and match to best suit their individual learning styles and increase their academic success. Further, such technologies are typically freely accessible, easy to incorporate, and have a minimal learning curve to master. Learning environments can become personalized, and faculty can enhance their pedagogical techniques by using tools to extend class engagement beyond designated class time and to increase the quality and quantity of participation in online courses. (p. 540)

While technology and social networking can supply students with these benefits, if not properly taught how to use them during the earlier years of school, the effort to differentiate to a specific learning style runs the risk of being ineffective. Students must enter higher education and employment opportunities with prior knowledge of how to use social networking to meet their individual learning style. By not being provided experiences with technology and social networking usage as a way of gathering information and communicating, students with disabilities are being denied crucial background information for their futures. This unequal access to social media results in possibly closing the door on a variety of different opportunities. As social media and technology usage continues to grow into a more widely used and expected set of skills, students with disabilities will be excluded from gaining necessary skills at a young age compared to their peers without disabilities. By not providing classroom instruction about technology and social networking to students of young ages with disabilities, there is a greater chance that students will be less prepared to meet the expectations their future will entail.

As the members of Generation Z grow up, there is a shift from having to teach children about the dangers of the world around them to teaching them about the dangerous of the physical world as well as the ones in the virtual world(s). It is no secret that the internet and social media can be dangerous places for individuals with and without disabilities. For the most part, individuals with disabilities will have access to social media whether they are taught how to properly use it or not. This includes all of the hazards on the internet and within social media. By denying students with disabilities the opportunity to learn about social media in a safe and supervised environment, they are being left to be taken advantage of or use the internet in an unsafe manner because others view them as vulnerable. Students with disabilities should not be placed in this position or excluded from the online community. According to research conducted by Power Up What Works (2014) about online safety and individuals with disabilities:

As young people spend an increasing amount of time online, much of the inappropriate behavior, language, and material they encounter is beyond the immediate view of parents, teachers, and guardians. As such, it is important to prepare all students for safe interactions online, and it is all the more critical to examine the special risks and issues that students with disabilities face online.

Without being taught how to safely use social media, students with disabilities are put at a greater risk for engaging in inappropriate or dangerous behaviors. The lack of supervision and strategies can result in the individuals being viewed as an easier target who is susceptible to cyber bullying. By not providing information about positive and negative internet experiences, students with disabilities are being denied the opportunity to safely use the internet and social media to their advantage.

SOLUTIONS AND RECOMMENDATIONS

There are a variety of strategies and concepts available that can and should be addressed in depth when teaching students with disabilities how to use social media effectively. Individuals with disabilities have the potential to become self-sufficient social media users after receiving proper instruction about the purpose of and opportunities offered by the internet. There are no reason students with disabilities should be excluded or placed in dangerous situations when the resources and necessary information are available through current institutions and organizations. Educators and parents should collaborate and work as a team to ensure students with disabilities are receiving the appropriate social media exposure and instruction in order to become a discerning and skilled member of the online community.

Before students with disabilities can begin using social media effectively, scaffolding should occur to show them the purpose of using a variety of websites or applications. The purpose of the social media must be clear and detailed. For scaffolding to occur, "The teacher initially provides substantial support and modeling. This support is gradually released as students develop proficiency" (Cuillo et al., 2017, p. 156). Parents and teachers should explicitly outline for the student how accounts and profiles can be used to communicate, create connections, access forms of entertainment and seek information. This can be done by using personal experiences and social media to explain strategies for navigation and implementation. Scaffolding the profile making process can be beneficial for students who are being exposed to social media for the first time. When being introduced to new topics and concepts, having an experienced individual who can answer questions or clarify misconceptions can be prevent further confusion from developing. According to Vogel and colleagues (2017):

A high level of collaboration is reached when groups of learners engage in certain socio-cognitive activities such as explaining, questioning, or arguing. Through an engagement in such activities, students are assumed to acquire both domain-specific knowledge (i.e., knowledge about the topic that is discussed within the group) and cross-domain skills such as collaboration skills or argumentation skills. (p. 477)

If the student is being supported and guided by another individual from the beginning of their social media experience, the opportunity to explain, question or argue is available. Parents and teachers should have the student explain what is occurring as the profile is being made to check for understanding. As well as, prompt the student to complete the profile, clarify any questions, and allow for the student to argue when appropriate. One of the main purposes of social media is to collaborate with others. Through scaffolding, students with disabilities can practice developing this skill within a new online setting.

Similar to academic content, social media should be introduced slowly, on a step-by-step basis, to avoid overwhelming the individual. Candice Evans stated (n.d.):

Students with special needs often have difficulty understanding long-winded or several instructions at once. For children with learning disabilities, it is best to use simple, concrete sentences. You might have to break down a step into a few smaller steps to ensure your students with special needs understand what you are asking.

Each student will have their own set of background information with social media, which will be important when considering how to proceed. As always, the parent or teacher should evaluate the student's present level of performance, meet the student at that point, and then work from there. Based on the student's prior knowledge, it may be beneficial for the student to hold off on creating their own personal social media account right away. A possible starting point for scaffolding could be to have the student explore the process using an alternative account. For example, having a parent use their social media with the child observing and practicing or by creating an account with the sole purpose of being for student practice. Some students with disabilities may benefit from supports that expand beyond the use of a tablet, phone or computer device. Students with disabilities who are categorized as visual learners could be supplied with checklists for signing in and navigating social media, rules for what should be or not be posted online, and images for guiding their online use. Students with disabilities who are categorized as auditory learners could benefit from using social media applications that can read directions and posts aloud to them.

It is important to supply students with disabilities with a variety of social media platform from which to choose. According to KidsMatter (n.d.), "allowing children's decision making provides many opportunities for children to practice their skills in the day-to-day activities of a service." By providing options, the student can develop a sense of independence toward what types of social media interest them the most. Additionally, different forms of social media serve multiple purposes. For example, the student may have no interest in creating an Instagram account for posting photographs, but could be fascinated by the idea of following Twitter accounts focused on a specific interest. The parent or teacher should emphasize the social media that interests the student the most. When teaching students with disabilities about social media, it is essential to present how individualized the website or application can be.

Once the student becomes interested and more familiar with the concept of social media, educators can begin showing the students with disabilities how strategies that have been learned in the classroom can be practiced, expanded upon and strengthened. By showing how classroom lessons can evolve into real life implications, students may become motivated and more interested. In comparison, the student with disabilities may not have a necessary reading or writing skill at the present moment and can use social media to develop them. It is will be helpful for students if social media, writing and reading skills are built upon one another. One way says Nicole Moskowitz (N. Moskowitz, personal communication, January 28, 2019), a 3rd grade special education teacher at P.S. 63 Old South in New York City, has brought together literacy concepts with social media is through the sharing of student's individual goals. Displayed in the classroom, there is a "Twitter Wall" of student's individualized education plan goals. At the beginning of the school year, Moskowitz has students write their goals for the academic school year using their own words on index cards. The purpose of the activity is for students to recognize how everyone in their community is working toward an achievement and by sharing them with each other, they can learn how to support their classmates. Moskowitz shared how having students share their goals is a yearly activity in her classroom. However, the concept of including Twitter is a more recent addition. Moskowitz found a higher percentage of students were engaged when the activity was related to their prior knowledge or the internet. While Moskowitz's students may be too young to begin creating social media accounts at this time, an early introduction and exposure can allow for the further development of these skills.

Although not prevalent in academic literature or teaching practice, a few strategies, methods and/or programs have been developed and implemented to assist students with disabilities with strategies that could help them successfully navigate social media applications. One method for developing social media and English language arts skills simultaneously is through the use of electronic pen pals or peer group chats. According to Wollak and Koppenhaver (2011):

Writing is particularly important for students with disabilities because it enhances communication, increases independence, and makes a unique contribution to literacy learning. Students with disabilities who can write clearly have enormous access to the world through the Internet. (p. 1)

By using writing skills to help develop social networking abilities, students are given the opportunity to build upon two important skills at once. Wollak and Koppenhaver (2011) stated that in order to successfully communicate in modern society, "students must be able to navigate, comprehend, analyze, synthesize, and construct digital texts and multimedia on the World Wide Web" (p. 5). When conducting their study, Wollak and Koppenhaver designed an e-pal program involving students with disabilities in junior high school and preservice teachers in undergraduate programs. This program gave the students with disabilities the opportunity to take information gathered about social networking in class and apply it to a real-life conversation through electronic mail (Wollak and Koppenhaver, 2011, p. 6). Everyone involved in the program was given a set of guidelines for how to properly respond to their e-pal. For example, preservice teachers were instructed to respond within 24 hours, using a certain format, with the overall goal of getting to know each other through writing (Wollak and Koppenhaver, 2011, p. 7). Additionally, the junior high school students were given a specific writing strategy for writing electronic mail. This strategy included phases for planning, translating, production, motivation and review of writing (Wollak and Koppenhaver, 2011, p. 3). There were members of the study with severe writing deficits that required additional support beyond the writing guidelines. This group of students was provided with assistive technology, the word predictor program *Co:Writer*, to promote their ability to become an independent writer (Wollak and Koppenhaver, 2011, p. 8). It is important for students to gain insight on how assistive technology can not only support their academics, but also their daily living and communication skills. Wollak and Koppenhaver (2011) found the program and writing strategy being implemented had multiple benefits for students with disabilities:

This format supported not only the planning process but also the pragmatic rules of social communication: (a) knowing to answer when a question has been asked; (b) being able to participate in a conversation by taking turns; (c) being aware of the need to introduce a topic of conversation in order to support listener understanding; (d) knowing which words or sentence types to use when initiating a conversation or response; and (e) maintaining or changing a topic appropriately. (p. 7)

Students were supplied with a checklist to look over before sending the electronic mail to their e-pal to double check that all guidelines were being followed. (Wollak and Koppenhaver, 2011, p. 10). The junior high school students with disabilities were given supplemental opportunities to practice writing skills, social networking and pragmatic rules through the use of Twitter accounts. Due to Twitter's 140 character maximum at the time, students were able to practice online communication without becoming overwhelmed with the task. By being introduced to Twitter, with the assistance of teacher instruction and observation, students gained information about the types of content that are appropriate to share with the public eye.

Typically, students with disabilities who experience communication or social skill deficits are taught how to interpret people's verbal and body language. Social media comes with its own style of communication that needs to be understood in order to comprehend the conversation or profile post. Aldridge, Jeffrey, Taylor and Barringer-Brown (2017) found, "...students with special needs text just like their abled peers and that girls typically text more than boys" (p. 35), leading to further research in how students with disabilities use social networking language. In order for social networking to be used to a student's advantage, if there needs to be explicit instructions about the language being used. The recent appearance of text message language, such as LOL being used as a substitute for "laugh out loud", may not always be clear to students with disabilities. Aldridge and colleagues (2017) found, that the inability to interpret and comprehend the language being used could leave a population of individuals isolated from the rest of society (Aldridge, Jeffrey, Taylor and Barringer-Brown, 2017, p. 36). Gabe Duverge (2016) states how "Both cognitive and neurological disabilities involve the nervous system or brain, impacting how people see, hear, move, speak and interpret information." Based on the specific needs of the individual with a cognitive or neurological disability, they may be someone who experiences difficulty interpreting social media lingo. Students who use screen readers may also be included in the population of individuals who have difficulty understanding the meaning behind abbreviations or slang. Duverge (2016) suggests using periods when incorporating abbreviations into online language because "Screen readers will be confused by any abbreviation without periods." It is necessary to inform students with disabilities of new vocabulary terms, abbreviations and phrases. As well as, the appropriate context to use social networking language in. Based on the research conducted by Aldridge and colleagues (2017):

The students were asked if they used text messaging language for their school assignments and 25% of the females and 22% of the males answered "yes." This was despite the fact that many teachers from the same schools opposed the use of texting lexicon in class assignments and many of the schools do not allow cell phones on campus. (p. 37)

Students should be aware of what language should be used formally and informally when using social networking to communicate. Educators cannot simply expect students to know that abbreviations are unacceptable to use in school work without teaching when it is adequate to use those terms. Developing a deeper understanding of social networking language will require teachers to incorporate skills needed to utilize technology into classroom curriculum (Aldridge, Jeffrey, Taylor and Barringer-Brown, 2017, p. 37).

In terms of teaching the concept of using social media to communicate and create bonding relationships, Common Sense Education (2018) focuses on teaching students to reflect on building positive relationships, avoiding risky online talk, and understanding why certain conversations and topics are better to not be discussed online. As well as, knowing the power of your words and actions when using the internet (Common Sense Education, 2018). The digital curriculum built around this concept includes being able to identify "online predator" behaviors and knowing how to create boundaries (Common Sense Education, 2018). It is essential for students to be able to distinguish between positive and negative interactions when using social media. As well as, how to properly respond to an online situation where they have been placed in an uncomfortable, risky or dangerous situation (Common Sense Education, 2018).

When academically preparing students with disabilities, it is important for parents and educators to hold them accountable to reach high expectations such as entering higher education programs and/or becoming a member of the workplace. It is critical that all students, including (and maybe especially) students with disabilities understand how social media can benefit their future life opportunities. It is not uncommon for higher education programs or professors to incorporate social media into a course. For example, the State University of New York: College at Plattsburgh campus uses a program called *Moodle* for submitting assignments, creating forums with peers, receiving feedback, taking online courses and more. For students with disabilities who are being exposed to social media at a younger age, it could be beneficial for childhood and adolescence education programs to find a similar type of program. It is difficult to determine what programs the students will be exposed to in their future. By having practice with the general concept of using social media alongside education the student can gain experiences to be generalized and adapted across settings. According to Hashim and colleagues (2018), the rise of social media in higher education stems from:

The new generation of students whom social media have heavily penetrated their lives has transformed the teaching delivery approaches. Higher education institutions integrated the use of social media with their existing learning management system platform to provide students with better learning experiences. This education transformation is essential as it helps to centre the effort to promote better engagement between students and learning activities. Through active engagement, it can help to improve students' academic performances. (pp. 4-5)

It is essential for higher education teachers to recognize how "Active interactions and engagement between students and faculty members made students feel that they are engaging themselves in learning activities. This is essential to provide students with positive learning experiences as they feel they are not left out in class" (Hashim et al., 2018, p. 12). By introducing the collaboration of social media and academic experiences prior to beginning higher education, there is a greater likelihood students with disabilities will be prepared to engage in a variety of new learning experiences and become active participants within their new environment and courses.

As an individual progresses into higher education, adulthood and become more familiar with social media, the ability to use the internet independently becomes an option. Students can increase online independence by creating references guides to help them navigate various social media. For example, writing down the steps for reaching their desired website or application and the logging in process. In terms of maintaining internet safety, the individual may benefit from having rules displayed near the computer or saved on a mobile device. These rules should be created in the individual's own words to reiterate the do's and don'ts of social media usage. For students who experience difficulty with interpreting language or abbreviations, graphic organizers with translations of social media lingo can be a helpful tool. It is important for students to gradually move towards using social media independently, there should also be a system developed between the individual, their parents and the teacher for progress monitoring. Parents should be encouraged to befriend and interact with their children on social media to monitor information shared on their page. As well as, having discussions to review the rules of using social media. In terms of using social media in the classroom, teachers can pair students in learning groups where they are encouraged or mandated to use of social media communication for their course. Teacher can meet with groups in a whole class or small group setting to discuss how social media has improved or prevented their understanding of class content. Hashim and colleagues (2018) found, "Although the communication is not at the personal level, social media application was proven to support open discourse between faculty and students" (Hashim et al., 2018, p. 14). Educators should provide students with and without disabilities with explicit guidelines for communicating with peer and faculty through social media. Teachers can also use social media as part of their course to create a learning environment where the student can become more familiar with the internet and online collaboration. One of the ways teachers can promote social media communication with students is to provide feedback to questions or assignment online (Hashim et al., 2018, p. 14).

Students with disabilities should be exposed to how social media can be a tool used for self-directing one's learning and accessing a variety of informational sources. An important concept to include during lessons about conducting research should focus around the idea of just because something was said online, that does not necessarily make it true. Students should be able to identify when a source is credible and trustworthy. Additionally, students need to understand the responsibility of using social media and how information they share online may be misinterpreted (Common Sense Education, 2018). Being able to identify and evaluate information sources will be an essential skill for applying social media to higher education and the workforce. Students with disabilities should be taught how social media can portray stereotypes, misrepresent information, use media that have been digitally altered and determine the purpose of information found online. In terms of higher educations, students should be informed about copyright rules and how to avoid plagiarism (Common Sense Education, 2018).

From the beginning and throughout an individual with disabilities experiences with social media, the importance of internet safety should be explained and reviewed. Parents and educators should compose a set of rules with the student to determine what behavior and information is appropriate or inappropriate to share with the online community. As well as, what are the red flags of negative social media usage to avoid and why certain information should not be shared. Students with disabilities who experience social skill deficits could be at greater risk for online dangers. There are multiple components of internet safety, all of which must be addressed, supervised and practiced extensively. Individuals with disabilities must be aware of how to maintain privacy and security when using social media. This includes being able to protect one's personal information and understanding privacy rights to advocate for themselves and others (Common Sense Education, 2018). It is important for individuals with disabilities to be made aware of their rights and what can be done to protect themselves. This includes creating a password for your profile or account that others will not be able to predict. By not making your account or profile accessible to others, the individual can guarantee that their personal information remains private (Common Sense Education, 2018). Alongside these lessons about privacy and security, individuals should be taught about the concept of creating a digital footprint and what that means for their identity. For example, students should be informed not to post information online that you do not want everyone to see and how once something is put on the internet it will be out there forever (Wollak and Koppenhaver, 2011, p. 12). Students with disabilities should be made aware of how the information shared online can and most likely will affect your life outside of the internet community. A individual's "digital persona" can influence "one's sense of self, reputation and relationships" (Common Sense Education, 2018). When teaching students with disabilities about digital footprints and identity, parents and educators should focus on: how images can lead people to make assumptions, ways we can and cannot control our footprint, and how unfair gender stereotypes online can influence your sense of self (Common Sense Education, 2018).

One of the largest issues surrounding social media usage for children and teenagers, stems from inappropriate cyberbullying behaviors. All students should be taught how to be an upstander who contributes to building more positive, supportive communities free from harmful behavior or harassment (Common Sense Education, 2018). For students with disabilities, this concept can be broken down into two categories. Parents and educators should consider how to avoid participating in cyberbullying activity and how to remove themselves for a situation where they are the one being cyberbullied. It is essential for the individual with disabilities to have a support system at home and in the school community to inform if or when they believe another individual is harassing them through social media. Individuals should be taught to only display positive messages online, how to properly react to others inappropriate behaviors and the power of our words. In terms of reacting to the behaviors presented by others, individuals should be taught the characteristics of being an upstander instead of displaying similar negative behaviors back at the person or group of people. Students with disabilities should be able to "Recognize similarities and differences between in-person bullying, cyberbullying, and being mean, empathize with the targets of cyberbullying and identify strategies for dealing with cyberbullying" (Common Sense Education, 2018).

Through consistent practice and implementation of strategies, students with disabilities have the opportunity to become actively engaged members of the online community. The instruction necessary for the teaching of specific strategies and skills will vary depending on the original level of performance and deficits of the individual. Students with disabilities should be taught how to use social media to serve many purposes, such as connecting with others and accessing information. Additionally, the ability to safely avoid risky or potentially dangerous situations is important for students with disabilities to acquire. By learning how to effectively use social media, individuals with disabilities have the ability to explore new forms of communication, gain independence and advocate for themselves.

FUTURE RESEARCH IMPLICATIONS

In the 21st century, school districts should be required to mandate a technology curriculum that includes strategies to assist students in practicing and implementing important social media skills within a safe, supervised environment. By developing a focused curriculum, educators can be provided with resources and additional information to share with parents to extend social media education into the home and community. A specific curricula, with a multi-pronged approach, will create a more cohesive and consistent way to teach students with disabilities about social media usage. Currently, there are general social media curricula available, however, they do not emphasize the additional instruction that may be necessary when teaching students with disabilities to use social media.

In order for school districts or personnel to create social media curricula for students with disabilities, additional research must take place to design new strategies, methods and programs. New research should focus on developing, implementing, and evaluating a set of guidelines and key concepts for social media education. Guidelines could include how to use social media effectively and how these skills will be used within the school environment. Previous research, such as studies by Shepley and colleagues (2016) on using SMART board technology for presenting academic content, Satsangi and colleagues (2016) on using technological manipulatives for mathematics instruction, and Rivera and colleagues (2017) on how to use iPads for story interventions and teaching content picture vocabulary, mainly provided insight on how to assist students with disabilities with general technology usage. There should be an advancement in the collection of strategies developed specific toward teaching individuals with disabilities how to use social media. Strategies could even be correlated with other academic skills learned in the classroom to promote the generalization, maintenance and self-directing of the recurring concepts. There should be strategies developed for the different processes and purposes of social media that explicitly outline essential information. As well, developing and evaluating strategies to support specific deficits or classifications would be beneficial.

Perhaps most importantly, development and investigation of programs of this nature is an excellent (and timely) opportunity for academic researchers and the special education community of practitioners to work together alongside social media creators in order to brainstorm ideas and create new ways to make their programs more accessible for individuals with disabilities. For example, one aspect to collectively consider is the specific accommodations or modifications that could be made to the social media application or website to make it more accessible or user friendly. By involving social media developers in research of this nature, new sources of information can be provided about the purpose and navigation of a specific application. This type of front-end knowledge can then inform the development of new strategies, methods, and programs specific to teaching students with disabilities how to effectively and safely participate in the online community. New research can increase the exposure, participation and opportunities offered through social media.

CONCLUSION

By ensuring individuals with disabilities are being granted opportunities provided through social media usage, new ways of connecting and participating as a member of a larger community can be achieved. Over the course of the 21st century, social media has grown to become an important and for the most part daily influence in people's lives. Especially for the members of Generation Z, who have grown up alongside the rise of technology and social media. When individuals are not provided with explicit social media instruction, an entire community of people are at risk for being left at a disadvantage compared to their peers without disabilities. By teaching students with disabilities how to use social media effectively and safely, they can then develop a deeper understanding of what social media can offer them. Whether or not the individual with disabilities chooses to use social media is a decision left entirely up to them. However, there should not be a smaller percentage of individuals with disabilities using social media because of lack of exposure or understanding.

Through further research and the development of social media curriculums, educators will not be left in the dark about where to start when teaching their students with disabilities this unique set of skills. Having varying methods and approaches to teach the concept and navigation of social media will give educators and parents opportunities to try a variety of ways to teach social media concepts to students with disabilities. By developing educational programs which focus on how to use social media, the opportunities for educators and parents to participate in professional development will hopefully increase. Currently, society, technology, and the field of special education is rapidly growing. All of these components must come together to offer individuals with disabilities equal and safe access to social media. While there is a need for more research on methods of teaching students with disabilities appropriate use of social media, the current information available should be used to the fullest extent possible to assist educators and parents when determining what approaches and sources of content to use.

REFERENCES

Chiu, M. H. P., & Juang, M. J. (2013). A Content Analysis of Facebook Pages for Children with Disability. *Journal of Educational Media & Library Sciences*, *50*(3), 383–392.

Ahmed, A. (2018). Perceptions of using assistive technology for students with disabilities in the classroom. *International Journal of Special Education*, *33*(1), 129–139.

Aldridge, P. R., Jeffrey, P., Taylor, G., & Barringer-Brown, C. H. (2017). Social skills training for students of color with disabilities through the use of social networking. *Multicultural Education*, *24*(2), 34–38.

Anderson, M., & Perrin, A. (2017, April 07). Disabled Americans less likely to use technology. *Pew Research Center*. Retrieved from http://www.pewresearch.org/fact-tank/2017/04/07/disabled-americans-are-less-likely-to-use-technology/

Carter, T. (2018). Preparing Generation Z for the Teaching Profession. *SRATE Journal*, *27*(1), 1–8.

Casey, G. (2013). Interdisciplinary literacy through social media in the mathematics classroom: An action research study. *Journal of Adolescent & Adult Literacy*, *57*(1), 60–71. doi:10.1002/jaal.216

Ciullo, S., & Dimino, J. A. (2017). The Strategic Use of Scaffolded Instruction in Social Studies Interventions for Students with Learning Disabilities. *Learning Disabilities Research & Practice, 32*(3), 155–165.

Coyne, J., Lane, M., Nickson, L., Hollas, T., & Potter, J. P. (2017). Assessing Pre-Service Teachers' Attitudes and Self-Efficacy in Using Technology in the Classroom. *Teacher Education and Practice*, *30*(4), 637–651.

DeLay, D., Zhang, L., Hanish, L. D., Miller, C. F., Fabes, R. A., Martin, C. L., ... Updegraff, K. A. (2016). Peer Influence on Academic Performance: A Social Network Analysis of Social-Emotional Intervention Effects. *Prevention Science: The Official Journal Of The Society For Prevention Research*, *17*(8), 903–913. doi:10.100711121-016-0678-8 PMID:27436291

Desai, S. P., & Lele, V. (2017). Correlating Internet, Social Networks and Workplace – a Case of Generation Z Students. *Journal of Commerce and Management Thought*, (4), 802-815.

Digital Citizenship Curriculum. (2018, October 24). Retrieved from https://www.commonsense.org/education/digital-citizenship/curriculum?topic=privacy--security

Duverge, G. (2016, June 15). Web Accessibility Standards for People with Disabilities. Retrieved from https://online.pointpark.edu/information-technology/web-accessibility-people-with-disabilities/

Ellahi, A. (2018). Social Networking Sites as Formal Learning Environments in Business Education. *Journal of Educational Technology & Society*, *21*(4), 64–75.

Evans, C. (n.d.). 5 Ways to Help Students with Special Needs. *Special Needs*. Retrieved from http://www.specialneeds.com/activities/general-special-needs/five-ways-help-students-special-needs

Friedman, L. (2014, April 22). 5 Benefits of Using Social Media. Retrieved from https://www.linkedin.com/pulse/20140422162738-44670464-5-benefits-of-using-social-media

Hashim, K. F., Rashid, A., & Atalla, S. (2018). Social Media for Teaching and Learning within Higher Education Institution: A Bibliometric Analysis of the Literature (2008-2018). *International Journal of Interactive Mobile Technologies*, *12*(7), 4–19. doi:10.3991/ijim.v12i7.9634

Hemsley, B., Balandin, S., Palmer, S., & Dann, S. (2017). A call for innovative social media research in the field of augmentative and alternative communication. *AAC: Augmentative & Alternative Communication*, *33*(1), 14–22. PMID:28121173

Hoffmann, M. M., & Ramirez, A. Y. (2018). Students' Attitudes Toward Teacher Use of Technology in Classrooms. *Multicultural Education*, *25*(2), 51–56.

Jonathon, R., & Victoria, Z. (2011). Social Networking in an Intensive English Program Classroom: A Language Socialization Perspective. *CALICO Journal*, (2), 326.

Kaplan, A., & Haenlein, M. (2010). Users of the world, unite! The challenges and opportunities of Social Media. *Business Horizons*, *53*(1), 53–68. doi:10.1016/j.bushor.2009.09.003

Kelly, S. M., & Smith, T. J. (2008). The Digital Social Interactions of Students with Visual Impairments: Findings from Two National Surveys. *Journal of Visual Impairment & Blindness*, *102*(9), 528–539. doi:10.1177/0145482X0810200903

Kim, E., & Drumwright, M. (2016). Full length article: Engaging consumers and building relationships in social media: How social relatedness influences intrinsic vs. extrinsic consumer motivation. *Computers in Human Behavior*, *63*, 970–979. doi:10.1016/j.chb.2016.06.025

Kind, T., & Evans, Y. (2015). Social media for lifelong learning. *International Review of Psychiatry (Abingdon, England)*, *27*(2), 124–132. doi:10.3109/09540261.2014.990421 PMID:25906988

Lough, E., & Fisher, M. H. (2016). Internet use and online safety in adults with Williams syndrome. *Journal of Intellectual Disability Research*, *60*(10), 1020–1030. doi:10.1111/jir.12281 PMID:27174494

Loveland, E. (2017). Instant Generation. *Journal of College Admission*, (234): 34–38.

Making decisions: Suggestions for schools and early childhood services. (n.d.). *Kids Matter.* Retrieved from https://www.kidsmatter.edu.au/mental-health-matters/social-and-emotional-learning/making-decisions/suggestions-schools-and-early

Masters in Special Education Degree Program Guide. (2018). *Is There a Role for Social Media in Special Education*. Retrieved from https://www.masters-in-special-education.com/faq/is-there-a-role-for-social-media-in-special-education

Media, H. H. (2018). Meet Gen Z: The social generation. Retrieved from http://thinking.hhcc.com/?utm_campaign=ThoughtLeadership—GenZ&utm_source=ppc&gclid=Cj0KCQiA8f_eBRDcARIsAEKwRGcKjpjl6Gw8rvoQfZD7_gmts7FmfvzHxrbvc0cgdzRDT2y1RJb5igwaAlNbEALw_wcB

MediaS. (2004). Retrieved from https://www.merriam-webster.com/dictionary/social-media

Miller, R. A. (2017). "My voice is definitely strongest in online communities": Students using social media for queer and disability identity-making. *Journal of College Student Development*, *58*(4), 509–525.

Park, H., & Lee, H. (2013). Show us you are real: The effect of human-versus-organizational presence on online relationship building through social networking sites. *Cyberpsychology, Behavior, and Social Networking*, *16*(4), 265–271. doi:10.1089/cyber.2012.0051 PMID:23363228

Probst, D. (2017). Social Media Literacy as an IEP Intervention for Social and Emotional Learning. *The Journal of Media Literacy Education, 9*(2), 45–57. doi:10.23860/JMLE-2019-09-02-04

Puiu, S. (2017). Generation Z -- an Educational and Managerial Perspective. *Revista Tinerilor Economisti [Young Economists Journal], 14*(29), 62–72.

Ranaldo, M. (2013). Communicating with 21st Century Bulletin Boards. *Exceptional Parent, 43*(2), 30–32.

Rivera, C. J., Hudson, M. E., Weiss, S. L., & Zambone, A. (2017). Using a Multicomponent Multimedia Shared Story Intervention with an iPad to Teach Content Picture Vocabulary to Students with Developmental Disabilities. *Education & Treatment of Children, 40*(3), 327–352. doi:10.1353/etc.2017.0014

Rodriguez, J. E. (2011). Social Media Use in Higher Education: Key Areas to Consider for Educators. *MERLOT Journal of Online Learning and Teaching, 7*(4), 539–550.

Rothman, D. (2016). A Tsunami of learners called Generation Z. Retrieved from http://www.mdle.net/JoumaFA_Tsunami_of_Learners_Called_Generation_Z.pdf

Satsangi, R., Hammer, R., & Hogan, C. D. (2018). Studying virtual manipulatives paired with explicit instruction to teach algebraic equations to students with learning disabilities. *Learning Disability Quarterly, 41*(4), 227–242. doi:10.1177/0731948718769248

Schlee, R. P., & Harich, K. R. (2013). Teaching Students How to Integrate and Assess Social Networking Tools in Marketing Communications. *Marketing Education Review, 23*(3), 209–224. doi:10.2753/MER1052-8008230301

Schwieger, D., & Ladwig, C. (2018). Reaching and Retaining the Next Generation: Adapting to the Expectations of Gen Z in the Classroom. *Information Systems Education Journal, 16*(3), 45–54.

Shepley, C., Lane, J. D., & Gast, D. L. (2016). Using SMART board technology to teach young students with disabilities and limited group learning experience to read environmental text. *Education and Training in Autism and Developmental Disabilities, 51*(4), 404–420.

Singh, A. (July. (2014). Challenges of Issues of Generation Z. *IOSR Journal of Business and Management, 16*(7), 59–63.

Smart Technologies and Teachers Complete Their First Global Collaboration Project. (2016). eParent.com.

Stevens, L. B. (2105, June 25). 5 Dangers of Social Media to Discuss With Your Kids. *Care*. Retrieved from https://www.care.com/c/stories/4275/5-dangers-of-social-media-to-discuss-with-you/

Teaching Students with Disabilities about Online Safety. (2014). *Power up what works*. Retrieved from https://powerupwhatworks.org/technology/teaching-students-disabilities-about-online-safety

Turner, A. (2015). Generation Z: Technology and Social Interest. *Journal of Individual Psychology*, *71*(2), 103–113. doi:10.1353/jip.2015.0021

U.S. population with a social media profile 2018. (2018). *Statista*. Retrieved from https://www.statista.com/statistics/273476/percentage-of-us-population-with-a-social-network-profile/

Vogel, F., Wecker, C., Kollar, I., & Fischer, F. (2017). Socio-cognitive scaffolding with computer-supported collaboration scripts: A meta-analysis. *Educational Psychology Review*, *29*(3), 477–511. doi:10.100710648-016-9361-7

Wang, K., Lv, Y., & Zhang, Z. (2018). Relationship between Extroversion and Social Use of Social Networking Sites. *Social Behavior and Personality*, *46*(10), 1597–1609. doi:10.2224bp.7210

Wollak, B. A., & Koppenhaver, D. A. (2011). Developing technology-supported, evidence-based writing instruction for adolescents with significant writing disabilities. *Assistive Technology Outcomes And Benefits*, *7*(1), 1–23.

Chapter 5
What's Seen and Unseen:
The Gen Z Experience in the Classroom

Claudia Marie Bertolone-Smith
State University of New York at Plattsburgh, USA

Ana Maria Spagna
Antioch University of Los Angeles, USA

ABSTRACT

Using the authors' varied experiences in the classroom with Gen Z and the next generation on its way, this chapter investigates an urgent and often unseen issue for students in higher education. With increased pressure to perform, a tension between time and technology, and lasting impacts from the Great Recession, Gen Z students suffer from a growing number of mental health issues. College coursework should challenge students; however, Gen Z often becomes impaired by what is a real and prevalent anxiety. The authors explore the ways Gen Z operates in the classroom, potential causes for this crisis, and solutions to improve Gen Z experiences in our institutions.

DOI: 10.4018/978-1-5225-7763-8.ch005

INTRODUCTION

Students in our higher institution courses face serious economic, academic, cultural, and personal challenges. As members of Generation Z they grew up during the Great Recession, a longer and deeper economic downturn than Americans had known for 70 years, the scope of which reached across the socioeconomic spectrum (Ariel, 2013). As a result, our students' families are more likely than in the past to have experienced the loss of employment, secure housing, and food sources. They also belong to the first generation to grow up entirely in the age of the internet with the associated pressures of near-constant digital engagement and the concurrent distractions of social media, texting, and video gaming. They've been educated in an era of ever-ratcheting academic expectations and high stakes testing, and they're more likely than ever before to have been victims of gun violence and/or sexual assault. Perhaps as result of one or more of these causes, in 2018, one in four college students had been diagnosed with anxiety (Lipka, 2018).

BACKGROUND

As authors and educators, we approach this topic from opposite ends of the spectrum of experience. One of us (Ana Maria) has no children and has been teaching writing to adults—baby boomers and Generation X students—for many years. The other (Claudia) has three children, two millennials and one a member of Generation Z, and has been teaching Gen Z students for a decade. Yet, our similar observations lead us to conclude that today's young adults face challenges that should be acknowledged and addressed with urgency. In both our situations, we notice an increased anxiety concerning the level of work required. We notice that students grow quiet when they feel they can't or don't understand. Too often, they suffer from the isolating envy of negatively comparing themselves to others. Twenge (2017) asserts that Gen Z is on the verge of the most severe mental health crisis for young people in decades, and it's not surprising. In this chapter, we unconventionally and intentionally choose to share our experiences in first person to highlight personal insights and the vulnerable voices of Gen Z. We offer possible solutions and suggestions for continued research for moving towards more hopeful and happier outcomes for Gen Z students.

MAIN FOCUS OF THE CHAPTER

Meeting Them on the Page: Ana Maria Spagna

I have written and published nonfiction books, essays, and stories. My passion lies in this kind of self-expression, and after many years teaching graduate students in MFA programs, I landed a job at a small liberal arts college in the Pacific Northwest. The students would be traditional age and relatively privileged, and while people warned me anecdotally, and predictably, about "kids today"—how they're addicted to technology, how they have no attention span, and goodness, their terrible manners! —when I arrived on campus, I found them delightful in every way. They were smart, earnest, polite, and eager to learn.

They were also suffering.

I didn't see it at first. Anxiety and depression did not always show on the surface; often it didn't show at all. But the assignments in a creative nonfiction writing class require a certain amount of self-disclosure, and when they turned in their journals for the first time, I was stunned. The students described, in specific detail and with a startling level of self-awareness, struggles that went far beyond nervousness about a test or sadness over a break-up. The symptoms they described were physical and acute, from shortness of breath to migraines, insomnia, irritable bowel syndrome, and debilitating chronic pain.

When I pushed them gently—the work of shaping a nonfiction story can brush dangerously, if necessarily, close to therapy—they shared more. The traced their troubles to trauma or to economic or academic anxiety; some couldn't name a source at all and that fact troubled them further. Some had been on medication for years, some never had. Ditto for counseling. Some self-medicated with drugs or alcohol; others tried diet and exercise. But most heartbreakingly, and in some ways most frighteningly, on campus many of them felt as though they couldn't talk to anyone about their problems, especially not to professors.

As much as I wanted to disagree, I could see what they meant. At a mid-semester conference with colleagues, a pall of exasperation pervaded, a sense that accommodations for anxious students—extra time for tests, presumably, and flexibility on deadlines—amounted to lowering academic standards. And I'd be lying if I said I didn't feel it occasionally myself, especially in my literature courses, which included more traditional (and to students, perhaps, more boring) assignments than creative writing did. The late papers, shoddily written, paired with the barrage of emails from the counseling center requesting extended deadlines did rankle. I could not help thinking: get with the program.

I learned later, by talking with other teachers, how common my experience was. An article in *The Chronicle of Higher Education* last year reported that one in four college students today suffer anxiety, and less than 40% get help. The same article pointed to a stigma around discussing mental health, resulting in isolation, and quoted students who claimed they could talk to other students, but not to professors "in part because professors are perceived as considering the anxiety a personal failing spawned by lack of preparedness" (Lipka, 2018, p. 14).

Gen Z to Gen Alpha: Buckle Your Seatbelts - Claudia Bertolone-Smith

I have been a classroom teacher for 25 years. I recently completed a doctoral degree in mathematics education, and this fall, I began working as an assistant professor. I have three children; two millennials and a Gen Z. The millennials left home to attend college and find themselves: to work in medicine, to work in cancer research, to change the world and the status quo. My Gen Z son carefully and persistently tightens his hold on "status quo." He would only consider one option for school, the university an hour away from home with no student or parent loans. The summer before he went to college, he decided to take an Emergency Medical Technician (EMT) course at a community college. Slowly, college faded into the background as he became enchanted with passing the course and testing to be an EMT with the local fire district. "I'll be making a great salary," he'd say, and when pressed, he'd admit, "I just hate money. It makes me so nervous." I thought we skated through the recession unscathed. My son, who was seven when it hit, nine when it ended, took on our anxiety about money; my husband's graphic design business folded, I had to go back to work full time, and we struggled to put his sisters through college. He absorbed this angst, and now I see it affecting his perception of his own ability to secure financial stability.

Last year, I taught a fifth-grade class in a small rural town. The school population consisted of many low socio-economic status families with plenty of trauma to go around. My students were born in 2008 and 2009, smack in the middle of the Great Recession. This population of students were toddlers during the economic downturn and heavily dependent on parent care. According to Ariel (2013), the stressors of the current time period have potentially an even greater negative effect on childhood development. Additionally, she reported that while parents who were not working had more time, this time was not likely spent on traditional parenting norms such as reading to your child, providing extracurricular experiences, and developing a family bond. Some parents managed stress levels by engaging in escape activities (i.e. social media, video games, alcohol and recreational drug use) to alleviate the constant economic worry. While some argue that the Great Recession ended in 2009, for this small rural town, the effects of housing, food, and job insecurity reverberated well into 2018. They have lived with the impact of the recession their entire lives.

These students do not remember a time when the internet was not available; I had students on free breakfast and lunch with smart phones in their pockets. They are over-stimulated by technology and often report unlimited access to video games and the internet. Parents who limit access often face an uphill battle. It is common for students to have internet access at school, in public places, and at friends' houses. Reducing access indicates the need to remove a laptop or phone, which has other necessary purposes. These students don't sleep enough; in a poll of 2,000 parents, one in six parents report their teens have trouble sleeping, and half of the parents blame the draw of electronic devices. Additionally, parents report that their teens stay up worrying about school (31%), and 23% report that they stay up worrying about their social lives (Fulton, 2018).

As an elementary school teacher, I increasingly dealt with issues caused by technology: cyber-bullying, cyber-sexting; gaming addiction, and access to pornography. Exposure to pornography is especially harmful for the maturation process. Pornography causes a desperate confusion about how to negotiate budding feelings of attraction that are appropriate, with sexually graphic images. The American College of Pediatricians (2016) reports that childhood use of pornography is associated with negative emotional, psychological, and physical health outcomes. Children who view pornography are more likely to exhibit depression, anxiety, violent behavior, promiscuity, engage in sexual acts at a younger age, and a have a distorted view of relationships between men and women. The adoption of one-to-one Chromebook policies in schools paired with students' creative ability to work around firewalls can be problematic. In my class, we dealt with students searching for pornographic photos and videos and sharing them with each other. Once, I had to reprimand two young boys who were on the swing set and calling out, "Nice vagina!" (except they were using slang terms) to girls as they passed by. When we questioned the boys, we found that an older brother was forcing one of the boys to watch pornography at home. Fortunately, I knew the brother and his high school principal. She brought him to my classroom and we spoke to the boys together. The principal unflinchingly addressed the inappropriate actions by the brother. We had a frank discussion about the addictive and destructive properties of pornography. While having a crush or "liking" someone is commonplace in classrooms, one could argue that access to pornography has changed the nature and the intent of a natural curiosity between boys and girls.

Many of my students were resilient and gritty, but not for academics. They expected multiple levels of distress in their own lives, in their families, and in others' lives. The stories of trauma shared at our morning meetings each day were heartbreaking, and over time, became commonplace. Jail, addiction, abuse, poverty, death, sexuality, racism, classism--we processed and held it all in our classroom community. This group of students was uniquely accepting of others' trauma and slow to judge. At the same time, those experiencing the deepest trauma were often the first to inflict it upon their classmates. Our class read *Wonder* by R.J. Palacio (2012). In this story, a young boy, Auggie, is mercilessly teased by his classmates with a game called the "Cheese Touch." Whenever anyone accidentally touched Auggie, his classmates would act as if they had been given the plague. I swear the whole class cried together when I read this aloud. "How could they?" they exclaimed. No less than three weeks later, I found myself having a stern conversation with four boys who had essentially done the same exact thing to a young woman in our class. This young woman was overwhelmingly distressed by the situation. When there was a consequence, the boys were angry and thought it unfair. Many of my students were quick to react, quick to give up, and slow to recognize their piece of the problem.

It can be difficult for some students in this generation to believe a math assignment or reading a text more deeply will alleviate the stress of their lives. They are up for quick fixes and big dreams: owning mansions and Lamborghinis funded by being a "YouTuber" (an occupation I still don't understand.) They benefit from small chunks of curriculum coupled with constant feedback. In my class last year, students were taught a district adopted curriculum on mindfulness, dealing with feelings, and calming down before acting. Recently, a Denver based elementary school substituted yoga practice with detention with tremendous success (Asmar, 2018).

One of our brightest students got off the bus one morning and walked towards me as I stood on guard for bus duty. He stopped by to chat. He told me he was tired because he stayed up late the night before. I asked him what was going on (with this generation it could be caused by a whole host of things.) He shared that he had stayed up until 3:00 am watching his parents pass a new level in popular online video game. Again, parents are not immune to the lure of technology as a way to escape, and it appears this may impact parental decision making. Using technology to avoid stress can lead to an underdeveloped ability to regulate emotions and deal with challenging situations. Experiencing and managing strong emotions are important skills developed in childhood and adolescence to develop internal regulatory processes, which are essential components of mental health (Hoge, Bickham, & Cantor, 2017).

Buckle your seatbelts, because the next generation of students entering secondary and higher education is going to be interesting.

ISSUES, CONTROVERSIES, PROBLEMS: WHAT'S AT THE ROOT?

Technology

Before Gen Z, the internet was considered a privilege, and in the transition to Gen Z, it is now considered a human right (Koulopoulos & Keldsen, 2014). Instead of working or playing outside, teens are more likely to remain tethered to their devices. In 2018, the World Health Organization classified gaming disorder as a diagnosable disease. Twenge (2017) argues that rather than "Gen Z", this generation could be labeled "iGen" to uniquely acknowledge the influence of internet and smartphones on their experiences so far. "Today's teens may go to fewer parties and spend less time together in person, but when they do congregate, they document their hangouts relentlessly — on Snapchat, Instagram, Facebook," Twenge wrote recently in *The Atlantic*. "Those not invited to come along are keenly aware of it." Twenge analyzed data collected from 1991 to 2015 and found the number of teens who report satisfaction with their 'lives as a whole' reached its lowest point in 2015, and the data show that teens are lonelier now than they have been since 1991. Feeling left out has reached an all-time high, and Twenge argues that increased screen time lowers in-person social interaction which results in increased loneliness. Additionally, more time on phones and social media with less person-to-person interaction is one possible reason the Gen Z is reported to be less sexually active than millennials or GenX. The percentage of sexually active high school students dropped from 54% in 1991 to 41% in 2015 (CDC, 2015).

Economic Anxiety

The extent to which Gen Z students have experienced economic strain varies, but few have been unaffected. In 2010, of the 17.2 million households that were food insecure, 3.9 million households included children (Coleman-Jensen, Nord, Andrews & Carlson, 2012). The long-term effects are only beginning to be understood. A "small but rigorous body of evidence" suggests that parental job and income losses, moving, and subjective perception of financial instability has a negative impact on human capital accumulation and emotional well-being (Ariel, 2013, p.245). One way this manifests on a practical level on college campuses is concern about job prospects. Having absorbed the fear of losing employment, many students place the quick path to security at higher value than exploring possibilities. They want to know from the outset what job they can expect to have and what the pay will be.

Even students who come from more affluent backgrounds face a more amorphous, but no less acute, kind of economic anxiety. Amid parents, teachers, and even their peers, they face a near constant demand for achievement, and by the time they reach college, the achievement may be less tied to specific outcomes. Earlier in their academic careers, they are trained to achieve broadly: in sports, music, student government, and a myriad of other activities, with the goal of admission to a "good" college. Once in college, the pattern of behavior remains. "There's a stigma around relaxing," one first-year student told me (Ana Maria) in my office. "When people ask what you plan to do on the weekend, they expect a list of activities, one after the next." The problem may intensify when they discover the choice of careers at which they can actually make a living is far more limited than the broad "well-rounded" artistic or esoteric avocations they've been nudged toward. It's a reality that's lurked under the surface for every generation of college graduates since Dustin Hoffman faced a future in plastics in 1968, but the weight of student loans, not to mention health care and housing costs, is considerably higher today.

Academic Anxiety

In *The Carpenter and the Gardener* (2016), Alison Gopnik argues that the carpenter model – training children to complete tasks with only one correct outcome – tends to be less effective than the gardener model making the soil fertile, so to speak, to allow for exploration of possibilities. The anxiety of these students can be traced, at least in part, to too much carpenter training, constantly doing the right thing at the right time for the right outcome. The 2018 National Teacher of the Year, Mandy Manning, tends to agree, advocating for less rigid classroom structure paired with time for exploration away from screens (M. Manning, personal communication, Oct. 3, 2018). Social media tends to increase negative self-comparison, especially since people post their successes. What is not often posted is the failure and essential learning that occurs on the way to success. This missing piece can lead vulnerable teens to become envious, depressed, and believing that they alone experience failure in their lives. It is not surprising that Gen Z scores lower in narcissism than the millennials who came before them (Twenge, 2017).

The Role of Medication

As far back as 2013, college counseling centers reported anxiety as the top presenting concern among college students (41.6%) followed by depression (36%). The same report stated that on average 24.5% of clients were taking psychotropic medications

(American Psychological Association, 2013). These data matched my (Ana Maria's) experience with Gen Z undergraduates in creative writing courses. Among the subjects, students wrote about with nuance and precision was the ways medication for anxiety and/or depression affected their lives. You cannot read a detailed description of young adult's experience of a panic attack on a city bus quelled, or a suicidal crisis averted, by taking a pill and be unmoved. Yet the students also worried about how prescription drugs dulled their senses, made them sleepy in class, and mixed poorly, if ill-advisedly, with alcohol. If they seemed more dependent on medication than previous generations of students, they also seemed more aware of the dangers of dependency, which, in turn, added to anxiety. This relative prevalence of mental illness diagnoses combined with prescription solutions may, in some cases, become a vicious circle when we consider the fact that between 1991-2010 the number of prescription stimulants to school age kids tripled, and side effects of the most commonly prescribed stimulants, Ritalin and Adderall, are anxiety and depression (Macy, 2018, p. 134).

The Role of Trauma

Gen Z students are more willing than students of our own generation to discuss sexual assault, from child abuse to date rape, and to display a general understanding of PTSD and its symptoms. Research supports this observation: one study found that two thirds of college students had experienced a traumatic event, a quarter of had suffered sexual assault, and 10% met the criteria for PTSD (Read et al., 2011). The students also specifically referenced school shootings; many of them had been in a school or a near a school when a shooting occurred. *The Washington Post* reported that as of early 2018, more than 187,000 students nationwide had been directly affected by school shootings since 1995 (Cox & Rich, 2018).

SOLUTIONS AND RECOMMENDATIONS

Some days, after the children had gone home, I (Claudia) felt like I had been hit by a school bus. While many teachers in my building felt the same way, we were reassured by the administration that what we dealt with was just "a bubble" of behavior, of high needs, and academic distress. It's not a bubble. It is what is here now; and we would be wise to firstly acknowledge it; and secondly get them the help they need. In a survey of more than 10,000 public school teachers in 2012, ninety nine percent of teachers reported they have students who need intervention for social, emotional, and behavioral challenges, while veteran teachers report increasing numbers of students living in poverty, who are hungry and homeless, and who have behavior issues (Bill & Melinda Gates Foundation, 2012). As Twenge (2017) reflects, "we all need to understand them, including friends and family looking out for them, businesses searching for new recruits, universities and colleges who will educate and guide them" (p. 4).

We know that overburdening young people with expectations can be counterproductive, and often it happens unknowingly. One group of students shared anecdotes about a counselor they admire who always greets them by asking if they've signed up yet for this activity or applied to be a resident advisor or to take a summer internship. They acknowledged the counselor's good intentions but claimed the pressure these expectations created had led to panic attacks. To be sure, counselors—and teachers—face a challenge in situations like this. How do we balance the task of meeting students' academic needs with caring for their mental health, especially when the underlying problem is not obvious? Training is surely part of the answer. We can learn to recognize the symptoms of anxiety and to help students recognize their own symptoms, so they can calm their bodies and prevent a panic attack before it occurs (Dwyer, 2014). On the most basic level, we must accept the fact that academic success requires good mental health. We can't nurture the former without the latter.

We also know overexposure to technology creates problems. While more research seems crucial, the need to cut back is both intuitive and urgent. A first-year student shared that her college recommends that they become present in their lives and in their experiences by avoiding technology and connecting with others. She is part of a college initiative to participate in a meditation practice each day. A cafe I recently visited had a sign, "We are a lap-top free facility. Please connect with others in your time here." As Twenge asserts, "there is a simple, free way to improve mental health, put down the phone, and do something else" (p. 118). If that "something else" takes a person outdoors, all the better, as a rash of research from around the world has shown time spent outdoors can improve mood, lower blood pressure, and increase attention span, reducing the need for medication for ADHD (Williams, 2017, p. 234). We can offer our students these mantras--get more sleep, spend time with friends, go outside and exercise. We can also heed the same in our own lives to model health. As healthier people, we will surely be better educators.

Where curriculum allows, include writing or art as self-expression. One irony and bright light of teaching creative writing at the liberal arts college was that rarely were these students, any students, late with expressive assignments. Their poems, stories, essays were original, complete, well-conceived, and compelling. The students' work was not perfect by any stretch, but most were excited to revise their work (a requirement of the course) and in doing so, often to delve even more deeply into their pain and the source(s) thereof. As teachers we can no longer stand and deliver curriculum. Instead, we need to use the curriculum as a vehicle for self-expression and self-understanding.

Another step to take is to acknowledge that the problem is bigger and more serious than it used to be. On the most basic level, this may mean believing a student who claims to have a problem. Twenge argues that "Teens are physically safer than ever, yet they are more mentally vulnerable" (2017, p. 3). Previous generations had these problems but not to the extent, not to the extreme. There has been a sharp rise in depression since 2010; 56% more teens reported experiencing a major depressive episode (MDE). In 2016, 2.2 million adolescents experienced an MDE with severe impairment in participating in home and school activities (Substance Abuse and Mental Health Services Administration, 2016). A primary risk factor for self-harm and suicide is depression, especially if it is severe. In fact, 46% more 15-19-year olds committed suicide in 2015 than 2007 (Twenge, 2017). The mental struggles of Gen Z have very serious consequences. Perhaps Gen Z is illustrating the effects of technology overuse, economic and academic anxiety, and overexposure to trauma. They are vulnerable and reaching out for help. We need to respond quickly and keep our wits about us as we do.

One simple step to take for those in higher education is to make time to listen and take them seriously. Within our institutions, a salient solution would be to set up reliable and timely intervention systems for students who seek professional intervention. Students may rely on and use a resource more regularly if it is quickly accessible. Googling teaches us to expect 2,000,000 results in .072 seconds. Students may reach out at critical points; it makes no sense to tell a student in crisis there is an available appointment in two weeks. Getting them help when they reach out is essential, as the window of opportunity may be closing quickly. When they finally call a counseling center or crisis line, they may have processed many of their feelings and decisions on social media; hence, they may be reaching out in person as a last step.

FUTURE RESEARCH

This generation has unique qualities and concerns. Yes, they need to be understood by those that help, guide, and hire them. Yet, they also need to understand themselves. As with climate change, turning the tide requires an immense institutional commitment in multiple directions, not all of them defined. For people on the ground, every day, some steps may be more manageable.

Further research into the tension between Gen Z needs and what we are currently providing is warranted. Long waiting lists for appointments may be a reality of budget cuts and lack of personnel. Future research can investigate the best way to offer real-time intervention with an educated and caring human being. Children are attending public schools that increasingly offer on-site counseling services, social services, and in-class instruction on resiliency, assertiveness, and mental well-being. The next generation of students is being taught to openly, and without shame, advocate for their mental health. Studies assessing how secondary and higher education institutions can match this trend are essential. Rethinking the stigma of mental health, and instead focusing on mental health and mindfulness may be the first steps in retooling for change. With further research, we may be able to find the best interventions to alleviate the suffering of Gen Z.

CONCLUSION

In closing, as urgent as these challenges are for today's young adults, it would be disingenuous to suggest we aren't all engaged in a grand negotiation with technology, wherein it's far too easy to lose track of what matters most. Gen Z retreats into technology, their lifelong companion, but it is an inaccurate mirror of a real life, one that reinforces insecurities and isolates vulnerable individuals in facsimiles of community. It falls on educators to counter this unreality, to rebuild confidence and connection. Yet we often feel flat-footed in addressing the complex problems that technology creates and amplifies, while still acknowledging the need for 21st century learning experiences. We struggle with the increase in mental health issues, problematic behavior, and decrease in achievement. Gen Z refuses to let us rely on what worked for other generations or on what seems to be a molasses pace of change in educational policies.

Yet, for all the angst, our schools are filled with young people cautiously putting a toe into uncharted waters. They are brave, they are stubborn, and they will eventually succeed. No doubt, Gen Z and what comes next will force a seismic shift in educational practices and policies, eventually leading to the discovery of interventions that work. The outcome may increase life satisfaction and happiness for us all.

REFERENCES

American College of Pediatricians. (2016). *The impact of pornography on children*. Retrieved from https://www.acpeds.org/the-college-speaks/position-statements/the-impact-of-pornography-on-children

American Psychological Association. (2013, June). College students' mental health is a growing concern, survey finds. *Monitor on Psychology*, *44*, 6. Retrieved from https://www.apa.org/monitor/2013/06/college-students.aspx

Ariel, K. (2013). Effects of the great recession on child development. *The Annals of the American Academy of Political and Social Science*, *232*. Retrieved from http://search.ebscohost.com.webdb.plattsburgh.edu:2048/login.aspx?direct=true&db=edsjsr&AN=edsjsr.24541684&site=eds-live&scope=site

Asmar, M. (2018, February 26). Why this Denver elementary school replaced detention with yoga. *Chalkbeat*. Retrieved from https://www.chalkbeat.org/posts/co/2018/02/26/why-this-denver-elementary-school-has-replaced-detention-with-yoga/

Bill & Melinda Gates Foundation. (2012b). Primary sources 2012: America's teachers on the teaching profession, a project of Scholastic and the Bill & Melinda Gates Foundation. Retrieved from http://www.scholastic.com/primarysources/pdfs/Gates2012_full.pdf

Centers for Disease Control and Prevention. (2015). *Trends in the Prevalence of Sexual Behaviors and HIV Testing National YRBS: 1991—2015*. Retrieved from https://www.cdc.gov/healthyyouth/data/yrbs/pdf/trends/2015_us_sexual_trend_yrbs.pdf

Centers for Disease Control and Prevention. (2018). *U.S. drug overdose deaths continue to rise; increase fueled by synthetic opioids* [Press Release]. Retrieved from https://www.cdc.gov/media/releases/2018/p0329-drug-overdose-deaths.html

Coleman-Jensen, A., Nord, M., Andrews, M., & Carlson, S. (2012). Household food security in the United States in 2011. Economic Research Report Number 141. Washington, DC: United States Department of Agriculture. Retrieved from https://www.ers.usda.gov/webdocs/publications/45020/30967_err141.pdf?v=41165

Cox, J. W., & Rich, S. (2018, March 25). Scarred by school shootings. *The Washington Post*. Retrieved from www.washingtonpost.com/graphics/2018/local/us-school-shootings-history/?utm_term=.fe7ba70c0eaf

Dwyer, L. (2014, October 3). When anxiety hits at schools. *The Atlantic*. Retrieved from https://www.theatlantic.com/health/archive/2014/10/when-anxiety-hits-at-school/380622/

Fulton, A. (2018). Teens sleeping too much, or not enough? Parents can help. *NPR*. Retrieved from https://www.npr.org/sections/health-shots/2018/09/23/650452971/teens-sleeping-too-much-or-not-enough-parents-can-help

Gopnik, A. (2016). *The Carpenter and the Gardener: What the New Science of Child Development Tells Us About the Relationship Between Parents and Children*. New York, NY: Farrar, Straus & Giroux.

Hoge, E., Bickham, D., & Cantor, J. (2017). Digital media, anxiety, and depression in children. *Pediatrics*, *140*(Supplement 2), S76–S80. doi:10.1542/peds.2016-1758G PMID:29093037

Koulopoulos, T., & Keldsen, D. (2014). *The Gen Z Effect: The six forces shaping the future business*. Brookline, MA: Bibliomotion Inc.

Lipka, S. (2018). 'I didn't know how to ask for help': Stories of students with anxiety. *The Chronicle of Higher Education*, *64*(22), 14. Retrieved from https://www.chronicle.com/article/I-Didn-t-Know-How-to-Ask/242412

Macy, B. (2018). *Dopesick: Dealers, Doctors, and the Drug Company that Addicted America*. New York, NY: Little Brown & Company.

Palacio, R. J. (2012). *Wonder*. New York, NY: Alfred A. Knopf Inc.

Read, J. P., Ouimette, P., White, J., Colder, C., & Farrow, S. (2011). Rates of DSM-IV-TR trauma exposure and posttraumatic stress disorder among newly matriculated college students. *Psychological Trauma: Theory, Research, Practice, and Policy*, *3*(3), 148–156. doi:10.1037/a0021260 PMID:25621098

Substance Abuse and Mental Health Services Administration. (2017). *Key substance use and mental health indicators in the United States: Results from the 2016 National Survey on Drug Use and Health* (HHS Publication No. SMA 17-5044, NSDUH Series H-52). Rockville, MD: Center for Behavioral Health Statistics and Quality, Substance Abuse and Mental Health Services Administration. Retrieved from https://www. samhsa.gov/data/

Twenge, J. M. (2017). *IGEN: Why today's super-connected kids are growing up less rebellious, more tolerant, less happy-- and completely unprepared for adulthood and (what this means for the rest of us)*. New York, NY: Atria.

Twenge, J. M. (2017, September). Have smart-phones destroyed a generation? *The Atlantic*. Retrieved from https://www.theatlantic.com/magazine/archive/2017/09/has-the-smartphone-destroyed-a-generation/534198/

Williams, F. (2017). *The Nature Fix: Why Nature Makes Us Happier, Healthier, and More Creative*. New York, NY: W.W. Norton & Company.

World Health Organization. (2018). *Gaming disorder. Online Q & A*. Retrieved from https://www.who.int/features/qa/gaming-disorder/en/

Chapter 6
Are We Part of the Problem?
Teacher Preparation Programs, Educational Technology, and the Mis-Education of Future Teachers

Heidi Lee Schnackenberg
State University of New York at Plattsburgh, USA

ABSTRACT

Do a quick search in Google Scholar and you will find overwhelming evidence that teachers both are and are not using technology in meaningful ways to enhance student learning. Actually, just do a simple Google search and you will find many news and magazine articles revealing the exact same confusing information. Yet despite all of the Internet traffic, are teachers any better at using technology to enhance student learning now than they were when educational technologies first arrived in schools? And are teacher preparation programs hindering or helping pre-service teachers in this endeavor? As Gen Z enters college and becomes practicing teachers, with their own particular characteristics and digital abilities and needs, it is important that we re-examine these questions and find out how to best serve the newest generation of teachers.

DOI: 10.4018/978-1-5225-7763-8.ch006

INTRODUCTION

At the time this chapter was written, teachers across the nation are striking for better working conditions and sorely needed pay raises. Tens of thousands of educators in West Virginia, Kentucky, Oklahoma, Arizona, and Colorado, just to name a few states, all walked off the job and did not return to teaching until their demands for better working conditions and compensation were met. Although the discontent had been brewing for a while – many teachers hadn't received raises in years – it's possible that the recent addition of Generation Z to the teaching force could have tipped the balance. Assuming that the oldest Gen Zers were born in the mid-1990's, some of them could very well be nascent teachers holding their first jobs. And what a way to begin your teaching career – by walking out of your first position!

Most of the older Generation Z are currently in college and presumably, some of them are studying to be teachers. It is no mystery that these young adults (and their younger compatriots) have grown up with various amounts and levels of digital technologies. Technology has always been in their world and so the idea of bringing it into their studies and using technology at the collegiate level is completely natural to them. Not so for the faculty complement who is preparing them to be future teachers.

The professors currently working in colleges and universities are primarily still Baby Boomers (born approximately between 1946-1964), Generation Xers (born approximately between 1965-1984), and the oldest Millennials (born between approximately 1984-mid-1990s). These are generations with very different characteristics from the one currently progressing through college, particularly with respect to technology. They utilize personal technologies, social media, etc. very differently from Gen Z in their personal lives, and markedly different in their teaching practices. It would stand to reason then that teacher technology-use in education preparation programs, and the technological expectations of Generation Z students, would clash.

BACKGROUND

Generation Z, or Gen Z, is the group of individuals born generally between the mid-1990s and the mid-2000's, although sources rarely agree on a specific timeframe. They are essentially the generation that was born subsequent to the Millennial generation and they hold their own sets of characteristics, wants, needs, fears, hopes, and ideas, different from the generations who have come before them. Gen Z has also been referred to as Generation Wii, iGeneration, Digital Natives, Gen

Tech, and Net Gen (Horovitz, 2012) - monikers which are likely very telling about the way the group sees and interacts with the world. Seemiller and Grace (2015) fascinatingly describe Gen Z as ascribing different characteristics to their peers than they ascribe to themselves. Gen Z considers their peer group as adventurous risk-takers, who are inquisitive and impulsive, as well as highly aggressive. However, when describing themselves, a Gen Z would typically label themselves as reliable and trustworthy, reflective and open-minded, as well as, kind yet possessing grit - a word that they may have learned through their KIPP character education program in school (Knowledge is Power Program [KIPP], 2018). Perhaps most notably, Gen Z is our first generation of true Digital Natives (Prensky, 2001) – individuals born into an age of computers, smartphones, high-speed Internet, WiFi, data plans, social media and a host of other hardware and software applications. Digital Natives are exposed to advanced technologies from birth and gain facility with them at a very early age, rather than learning to use digital technologies as an adult. Although some Millennials could arguably be characterized as Digital Natives, Generation Z is the first full generation to truly be Digital Natives. Their use of, need for, and perceptions about technology are like nothing educators have ever encountered before. Thus, an examination of technology, specifically educational technology, and how it interplays in the teaching and learning of Generation Z is critical.

Per the Association for Educational Communications and Technology, educational technology is "the study and ethical practice of facilitating learning and improving performance by creating, using and managing appropriate technological processes and resources" (Januszewski & Molenda, 2007). Though generally applicable to all ranges of schooling, this definition takes on different flavors at different grade levels and in different contexts. For instance, P-12 schools, particularly public schools, have many more Internet safety measures in place than would a college or university. The online safety of P-12 students is paramount, whereas in higher education all of the students are legal adults and as such, institutions do not need to monitor the appropriateness of the content that they view, however restrictions may be in place when using university-owned hardware. (Note that all educational spaces do keep securities in place to protect from identity-theft, hacking, and viruses.) Also, colleges and universities often require that their students bring technologies such as laptops and/or tablets to be utilized for class activities, whereas some P-12 schools actively prohibit students from bringing in such technologies, even for educational purposes. (Many P-12 schools provide their own computer access, in some form, at present.) Therefore, the types of things and ways in which instructors can utilize technologies for teaching and learning differs greatly by type of educational institution, and even within category of institution/school. Here we will focus on the use of educational technology at the collegiate level in order to explore professional teacher preparation programs and pre-service teachers needs and experience with educational technology.

MAIN FOCUS OF THE CHAPTER

The use of educational technologies in teacher education programs has long been established as an important component of preservice teacher professional preparation. Organizations such as the International Society for Technology in Education (ISTE) have published several sets of standards for students, teachers, administrators, computer science educators, and technology coaches. Referred to as the "ISTE Standards for Educators" (ISTE, 2018), this set of guidelines is well-respected by schools and practitioners, and the broad categories of standards for teachers are as follows (note that there are behavioral indicators under each standard, but they won't be listed here):

- **Learner:** Educators continually improve their practice by learning from and with others and exploring proven and promising practices that leverage technology to improve student learning.
- **Leader:** Educators seek out opportunities for leadership to support student empowerment and success and to improve teaching and learning.
- **Citizen:** Educators inspire students to positively contribute to and responsibly participate in the digital world.
- **Collaborator:** Educators dedicate time to collaborate with both colleagues and students to improve practice, discover and share resources and ideas, and solve problems.
- **Designer:** Educators design authentic, learner-driven activities and environments that recognize and accommodate learner variability.
- **Facilitator:** Educators facilitate learning with technology to support student achievement of the ISTE Standards for Students.
- **Analyst:** Educators understand and use data to drive their instruction and support students in achieving their learning goals.

Based on these standards, it is clear that practicing teachers are expected to play many roles and have facility with many types of learning technologies in order to be considered professionally competent. It's also important that attainment of these skills, knowledge, and abilities must begin in college and university teacher preparation programs so that practicing teachers can attain the performance standards early in their careers. Accordingly, Darling-Hammond, Kammerness, Grossman, Rust, and Shulman (2005) posited that there may not be one best way to design teacher preparation programs, but that elements common to successful program designs do exist. These elements generally include student teaching and field experiences, portfolios and performance assessments, case studies, action research, analyses of teaching and learning, and autobiographies. While these common elements widely exist in most teacher preparation programs today, the ways in which specific areas of foci within teacher education are implemented in programs of study are less widely agreed upon. Despite research indicating best practice and specific types of effective learning experiences with regard to educational technology (Hsu, 2012), the ways in which educational technology is taught to preservice teachers varies greatly, and without consistent lasting impact.

Perhaps the two most common ways to teach preservice teachers about and with educational technologies are either to 1) utilize distinct classes within the college curriculum, colloquially referred to by preservice teachers and faculty alike as the "tech courses" (Hargrave & Hsu, 2000; Hofer, 2005), or 2) to interweave or spiral educational technology content, concepts and practices throughout all of the education courses in a preservice teacher's curriculum (Hofer, 2005). Given the lack of and/or highly sporadic use of educational technologies by practicing teachers, neither model of pre-service teacher educational technology preparation is highly effective. However, in their studies, both Foulger, Buss, Wetzel, and Lindsey (2012), and Schnackenberg and Still (2014), found that college curricula that make use of discrete courses in educational technology, taught by individuals with focused academic preparation in that area, are indeed more effective than a more spiraled type of course structure. Unfortunately, these studies were performed with preservice teachers in the Millennial Generation, so best practice with regard to educational technology and professional teacher preparation with Generation Z is still largely unknown. Yet, the earliest research that has been done with the oldest of Gen Z reveals some clear challenges to the current ways higher education prepares the newest crop of college students to become teachers.

ISSUES, CONTROVERSIES, PROBLEMS

Since Generation Z is the present student population in P-16 education, a fair amount has been written about how to connect with them and the best strategies to use to facilitate their learning (Berk, 2009; Cilliers, 2017; Geck, 2007). Unfortunately, much of the scholarly research in this area is focused on teaching Generation Z students in P-12 schools. Less has been written about teaching and learning strategies for Generation Z students in colleges and universities, likely because the very first wave of Gen Z has just graduated college. They are a group that is relatively new to higher education. Nevertheless, some research has been done investigating the teaching and learning styles and preferences of Generation Z.

Focusing on college students, Zorn (2017) discusses the highly collaborative approach toward work that Gen Z prefers. Nichols and Wright (2018) state, as many, many, others have, that Generation Z is more highly advanced with electronics and technology than any previous generation and that this will affect the way classes at universities function. Salubi, Ondari-Okemwa, and Nekhwevha (2018) investigated the Net Generation's university library usage and found that although these students are Digital Natives, they prefer print resources to e-books and rarely/barely use electronic databases for scholarly research. They did seem to like the college library's WiFi, however. Also, Gütl, Cheong, Cheong, Chang, Nau, and Pirker (2015) researched approaches to student engagement and found that Gen Z has the shortest attention span yet of any group entering higher education and that college faculty need to develop methods for retaining student focus in the classroom. Finally, Seemiller and Grace (2017) offer that GenNext view and interact with the world through social media and that professors need to contextualize information both within and outside of that lens when teaching.

While these strategies are clearly applicable to wide variety of degree programs and professional preparation at the collegiate level, their impact on teacher education is unique. Carter (2018) posits four strategies that teacher preparation programs can employ to help reach preservice teachers in Generation Z. These strategies include: 1) the use of "blended" learning environments where there is a mix of both social and individual learning activities, 2) real world problem-solving where students have as many experiential learning opportunities as possible, 3) entrepreneurial and transformational experiences (i.e. opportunities for students to make positive changes to their environment and/or make money), and 4) the incorporation of mobile devices into teaching practices. While precious little has been written that assists in the revamping of teacher preparation programs to more successfully meet the needs of Generation Z preservice teachers, what has been written mostly focuses on the use of media and digital media in teaching practices.

For decades, teacher education programs have attempted to infuse technology into their own teaching practices and, more importantly, teach preservice teachers' strategies for using educational technology in ways that are more than just cursory, and extend throughout the life of their career. Currently, our first generation of true Digital Natives is graduating from teacher education degree programs and their need for and consumption of digital technologies is no match for the curricula and structure of present-day professional educator preparation. In their 2016 study, Fernández-Cruz and Fernández-Díaz (2016) found that the educational technology skills of present-day teachers, including the newest group of Generation Z teachers, are lacking far beyond what professional groups and associations deem optimal (Fernández-Cruz &Fernández-Díaz, 2016). Research is clear that Gen Z needs and expects to use digital technologies in their higher education experiences, teacher education programs included (Berk, 2009; Gütl, et al., 2015; Prensky, 2001; Seemiller & Grace, 2015; Seemiller & Grace, 2017; Zorn, 2017). And the Net Generation are more than capable of doing so when presented with the opportunity – Vu and Gaskill (2018) found that teacher education majors could create effective digital games even without prior coding knowledge. So, it is possible, when structured appropriately, to teach and challenge Generation Z with educational technologies. Yet teacher education programs lag far behind what Gen Z needs to fulfill their appetites for learning with and about educational technologies. Therefore, it is incumbent upon institutions of higher education to move quickly and rectify this situation. The following are some recommended solutions to improve the professional preparation of future teachers.

SOLUTIONS AND RECOMMENDATIONS

The January 2017 update to the National Education Technology Plan (Department of Education, 2017) took to task teacher professional preparation programs in higher education. While it doesn't overtly state that preparation programs are failing to fully prepare pre-service teachers to use educational technologies in their teaching practices, the report does set forth four guiding principles for advancing educational technology in teacher preparation. The guiding principles are as follows:

1. Focus on the active use of technology to enable learning and teaching through creation, production, and problem-solving.
2. Build sustainable, program-wide systems of professional learning and teaching.
3. Ensure pre-service teachers' experiences with educational technology are program-deep and program-wide, rather than one-off courses separate from their methods courses.
4. Align efforts with research-based standards, frameworks, and credentials recognized across the field.

Though hardly new, the principles are novel in the clarity of their language about what should happen in pre-service teacher preparation programs and what, it could be assumed, is not currently happening now.

The first principle is clear in that technology should be student-centered and revolve around the creation of knowledge through activities such as problem-solving and formation of a product. Too often, teacher preparation programs focus on software, hardware, apps, and activities that enable pre-service teachers to enhance their own teaching practices by making their own lesson preparation more efficient. Be it through ways to create activities or (god help us) worksheets for children to use, cloud storage for grades or presentations, online research, or similar activities, pre-service teachers graduate from college with a vast and current arsenal of ways to better prep for the lessons that they teach. What these newly minted graduates don't leave with however is a conception of how to enable P-12 students to interact with technology in a way that deepens and furthers their learning.

The second and third principles set forth by the National Educational Technology Plan address the idea that educational technology preparation in university-level teaching programs needs to happen throughout a curriculum, rather than simply in one or two "tech courses.". Though the spirit of this principle hits the mark in what indeed should happen, it is almost an unfathomable task to actually *make* it happen in most current teacher education programs. To do so would mean most if not all faculty in teacher preparation programs would need to undergo extensive professional development in order to gain the skills needed to implement technology into both college curricula and active coursework in a meaningful way. Perhaps even more daunting is the need to change some faculty member's lingering old-school beliefs that preparing future teachers to use technology in their teaching practices is unnecessary because a) there is enough for teachers in schools to do and utilizing technology isn't truly necessary for successful student learning; b) research in educational technology has been occurring since the 1980s and no definitive, un-refuted learning gains have been reported; or, most troubling, c) college students interact constantly with technology in their personal lives so they don't need any further instruction on how to use it for learning and/or in their classroom practices. This third rationale is so prevalent and so dangerous to professional teacher preparation that the National Education Technology plan cites it specifically as a pitfall of which to beware. Yet, the broadly-held opinion still exists among teacher education faculty. (Who are, notably, Digital Immigrants [Prensky, 2001] for the most part. Unlike the Generation Z students – Digital Natives - whom they are now teaching, and the students that those students will educate.)

The fourth and final principle discusses the need for current, research-based, practices to be utilized throughout college curricula. In some respects, this goes right to the heart of the need for current teacher education faculty in higher education to receive intensive professional development so that they can, in fact, discover and understand such practices. It also speaks to the need for teacher education faculty to listen to the educational technologist, or technologists, on staff and to value their expertise. Often, teacher education faculty complements only include one faculty member (two if they are lucky) who has engaged in any sort of deep study in educational technology (a Ph.D., Ed.D. or a master's degree). All too often this individual is somewhat professionally isolated and simply teaches technology classes and isn't really consulted on how to incorporate cutting-edge technological practices throughout the curricula (see principles two and three). In a few unfortunate situations, technology experts can often be told what and how to teach by other teacher education faculty thinking they know better either through a small amount of selective research on the topic, or having recently been in P-12 classrooms and observing what practicing teachers are doing with technology. The ultimate rub in this sort of instance is that insisting that teacher candidates be taught exclusively what currently occurs with technology in classrooms is exceedingly short-sighted, poor and/or even harmful professional practice, and is a small scale deprofessionalization of educational technology in general. In short, when it comes to current practice with technologies in teaching, the educational technologist(s) on staff probably does know best.

FUTURE RESEARCH DIRECTIONS

Interestingly, the direction research on teacher preparation programs, Gen Z, and educational technology needs to take is not necessarily one where initially, there is direct study. Of course, qualitative and quantitative research needs to continue on the wants and needs of Gen Z with respect to technology use and integration in teacher preparation programs. However, conclusive research also needs to finally happen on why and how practicing teachers use technology for teaching and learning in their classrooms. Unlike other aspects of education, such as direct instruction, packaged reading and math programs, and homework, educational technology is something that is inconsistent and sporadic, yet much more meaningful, in teacher professional practice. Some teachers utilize educational technology well, while others don't use it at all. And recommendations are clear that the effective use of educational technologies is integral to P-12 students learning. For years, researchers in the field of educational technology have tried to determine what makes teachers hesitant to incorporate technology into classroom practice, and what makes teachers innovative with teaching technologies. Research of this nature has been occurring for decades, with multiple generations of practitioners, and while many conclusions have been drawn, none of them have been utilized and implemented in such a way as to help teachers use technologies consistently and effectively in their teaching practices throughout the course of their careers. Until the broader education profession can solve the problem of teacher mis-use or non-use of educational technology with P-12 students, then college and university teacher preparation programs will continue to have an uphill battle preparing future teachers, regardless of the generation to which they belong.

CONCLUSION

Despite a wide variety of curriculum designs, course delivery methods, and practical experiences over several generations (the youngest Baby Boomers, Gen Xers, Millennials, and now Gen Z), educational technologies still have not made their way into teacher preparation programs in a long-standing and continuously impactful way. While professional associations, such as the Association for Educational Communications and Technology (AECT) and the International Society for Technology in Education (ISTE) have long supported the use of technology in teaching and learning, and produced important research, definitions, and standards for both students and teachers, it appears that there is a disconnect between scholarly organizations, teacher preparation programs, and the actual practice of teachers. Whether it's Gen Z, or Millennials, or Gen Xers, it's time to truly figure out how to teach preservice teachers to use technology in their teaching practice so that it becomes as second nature in their careers as developing objectives or creating meaning learning activities. This problem has gone on long enough and it's time for higher education and teacher educators to finally figure out where the roadblocks are, and then fix them permanently.

REFERENCES

Berk, R. A. (2009). Teaching strategies for the net generation. *Transformative Dialogues. Teaching & Learning Journal*, *3*(2), 1–23.

Carter, T. (2018). Preparing Generation Z for the teaching profession. *SRATE Journal*, *27*(1), 1–8.

Cilliers, E. J. (2017). The challenge of teaching generation Z. *PEOPLE. The International Journal of Social Sciences (Islamabad)*, *3*(1), 188–198.

Darling-Hammond, L., Kammerness, K., Grossman, P., Rust, F., & Shulman, L. (2005). The design of teacher education programs. In L. Darling-Hammond & J. Bransford (Eds.), *Preparing teachers for a changing world: What teachers should learn and be able to do*. San Francisco, CA: Jossey-Bass.

Department of Education. (January, 2017). *Reimagining the role of technology in education: 2017 national education technology plan update*. Retrieved from https://tech.ed.gov/files/2017/01/NETP17.pdf

Fernández-Cruz, F. J., & Fernández-Díaz, M. J. (2016). Generation Z's Teachers and their Digital Skills. *Comunicar*, *24*(46), 97–105. doi:10.3916/C46-2016-10

Foulger, T. S., Buss, R. R., Wetzel, K., & Lindsey, L. (2012). Preservice teacher education benchmarking a standalone ed tech course in preparation for change. *Journal of Digital Learning in Teacher Education*, *29*(2), 48–58. doi:10.1080/21532974.2012.10784704

Geck, C. (2007). The generation Z connection: Teaching information literacy to the newest net generation. *Toward a 21st-Century School Library Media Program, 235*-241.

Gütl, C., Cheong, C., Cheong, F., Chang, V., Nau, S. Z., & Pirker, J. (2015). Expectations of the generation NeXt in higher education: Learning engagement approaches in information sciences subjects. In *Proceedings of the Annual Meeting of the International Conference on Interactive Collaborative Learning (ICL)* (pp. 205-214). 10.1109/ICL.2015.7318027

Hargrave, C., & Hsu, Y.-S. (2000). Survey of instructional technology courses for preservice teachers. *Journal of Technology and Teacher Education*, *8*(4), 303–314.

Hofer, M. (2005). Technology and teacher preparation in exemplary institutions: 1994-2003. *Journal of Computing in Teacher Education*, *22*(1), 5–11.

Horovitz, B. (2012). After Gen X, Millennials, what should next generation be? *USA Today*. Retrieve May 9, 2018 from http://usatoday30.usatoday.com/money/advertising/story/2012-05-03/naming-the-next-generation/54737518/1

Hsu, P.-S. (2012, June). Examining the impact of educational technology courses on preservice teachers' technological pedagogical content knowledge. *Teaching Education*, *23*(2), 195–213. doi:10.1080/10476210.2011.622041

International Society for Technology in Education. (2018). ISTE Standards for Educators. *ISTE*. Retrieved from https://www.iste.org/standards/for-educators

Januszewski, A., & Molenda, M. (2007). *Educational technology: A definition with commentary* (2nd ed.). New York, NY: Routledge.

Knowledge is Power Program (KIPP) (2018). Focus on Character. *KIPP*. Retrieved from http://www.kipp.org/approach/character

Nichols, T., & Wright, M. (2018). Generational differences: Understanding and exploring generation z. In *Proceedings of the Annual Meeting of the Southwest Academy of Management* (pp. 177-185).

Prensky, M. (2001). Digital natives, digital immigrants. *On the Horizon*, *9*(5), 1–6. doi:10.1108/10748120110424816

Salubi, O. G., Ondari-Okemwa, E., & Nekhwevha, F. (2018). Utilisation of Library Information Resources among Generation Z Students: Facts and Fiction. *Publications*, *6*(2), 16. doi:10.3390/publications6020016

Schnackenberg, H. L., & Still, G. III. (2014). Teacher preparation programs and technology integration: Best practices for curriculum design. *International Journal of Education and Practice*, *2*(7), 147–158. Retrieved from http://www.pakinsight.com/?ic=archive&journal=61&month=07-2014&issue=7 doi:10.18488/journal.61/2014.2.7/61.7.147.158

Seemiller, C., & Grace, M. (2015). *Generation Z goes to college*. San Francisco, CA: Jossey-Bass.

Seemiller, C., & Grace, M. (2017). Generation Z: Educating and Engaging the Next Generation of Students. *About Campus: Enriching the Student Learning Experience*, *22*(3), 21–26. doi:10.1002/abc.21293

Vu, P., & Gaskill, M. (2018). Can pre-service teachers create digital game-based activities without coding knowledge? In Gamification in education: Breakthroughs in education and practice (pp. 159-173). Hershey, PA: IGI Global. doi:10.4018/978-1-5225-5198-0.ch009

Zorn, R. (2017). Coming in 2017: A new generation of graduate students – The generation Z. *College and University*, *92*(1), 61–63.

ADDITIONAL READING

Fromm, J., & Reid, A. (2018). *Marketing to Gen Z: The Rules for Reaching This Vast--and Very Different--Generation of Influencers*. New York, NY: AMACOM.

Kimmons, R., & Hall, C. (2018). How Useful are our Models? Pre-Service and Practicing Teacher Evaluations of Technology Integration Models. *TechTrends*, 1–8.

Madden, C. (2018). *Hello Gen Z: Engaging the Generation of Post-Millennials*. Seattle, WA: Amazon Digital Services LLC.

Niederhauser, D. S., & Lindstrom, D. L. (2018). Instructional Technology Integration Models and Frameworks: Diffusion, Competencies, Attitudes, and Dispositions. In Handbook of Information Technology in Primary and Secondary Education (pp. 1-21).

Roblyer, M. D., & Doering, A. H. (2009). *Integrating educational technology into teaching*. Boston, MA: Allyn & Bacon.

Seemiller, C., & Grace, M. (2016). *Generation Z Goes to College*. San Francisco, CA: Jossey-Bass.

Stillman, D., & Stillman, J. (2017). *Gen Z Work: How the Next Generation Is Transforming the Workplace*. New York, NY: Harper Collins.

Uerz, D., Volman, M., & Kral, M. (2018). Teacher educators' competences in fostering student teachers' proficiency in teaching and learning with technology: An overview of relevant research literature. *Teaching and Teacher Education*, *70*, 12–23. doi:10.1016/j.tate.2017.11.005

KEY TERMS AND DEFINITIONS

Digital Immigrant: A person born or brought up prior to the proliferation of digital technology.

Digital Native: A person born or brought up during or into the age of digital technology.

Educational Technology: The field of study that facilitates learning through the effective and appropriate/ethical use of technological resources.

Generation Z: People born from the mid-1990s to early 2000s; the generation after Millennials.

Google: (For the purposes of this chapter) an internet search engine.

Instagram: An online social networking service where users can share photos and videos.

Technology: (For the purposes of this chapter) machinery and equipment developed from scientific knowledge.

Twitter: An online social networking and news service where users post 140 character messages called "tweets."

Chapter 7
Connecting With Generation Z Through Social Media

Brian Bourke
https://orcid.org/0000-0002-1323-993X
Murray State University, USA

ABSTRACT

When it comes to Generation Z's participation in higher education, few topics receive as much attention as their use of social media. However, much of the focus rests on marketing to Generation Z through social media. The connectedness of Generation Z is accompanied with assumptions about their technological abilities. Although they are generally comfortable with technology, their tech acumen is likely limited. Members of Generation Z are often labeled as "digital natives," a term that suggests that because of the omnipresence of technology in their lives from birth, that they are naturally skilled and competent with many, if not all, forms of technology. The purpose of this chapter is to offer strategies for higher education professionals in connecting with members of Generation Z through social media.

DOI: 10.4018/978-1-5225-7763-8.ch007

INTRODUCTION

Students expect that those with whom they will work have an understanding of social media. - Study participant

When it comes to Generation Z's participation in higher education, few topics receive as much attention as their use of social media. However, much of the focus rests on marketing to Generation Z through social media (e.g. Patel, 2017a). Tips for marketing and lists of social media habits/traits are useful in painting a picture of the prevalence of social media in the lives of the members of Generation Z. It certainly makes sense to focus on social media use by Generation Z. Study results have shown that 98 percent of college students utilize social media (Griffin, 2015). Not only do members of Generation Z utilize social media, but it is also part of their daily lives, with 76 percent of adults age 18-29 checking Facebook at least once per day (Greenwood, Parrin, & Duggan, 2016).

The connectedness of Generation Z carries assumptions about their technological abilities. Although they are generally comfortable with technology, their tech acumen is likely limited (Parker, 2015). Some refer to members of Generation Z as "digital natives," a term that suggests that because of the omnipresence of technology in their lives from birth, that they are naturally skilled and competent with many, if not all, forms of technology (Kirschner & Bruyckere, 2017). However, this assumption is a myth, which can result in short-changing development (Kirschner & Bruyckere, 2017). The purpose of this chapter is to offer strategies for higher education professionals in connecting with members of Generation Z through social media, and the potential for other Web 2.0 technologies.

BACKGROUND

In order to dig into perspectives and strategies to connect with members of Generation Z through social media, a few things need to happen. It is important to clarify how the author frames Generation Z. From there, the author offers perspectives on the current state of social media, and they ways in which members of Generation Z utilize and connect through it. That discussion of social media helps provide a backdrop to discuss a study looking at how higher education professionals live their digital lives, and subsequently approach connecting with students on social media. The author uses the findings from the study to help frame strategies for connecting with members of Generation Z through social media. Finally, the chapter wraps-up with some implications for practice; in other words, some helpful tidbits higher education professionals should keep in mind.

Who Are Generation Z?

Members of Generation Z were born between the years 1995 and 2010 (Patel, 2017b). Generations are not only marked by the years of their birth, but by common culture events and experiences. Generational scholars use those culture events and experiences in an attempt to identify key characteristics of a generation. Generation Z has lived their lives in a technologically-rich world, leading them to be labeled as digital natives (Kirschner & De Bruyckere, 2017), developing preferences to utilize technology first, then seek other forms of communication (Thompson, 2015), and have developed keen approaches to multi-tasking (Cameron & Pagnattoro, 2017).

Digital Natives

Prensky (2001a; 2001b; 2001c) coined the term in referencing technology proclivities and preferences of members of today's youth. It is not simply that members of more recent generations have preferences toward technology, but that they have never not known a world without technology. This fact of growing up surrounded by and using technology is what has led to the adoption and application of the term digital natives (Kirschner & De Bruyckere, 2017).

Members of Generation Z are not the first generation labeled as digital natives. Prensky's (2001a; 2001b; 2001c) work focused on members of the Millennial Generation, who were born between 1977 and 1994 (Zorn, 2017). Unlike preceding generations, members of Generation Z are both consumers and producers of online content (Conefrey, 2016). This places Generation Z in a unique space, as members of preceding generations make assumptions, about not only Generation Z as digital natives, but also the expectations of their abilities to produce high-quality content.

Nikou, Mezei, and Brännback (2018) introduce an interesting perspective on digital natives in their consideration of social media mavens. The authors characterize mavens as those who are adept at social media platforms, demonstrates identifiable traits and characteristics, traits and behavior, which are akin to those of digital natives, and motivated to encourage and inform others about social media. Social media mavens feel a personal connection with one or more specific social media platforms, and feel an obligation to bring others online, cultivating a richer online experience for themselves (Lester, Tudor, Loyd, & Burton, 2012).

Myths and False Assumptions

While many working in higher education are quick to label members of Generation Z as digital natives, it is important to address myths that are abundant about assumed digital natives.

Expectations

Despite issues and myths around the digital native label, there are some truths to the ways in which members of Generation Z experience through world mediated through technology. Through their technologically mediated experiences, they have developed preferences and expectations that they bring to college campuses. Although many faculty and administrators in higher education expect today's students to be technology experts, the reality is that supposed digital natives' technological expertise is superficial (Kirschner & De Bruyckere, 2017).

Members of Generation Z look for ways to connect their online experiences to future successes. In fact, they tend to view online experiences and connections with others as a path to academic success while in college (Swett, 2016). Members of Generation Z might see and seek these connections because of the ways in which technology has been a part of the education experiences. Not only have students been immersed in technologically connected learning experiences (Xiaoqing, Yuankun, & Xiaofeng, 2013), but hybrid and online approaches to teaching and learning have been part of their lives (Zorn, 2017).

Great Multitaskers

As scholarship about Generation Z continues to emerge, one of their generational hallmarks is an innate ability to multitask, and multitask efficiently. The assignment of this generational trait is often met with a raised eyebrow of wonder and doubt, as prior research has suggested that multitasking is a myth (Wang & Tchernev, 2012). When considering multitasking by members of Generation Z, they tend to have attention spans of roughly eight seconds (Cameron & Pagnattoro, 2017).

Non-Universal Traits

Any treatment of a generation should be taken with a grain of salt. When assumptions of generational traits and behaviors are treated as universal, the influences and nuances of culture are ignored. When it comes to members of Generation Z, assumptions about digital fluency are also problematic. Not all members of Generation Z have access to social media in the home, and some lack it school settings (Li, Snow & White, 2014).

Social Media

The term social media represents a wide range of Web 2.0 and other interactive technologies. While platforms like Facebook and Twitter dominate the conversations about social media use among Generation Z, myriad tools and platforms exist that allow people to connect virtually. From the sharing of pictures on Instagram to connecting workout goals and personal records on fitness trackers, today's college students are more virtually-connected than ever. Regardless of how they connect, "college student social media use is driven by emotional, informational, social, and habitual needs" (Smith & Gallicano, 2015, p. 87)

Despite increases in virtual connections among students, higher education professionals, particularly those who work in student affairs and student services areas struggle to unlock the secrets of getting Generation Z to put down their devices and interact face to face. As these professionals struggle and ponder potential strategies, they lament about the days of old, when students would wander into the program and service offices. And while the students may have been lost and came in to ask for directions, it still counted for student contact, and went in the monthly report. Today, those same higher education professionals shrug their shoulders when tasked with developing strategies to connect virtually with Generation Z. Through this chapter, I draw on an empirical study to offer proven strategies to connect virtually with Generation Z.

Beyond attempting to conjure ways to get Gen Z students to put down their devices and interact face to face, higher education professionals also struggle with choices about engaging with students on social media. Higher education professionals are sometimes encouraged to avoid online spaces that students inhabit (Gin, Martínez-Alemán, Rowan-Kenyon & Hottell, 2017).

STUDY OVERVIEW

In order to provided sound strategies for engaging with Generation Z online, the author of this chapter draws upon a survey-based study, in which 420 participants who work in higher education administration responded to questions about digital leadership and their digital lives as higher education professionals. One component of the survey was a section devoted to connecting with students online. Although the focus of the chapter is one of multiple sections of the survey, results from across the dataset cast light on the topic of connecting with students through social media. The author uses the analysis of the quantitative data to undergird proposed strategies for connecting Generation Z through social media.

Instrument

The author and a colleague, Dr. Josie Alquist, administered the survey online via SurveyMonkey. The author developed the instrument with Dr. Josie Ahlquist, drawing on Dr. Alquist's previous work (Alquist 2014; 2015; 2016; 2017). Questions included provide demographic information, including years in the field, education level, and area of focus within higher education administration. From there, questions shifted to the social media platforms that participants use, those with which they feel proficient, and the types of devices used to access those platforms. Participants were then asked to respond to questions divided into some key categories: with whom participants connect online, and through which platforms; digital identity; participation in online communities; connecting with students and role modeling; intersections with online use/presence and professional competencies; leadership via digital tools; digital education, and; future needs and professional development. Finally, the survey concluded with an opportunity to provide comments through a textbox at the end of the survey instrument.

Participants

The author and his colleague recruited participants through social media and email. The sampling media was most analogous with snowball sampling, as potential participants were asked to share the call to participate with colleagues (Lewis-Beck, Bryman, & Futing Liao, 2004). The total number of responses logged was 419, but 306 participants completed the survey in its entirety. The remaining 113 people started the survey but did not complete the full instrument. In some cases, did not fully complete the demographic information. The Results section of this chapter draws only on data from the 420 participants who completed the full survey instrument.

Tables 1-7 offer a glimpse of who the participants are as a group.

Researcher Positionality

Although more commonly associated with qualitative research designs, it is important to note the potential influences of researcher positionality in this research study. The author identifies as a White, cisgender, heterosexual man. The author previously worked in student affairs, presently teaches in a student affairs and higher education administration graduate preparation program, and identifies as a student affairs educator. He has been active on social media for a number of years, and served on committees within professional associations related to technology

Table 1. Gender

Gender		
Answer Options	**Response Percent**	**Response Count**
Female	62.8%	263
Male	34.1%	143
Trans*	1.2%	5
Gender fluid	0.0%	0
Non-binary	0.2%	1
Genderqueer	0.2%	1
Gender nonconforming	0.2%	1
Other	0.0%	0
Prefer not to respond	1.2%	5

Table 2. Ethnicity

Ethnicity		
Answer Options	**Response Percent**	**Response Count**
American Indian or Alaska Native	0.0%	0
Asian	4.8%	20
Black or African American	6.4%	27
Native Hawaiian or Other Pacific Islander	0.2%	1
White	76.2%	321
Hispanic or Latino or Spanish Origin	6.7%	28
Not Hispanic or Latino or Spanish Origin	0.2%	1
Other	4.3%	18
Prefer not to state	1.2%	5

in student affairs. Finally, the author has taught online since 2011. Each of these identities and experiences has the potential to shape and frame the author's biases and perceptions. Further, these biases and perceptions can affect both the research process, and resulting product. Despite efforts to bracket oneself from the research, a possibility always exists for the researcher to influence the research (Charmaz, 2006; Tufford & Newman, 2012).

Table 3. Years in the field

Years in the Field		
Answer Options	**Response Percent**	**Response Count**
1-5 Years	28.5%	120
6-10 Years	27.1%	114
11-15 year	15.4%	65
16-20 Years	12.4%	52
21-25 years	7.4%	31
26-30 years	4.5%	19
31-35 Years	2.4%	10
36+ Years	2.4%	10

Table 4. Level in the field

Level in the Field		
Answer Options	**Response Percent**	**Response Count**
Graduate Student	9.1%	38
Entry/New Professional	24.8%	104
Mid Level (supervising other pro staff)	30.8%	129
Senior Level (e.g. Director)	19.3%	81
Executive/Cabinet (e.g. VP, AVP, Dean)	7.9%	33
Faculty	8.1%	34

Table 5. Current division

Current Division		
Answer Options	**Response Percent**	**Response Count**
Student Affairs	63.4%	262
Human Resources	1.2%	5
Enrollment Management	6.3%	26
Academic Affairs	21.5%	89
University Relations	2.7%	11
Advancement/Fund-Raising	4.4%	18
Athletics	0.5%	2

Table 6. Institution type

Institution Type		
Answer Options	**Response Percent**	**Response Count**
Two-year, very small (<500 FTE)	1.7%	7
Two-year, small (500-1,199 FTE)	1.2%	5
Two-year, medium (2000-4,999 FTE)	1.0%	4
Two-year, large (5,000-9,999 FTE)	1.9%	8
Two-year, very large (10,000 or more FTE)	2.4%	10
Four-year, very small, primarily nonresidential (<1,000 FTE, < 25-49% live on campus)	2.4%	10
Four-year, very small, primarily residential (<1,000 FTE, 50% or more live on campus)	1.0%	4
Four-year, very small, highly residential (<1,000 FTE, < 25% live on campus)	0.0%	0
Four-year, small, primarily nonresidential (1,000-2,999 FTE, < 25% live on campus)	2.6%	11
Four-year, small, primarily residential (1,000-2,999 FTE, 25-49% live on campus)	3.6%	15
Four-year, small, highly residential (1,000-2,999 FTE, 50% or more live on campus)	2.4%	10
Four-year, medium, primarily nonresidential (3,000-9,999 FTE, < 25% live on campus)	7.7%	32
Four-year, medium, primarily residential (3,000-9,999 FTE, 25-49% live on campus)	**10.6%**	44
Four-year, medium, highly residential (3,000-9,999 FTE, 50% or more live on campus)	4.3%	18
Four-year, large, primarily nonresidential (10,000 or more FTE, < 25% live on campus)	**23.0%**	96
Four-year, large, primarily residential (10,000 or more FTE, 25-49% live on campus)	**22.5%**	94
Four-year, large, highly residential (10,000 or more FTE, 50% or more live on campus)	9.1%	38
Exclusively graduate/professional	2.6%	11

Table 7. Highest level of education

Highest Level of Education		
Answer Options	**Response Percent**	**Response Count**
Associate degree	1.0%	4
Associate degree in progress	0.0%	0
Bachelor's degree	8.1%	34
Bachelor's degree in progress	0.2%	1
Master's degree (in higher education, student affairs, or related field)	31.4%	132
Master's degree in progress (in higher education, student affairs, or related field)	11.9%	50
Master's degree (in other fields)	9.5%	40
Master's degree in progress (in other fields)	2.6%	11
Juris doctorate	0.7%	3
Juris doctorate in progress	0.0%	0
Earned doctorate (Ed.D, Ph.D. in higher education, SA, or related)	14.7%	62
Doctorate in progress (Ed.D, Ph.D. in higher education, SA, or related)	15.7%	66
Earned doctorate (in other fields)	3.6%	15
Doctorate in progress (in other fields)	0.7%	3

Data Analysis

The author analyzed data using a mixture of correlation analysis, cross-tabs, and Chi Square analysis to examine relationships between demographic variables and responses to instrument items. Correlation analysis is useful because it provides a means to assess relationships between two variables, leading to the ability to draw inferences about those statistical relationships (Biddix, 2018). The author utilized Chi Square analysis for a few items in the instrument where the point of analysis was to test for statistical relationships between two categorical variables, primarily where each variable contained exactly two variables (Field, 2013). The author then populated in some cases to generate binary categorical variables. Cross-tabs can be used to help further explore and explain correlation results because it provides a means to combine two or more variables or categories within variables (e.g. collapsing positive response items together) (Biddix, 2018).

RESULTS AND DISCUSSION

After completing data analysis, the following results are most pertinent to engaging with Generation Z online. The author found statistical significance in examining a number of survey items and their relationship to demographic categories. Of most importance to this chapter are the results that indicate a statistical relationship between an item and Current Division, along with Level in the Field. The author focuses on the textual data from participant comments in the open-ended text box at the end of the survey instrument to provide nuance for the focus of this chapter.

Role Modeling

Multiple pieces connect with engaging on social media and role modeling among higher education professionals. One such connection came in response to questions about personal learning networks. Participants who responded with agree or strongly agree to questions about connecting with students as a means to role model appropriate social media use also identified using social media as a component of their own approaches to ongoing personal and professional development.

Participants also demonstrated connections between role modeling social media activity through student connections and their perspectives on leadership. Role modeling can be a bit of a nebulous term, but the following participant quote situates it nicely in the context of setting a good example.

I find that my use of social media blends the personal and professional - I have solely personal social media accounts (Instagram, Tumblr) and solely professional accounts (LinkedIn), but most of my platforms and accounts blend my personal and professional identity. I really see my digital identity as reflective of my in-person identity, which blends the personal and professional. i.e., I'm not a different person at work than I am outside of work! To that end, I am conscious of the platforms on which students follow me - although I am authentic on social media, I also want to set a good example of being an ethical person of integrity (since ethics and integrity are both personal and professional values of mine).

Part of setting a good example can come in the form of demonstrating congruence between one's offline and online personas. For the following participant, such congruence is important in terms of modeling integration of one's offline with one's online self.

Like with everything in life, there is a balanced approach to integrating the personal and professional in the social media environment. As an advisor to student leaders (one the hats I wear), being accessible online is important. Also, they see that I have a life that includes work and other things. Working with them to help in their learning around boundaries, choices, and opportunities, means I am challenged to represent the honest truth in my SoMe [social media] world. That is good - it makes me think twice about the way I live my life and if it's congruent with my values.

Being accessible to students through social media was important to this participant, but they also note the importance of helping students see that they (the higher education professional) have a life beyond work responsibilities.

In addition to helping students see the higher education professionals they rely upon as people with full lives beyond work, there is also an important aspect of role modeling through online connections that revolves around appropriate behavior.

I see that I need to use SM [social media] to role model how to have civilized conversations. With the recent election and the general unrest among groups, I am seeing SM platforms used to argue more than listen and reflect. I am hopeful that the hatred and vitriol that seems to be modeled at the highest level with our POTUS [President of the United States, Donald J. Trump] will be tempered over time. SM [social media] is a powerful platform and communication tool.

As the participant above noted, social media offers tremendous potential as a communication tool. In the section that follows, the author draws on participant quotations to explore the ways in which participants addressed online connections as benefiting students.

Benefiting Students

As one participant shared, "social networking is an essential tool to nowadays educational development." As more and more students are actively engaged in social media, there are myriad opportunities for higher education professionals and other educators to explore connecting with students in meaningful ways that can foster out-of-class learning.

Because of the ubiquitous nature of social media, it is becoming increasingly critical for higher education professionals to not only share information (broadcast) but also to use social media and online connection to listen to students.

Social media has provided opportunities to share content and programs that benefit students. I am able communication perspectives experiences and resources that I believe are valuable to personal development. I also use social as a student voice. We know students use it as a medium to communicate experiences, challenges and success with higher education and need to monitor and engage with those expressions as much as face to face.

By using social media to listen, higher education professionals are able to use that information to provide more targeted content and programs that reflect the needs students have expressed. Likewise, listening via online connections can have very direct and profound impacts on students.

I believe that it is essential to blend my public/private role in higher education with social media. I think that otherwise there are certain power dynamics, which can get in the way of developing authentic relationships with students, colleagues, etc.... I have used social media to save students who are struggling academically, to reach out to get former students to return to finish their degrees, to show solidarity with student protesters, model appropriate social media use and to occasionally help students who are depressed or suicidal to seek help or connect with crisis services.

Use With Caution

While the quotes above highlight some promising practices for role modeling appropriate behavior on social media through connections with students, some participants shared some cautionary perspectives.

I have had my social media usage referenced as the basis for an appeal in a student organization's conduct process. It made me more conscious of how I use social media and what I post in online spaces.

Part of a perspective of using caution when connecting with students online is reflected in the following participant quotation.

It's important to me not to air personal issues on social media--especially if students can see it. I like to share surface level information that humanizes me to students and staff while also showing part of my life. I use social media for personal purposes mostly.

This participant expressed a value in being present on social media and connecting with students online, but does so cautiously. In an effort to "humanize," the participant demonstrated seeing a value in online connections with students, but has established boundaries in doing so.

One participant takes the role of boundaries so seriously, that they shared their utilization of the technology in specific ways to automate part of the process of determine who can see what content.

I have a blend of personal and professional usage in my social media platforms. I make it a point to have strong filters that determine what is displayed to which population, and I make sure that I am appropriate in my social media postings.

Another participant reflected a similar perspective, which the author describes as self-policing.

As a general rule I never put anything online that could reflect poorly on me or the university. I keep my opinions to myself, and only post news articles or informational information that make no evaluative commentary. It's all completely neutral.

Part of what the author presents in this chapter related to connecting with students online is being cognizant of how higher education professionals approach social media, and then consider choices of connecting with students.

Social media is an extension of who I am on another plane. I engage with both personal and professional connections on my profiles and I have one profile per platform. I do hold myself to policies with student that I myself have created in never adding a student unless the invited me to the connection first.

Sometimes higher education professionals choose to have separate social media accounts. "I maintain separate social media accounts for personal and professional use." Such an approach demonstrates a measured approach to engaging with students online, but in a way that ensures clear boundaries between personal and professional domains.

Passive Engagement

Sometimes higher educational professionals take a less active approach to connecting with students online. As one participant shared, "I like to advertise on social media as well as use other forms of social media . . . to connect students to opportunities on campus." Another participant stated, "I think social media should be used to promote and market events for campuses as well as job openings for students." For these higher education professionals, social media represent more of an online bulletin board than a space for active interaction. "I work in student activities, therefore all our events are marketed mainly through social media. We have an organization Facebook, Snapchat, Twitter, and Instagram that we update regularly." These participants see the utility of social media in sharing information, with the hope it will be useful for students.

Looking Ahead With Social Media

Some participants shared perspectives on social media that reflect looking to the future. This forward thinking demonstrates an old adage of meeting students where they are.

I encourage students, my professional staff and colleagues to not only use social media that I am aware of, but to explore social media outlets that are popular "in the moment" or that might assist in either marketing or research objectives that we are working on. We do consider pros and cons of generally known as well as unknown social media outlets, as to how those would both assist or create a negative impact on our overall purposes.

In the digital age, it can be very difficult to meet students where they are if higher education professionals do not seek out opportunities to learn about and engage in those spaces. Another participant noted this perspective of having dire consequences for not connecting with students through social media: "Social media is essential in higher ed. If we're not using it as a department, it could actually hurt us." Finally, a participant shared, "Our VPSA [Vice President for Student Affairs] and our President [of the institution] are very active on social [media]. Sets a good example to not be afraid to engage."

STRATEGIES FOR ENGAGING WITH GENERATION Z ONLINE

Strategies for using social media to connect with Generation Z in higher education fall into the following categories. First, professionals are role models for what they see as appropriate social media use. This can involve efforts around crafting an online persona that is congruent with their offline persona, setting personal boundaries and limits for using and connecting through social media, and engaging with others responsibly on social media. The second group of strategies relate to using social media to reach out. As a strategy category, reaching out is a bit nebulous, because it can involve pushing out content and announcements, but also as a tool to check in with students.

While responses to the survey help shed some light on how higher education professionals do or do not choose to connect with members of Generation Z online, this would only provide one view into potential strategies. The author also draws strategies from current and emerging literature, as well as resources from professional associations and companies specializing in helping higher education administer meet students online.

Members of Generation Z expect access to information, and the people who create content, to be instantaneous (Cameron & Pagnattaro, 2017). A common adage among higher education professional is to "meet students where they are." However, in many ways, and engagement with students through social media has been no exception, higher education professionals often take an "in you build it, they will come" approach to anticipating and responding to student needs. It would be unreasonable to suggest that social media represents a panacea for better serving students who are part of Generation Z.

Cameron and Pagnattaro (2017) note that effective faculty good a good job of bridging content knowledge and teaching ability. The same can be said for higher education professional who are effective at connecting with students and anticipating their needs. The higher education professional needs to have sound training in meeting students' needs and fostering out of class learning and engagement, all while working to connect with students individually. It would be foolish to suggest that all members of Generation Z engage with social media; even if that were true, it would be equally foolish to assume that they want to connect with higher education professionals. This is why it is important to vary technological approaches in learning environments (Cameron & Pagnattaro, 2017).

IMPLICATIONS

Strategies are often helpful, and the idea of being able to provide empirically-based strategies was a motivator for writing this chapter. However, with any set of strategies, there are important implications that bear out. In the case of engaging with members of Generation Z in online spaces, the implications that arise are largely key reminders. These reminders are things not only to be cognizant of, but for which higher education professionals must remain vigilant in not losing sight.

Increased online interaction is forcing faculty and staff alike in higher education to confront what it means to be truly student-centered. Because of their experiences with being both content consumers and producers, students are increasingly pushing back at decades-old approaches to teaching, and the provision of out-of-class expectations. By shifting to more true student-centered approaches, students are empowered and expected to make more choices about "what they need to learn, how they can best learn it, [and] where they can get the information and skills they need" (Conefrey, 2016, p. 39).

In order to members of Generation Z to see the educational work of higher education professionals as being relevant to their lives, those higher education professionals have to work to make sure students see that relevance. Educators, including higher education professionals, have to work to engage students through digital means (Oriji & Efebo, 2103). Even then, Oriji and Efebo (2013) note that educators have to move away from text-centric approaches with students. Higher education professionals have to explore ways to utilize interactive media to connect with students, and looks for opportunities to allow students to be content creators, rather than simply receptors of information.

Engaging Online Communicates Availability Beyond Physical Spaces

Higher education professionals, particularly those in student affairs, see the greatest potential for engaging with students, and helping students engage with one another, as taking place in physical spaces. While this has been the mode of operating for those professionals for the entire history of the student affairs profession (which can be traced to the late 19th Century), students have increasingly sought opportunities to seek out information and engage via technology. Research suggests that college students coming to college directly from high school today are likely to look at technology, especially social media, as a community-building tool (Davis, Deil-Amen, Rios-Aguilar, & González Canché, 2014).

Thinking Across Institutional Types

So much of the literature about higher education focuses on four-year institutions, despite the fact that more than one-third of all undergraduates attend two-year institutions (Community College Research Center, 2017). Nearly half of all who graduate from four-year institutions completed at least some coursework at two-year institutions (Smith, 2015). The work of Davis III and his colleagues highlights the dearth of literature addressing the experiences of students in online spaces beyond four-year institutions. However, very little of the scholarship about members of Generation Z or social media usage among college students focuses on those attending two-year institutions.

Harsh Realities

Despite student preferences to engage online, higher education professionals do need to explore paths to help students bridge their online experiences with face to face experiences. Research shows that frequent use of social media has negative effects on mental health among adolescents (Sampasa-Kanyinga & Lewis, 2015). It can be tempting to dismiss research about adolescents when addressing college students, but as Arnett (2007) notes, college students, including those in their early twenties, can exhibit behaviors and traits more closely associated with adolescence, attributable to a stage of development labeled emerging adulthood.

One specific mental health concern with social media use is addictive behaviors. Social media addiction can take the form of compulsively checking for updates, mindlessly browsing news feeds and posts, and thinking about social media activity when not actively engaged with social media (Zaremohzzabieh, Samah, Omar, Bolong, & Kamarudin, 2014).

Great Potential

While there are certainly potential concerns for which higher education professional need to be mindful, connecting with members of Generation Z online represents practices with tremendous potential. Higher education professionals have the potential to positively impact college students' development in a number of realms (Patton, et al., 2016). The same is true of technology literacy. When educators model appropriate online behavior and function as role models in online spaces (Bers, 2010).

Potential does not only exist through reinforcing positive one-on-one relationships in online spaces. By maintaining both positive online relationships and a positive visible and active presence, educators can aid students in forming online communities for a range of educational and social ends (Bers, 2010). The communal potential of online engagement is a piece where higher education professionals have countless opportunities to help students think critically about their online interactions and the choices they make (Bourke, 2014).

CONCLUSION

Connecting with members of Generation Z via social media not only represents an area of growing importance in higher education, but a professional practice that cannot be neglected. These connections do not require higher education professionals to spend their entire days online, or invite everyone who uses the Internet into their personal lives through social media. Regardless of how higher education professionals choose to connect online with members of Generation Z, there are some evidence-based strategies to use. Higher education professionals should role model appropriate online behavior. This goes hand in hand with helping students learn to set boundaries and make choices about how they live their lives in online spaces. Higher education professionals to make choices about the ways in which they meet students where they are in online spaces, including the role of social media in pushing information out versus interacting with members of Generation Z through social media.

Limitations

There are a few things that represent potential limitations to drawing inferences from the data. First, the sample was heavily skewed toward those who identify as working in student affairs, with 63.4% of respondents selecting that as the closest match to their current division. This could mean that the sample is not representative of the breadth of higher education administration. While the author took great care to provide a breadth of options for gender identity, the author failed to include multiracial as a possible category under racial identity. Across demographic questions, participants were unable to select more than one option. These issues in the demographic questions could have led some respondents to choose to not complete the survey, and/or not share it further with other colleagues.

There are also limitations when it comes to analysis. The size of the sample resulted in statistical significance being associated with low *r* scores in correlation analyses. Participants were also heavily skewed toward four-year institutions (89.2% of respondents selected a four-year institution type). This means few inferences can be drawn in relating participant responses and institutional type. Despite these limitations, the presence of a number of statistically significant results and the richness of the textual data from participant comments offer opportunities to draw inferences and conclusions from the dataset as a whole.

REFERENCES

Ahlquist, J. (2014). Trending now: Digital leadership education using social media and the social change model. *The Journal of Leadership Studies*, *8*(2), 57–60. doi:10.1002/jls.21332

Ahlquist, J. (2015). *Developing digital student leaders: A mixed methods study of student leadership, identity, and decision making on social media*. California Lutheran University.

Ahlquist, J. (2016). The digital identity of student affairs professionals. *New Directions for Student Services*, *2016*(155), 29–46. doi:10.1002s.20181

Ahlquist, J. (2017). Digital Student Leadership Development. *New Directions for Student Leadership*, *2017*(153), 47–62. doi:10.1002/yd.20229 PMID:28199059

Arnett, J. J. (2007). Emerging adulthood: What is it, and what is it good for? *Child Development Perspectives*, *1*(2), 68–73. doi:10.1111/j.1750-8606.2007.00016.x

Bers, M. U. (2010). Beyond computer literacy: Supporting youth's positive development through technology. *New Directions for Student Leadership*, (128), 13–23. PMID:21240949

Bonilla, Y., & Rosa, J. (2015). # Ferguson: Digital protest, hashtag ethnography, and the racial politics of social media in the United States. *American Ethnologist*, *42*(1), 4–17. doi:10.1111/amet.12112

Bourke, B. (2014). Adult Millennials: Conceptualizing a student subpopulation with implications for online teaching and learning. In J. Keengwe & K. Kungu (Eds.), *Cross-cultural online learning in higher education and corporate training* (pp. 62–78). Hershey, PA: IGI Global Publishing. doi:10.4018/978-1-4666-5023-7.ch003

Cameron, E. A., & Pagnattaro, M. A. (2017). Beyond millennials: Engaging generation Z in business law classes. *Journal of Legal Studies Education*, *34*(2), 317–324. doi:10.1111/jlse.12064

Charmaz, K. (2006). *Constructing grounded theory: A practical guide through qualitative analysis*. Los Angeles, CA: SAGE Publications.

Community College Research Center. (2017). Community college enrollment and completion. Retrieved from https://www.ccidinc.org/single-post/2017/05/04/Community-College-Enrollment-and-Completion

Conefrey, T. (2016). Technology in the college classroom: Crisis and opportunity. *Educational Technology*, *56*(4), 37–40.

Davis, C. H. III, Deil-Amen, R., Rios-Aguilar, C., & González Canché, M. S. (2015). Social media, higher education, and community colleges: A research synthesis and implications for the study of two-year institutions. *Community College Journal of Research and Practice*, *39*(5), 409–422. doi:10.1080/10668926.2013.828665

DeAndrea, D. C., Ellison, N. B., LaRose, R., Steinfield, C., & Fiore, A. (2012). Serious social media: On the use of social media for improving students' adjustment to college. *The Internet and Higher Education*, *15*(1), 15–23. doi:10.1016/j.iheduc.2011.05.009

Field, A. (2013). *Discovering statistics using IBM SPSS statistics* (4th ed.). Los Angeles, CA: Sage.

Gin, K. J., Martínez-Alemán, A. M., Rowan-Kenyon, H. T., & Hottell, D. (2017). Racialized aggressions and social media on campus. *Journal of College Student Development*, *58*(2), 159–174. doi:10.1353/csd.2017.0013

Greenwood, S., Perrin, A., & Duggan, M. (2016). Social media update 2016. Pew Research Center. Retrieved from http://assets.pewresearch.org/wp-content/uploads/sites/14/2016/11/10132827/PI_2016.11.11_Social-Media-Update_FINAL.pdf

Griffin, R. (2015, July 21). Social media is changing how college students deal with mental health, for better or worse. *Huffington Post*. Retrieved from https://www.huffingtonpost.com/entry/social-media-college-mental-health_us_55ae6649e4b08f57d5d28845

Hawkins, D. (2015). *Here comes generation Z. What makes them tick*. NEA Today.

Issa, T., & Isaias, P. (2016). Internet factors influencing generations Y and Z in Australia and Portugal: A practical study. *Information Processing & Management*, *52*(4), 592–617. doi:10.1016/j.ipm.2015.12.006

Kirschner, P. A., & De Bruyckere, P. (2017). The myths of the digital native and the multitasker. *Teaching and Teacher Education*, *67*, 135–142. doi:10.1016/j.tate.2017.06.001

Lester, D., Tudor, R. K., Loyd, D. D., & Mitchell, T. (2012). Marketing mavens' fusion with social media. *Atlantic Marketing Journal*, *1*(1), 79–94.

Lewis-Beck, M. S., Bryman, A., & Liao, F. T. (2004). The SAGE encyclopedia of social science research methods. Thousand Oaks, CA: SAGE Publications. doi:10.4135/9781412950589

Li, J., Snow, C., & White, C. (2015). Urban adolescent students and technology: Access, use and interest in learning language and literacy. *Innovation in Language Learning and Teaching*, *9*(2), 143–162. doi:10.1080/17501229.2014.882929

Loader, B. D., Vromen, A., Xenos, M. A., Steel, H., & Burgum, S. (2015). Campus politics, student societies and social media. *The Sociological Review*, *63*(4), 820–839. doi:10.1111/1467-954X.12220

Muzamil, M., & Shah, G. (2016). Cyberbullying and self-perceptions of students associated with their academic performance. *International Journal of Education and Development Using Information and Communication Technology*, *12*(3), 79–92.

Oriji, A., & Efebo, P. I. (2013). New technology, new methodology: The "digital natives" and "digital immigrants" debate. *Journal of Educational Review*, *6*(2).

Patel, D. (2017a, April 8). 10 tips for marketing to Gen Z on social media. *Forbes Magazine*. Retrieved from https://www.forbes.com/sites/deeppatel/2017/08/08/10-tips-for-marketing-to-gen-z-on-social-media/#765056a32718

Patel, D. (2017b, September 21). 8 ways Generation Z will differ from Millennials in the workplace. *Forbes Magazine*. Retrieved from https://www.forbes.com/sites/deeppatel/2017/09/21/8-ways-generation-z-will-differ-from-millennials-in-the-workplace/#7527d56b76e5

Piwek, L., & Joinson, A. (2016). "What do they snapchat about?" Patterns of use in time-limited instant messaging service. *Computers in Human Behavior*, *54*, 358–367. doi:10.1016/j.chb.2015.08.026

Prensky, M. (2001a). *Digital game-based learning*. New York: McGraw-Hill.

Prensky, M. (2001b). Digital natives, digital immigrants. *On the Horizon*, *9*, 1–2.

Prensky, M. (2001c). Immigrants part 2: Do they. *On the Horizon*, *9*, 2–6.

Rickes, P. C. (2016). Generations in flux: How gen Z will continue to transform higher education space. *Planning for Higher Education*, *44*(4), 21.

Sampasa-Kanyinga, H., & Lewis, R. F. (2015). Frequent use of social networking sites is associated with poor psychological functioning among children and adolescents. *Cyberpsychology, Behavior, and Social Networking*, *18*(7), 380–385. doi:10.1089/cyber.2015.0055 PMID:26167836

Smith, A. A. (2015, March 26). Community college to bachelor's. *Inside Higher Ed*. Retrieved from https://www.insidehighered.com/news/2015/03/26/nearly-half-four-year-college-graduates-attended-two-year-college

Smith, B. G., & Gallicano, T. D. (2015). Terms of engagement: Analyzing public engagement with organizations through social media. *Computers in Human Behavior*, *53*, 82–90. doi:10.1016/j.chb.2015.05.060

Swett, D. (2016). Online student orientation: Guerrilla style. *Change: The Magazine of Higher Learning*, *48*(5), 26–35. doi:10.1080/00091383.2016.1227673

Thompson, P. (2015). How digital native learners describe themselves. *Education and Information Technologies*, *20*(3), 467–484. doi:10.100710639-013-9295-3

Tufford, L., & Newman, P. (2012). Bracketing in qualitative research. *Qualitative Social Work: Research and Practice*, *11*(1), 80–96. doi:10.1177/1473325010368316

Turner, A. (2015). Generation Z: Technology and social interest. *Journal of Individual Psychology*, *71*(2), 103–113. doi:10.1353/jip.2015.0021

Wang, Z., & Tchernev, J. M. (2012). The "myth" of media multitasking: Reciprocal dynamics of media multitasking, personal needs, and gratifications. *Journal of Communication*, *62*(3), 493–513. doi:10.1111/j.1460-2466.2012.01641.x

Xiaoqing, G., Yuankun, Z., & Xiaofeng, G. (2013). Meeting the "digital natives": Understanding the acceptance of technology in classrooms. *Journal of Educational Technology & Society*, *16*(1), 392–402.

Zaremohzzabieh, Z., Samah, B. A., Omar, S. Z., Bolong, J., & Kamarudin, N. A. (2014). Addictive Facebook use among university students. *Asian Social Science*, *10*(6), 107–117. doi:10.5539/ass.v10n6p107

Zorn, R. L. (2016). Coming in 2017: A new generation of graduate students - The z generation. *College and University*, *92*(1), 61–63.

KEY TERMS AND DEFINITIONS

Generation: A collective group of people born during the same span of years, influenced by world and geopolitical events, and shared/common experiences and cultural elements.

Generation X: A generation born between the years 1964 and 1982.

Generation Z: A generation born between the years 1995 and 2010.

Higher Education Professional: Professional-level staff at a postsecondary educational institution whose primary responsibilities are not connected to formal teaching/research roles.

Millennial Generation: A generation born between the years 1982 and 1994.

Social Media: World Wide Web-based applications designed to facilitate interpersonal connections among users.

Chapter 8
Using Social Media in the Classroom:
Preparing Faculty for Change

Victoria Reynolds
State University of New York at Plattsburgh, USA

ABSTRACT

This chapter focuses on the unique problem of preparing faculty to meet students by crossing the divide of the digital media native generation. Members of Gen Z, the first of whom are just matriculating to college, hold certain expectations about the availability of information in digital forms, among other things. There is a growing realization, in the higher learning space, that traditional classroom practices are unlikely to meet the needs of Gen Z. Student learning preferences and styles have evolved. It is essential for faculty to investigate ways in which their teaching practices can develop to meet the needs of this generation. This chapter discusses the use of social media to engage students in a topic in the communication sciences and disorders that are seen as difficult and unengaging, augmentative and alternative communication systems. Students were encouraged to challenge their pre-conceptions around ability, and utilizing a digital medium, which in turn incentivized every student to become comfortable with digital technology and familiar with the principles of universal design.

DOI: 10.4018/978-1-5225-7763-8.ch008

INTRODUCTION

Who Are Gen Z?

A single, universally-agreed definition of a "generation" is elusive. In defining a generation, sociological theory suggests that there is a time and history component: this is generally interpreted to mean that a generation is a group of people who occupy the same place in time and have a shared knowledge of a memorable historical event (Jansen, 1974). Yet, the term "shared knowledge" is also subjective. It may refer to an awareness, an intimate knowledge or to having been profoundly affected in some way. One possibility is that these phenomena exist on a continuum, in which case each so-called generation will be affected, and therefore shaped, by that "shared knowledge" to different degrees.

Despite the abundance of research about the characteristics of Gen Z, even the major dictionaries of the Anglophonic nations cannot agree on a single definition of this generation. The Macquarie Dictionary, Merriam Webster and the Oxford English Dictionary, generally held to be the authoritative sources for Australian, American and British English, respectively, do not agree on a definition for the "place in time". Two sources define the birth of Gen Z as occurring in "the late 1990s and early 2000s" and "the early 2000s" (Macquarie Dictionary Online, 2016; Merriam-Webster.com, n.d.); one source neatly sidesteps the challenges of agreeing on a birth decade by defining Gen Z as "reaching adulthood in the second decade of the 21st century" (Oxford English Dictionary, n.d.). No source specifically cites a historical event – but all mention technology. Each definition cites one or more different characteristics of Gen Z, ranging from economic behavior (consumerism) to ethical and moral behavior (a sense of social responsibility).

The one common characteristic is a high level of comfort and/or proficiency with technology, defined as "being at ease", "being familiar" and "tech-savvy" (Macquarie Dictionary Online, 2016; Merriam-Webster.com, n.d.; Oxford English Dictionary, n.d.). Is the information age the historical event of Gen Z? This would represent a shift in the nature and duration of occurrences traditionally accepted as "historical events" for the purposes of attempting to define a generation. The information age represents a paradigm shift, similarly to the agrarian and industrial revolutions of the 18th and 19th centuries. Fundamental changes in ways of living, interacting, and in world concepts are experienced by those who live through such events. For those who are born afterwards, those ways are simply the norm.

Gen Z is, like all generations, somewhat nebulous – yet commonalities can be agreed from the wide variability in defintions. Gen Z are becoming adults in this decade (the 2010s) and technology is integrated into their lifestyles, perhaps even into their identities.

By generational definition, faculty and students will always clash. Despite the best of intentions, the age differential between students and faculty means that there is an aspect of the relationship that mirrors that of the "generation of initiation" and the "generation of domination", respectively (Jansen, 1974, p. 95). Students, who are the younger relation, seek to change societal norms and structures, as every generation before them has done. Faculty, having had the adventure and excitement of enacting change in their younger days, are now resistant to change – having forgotten their own frustrations.

This generational divide is not new, and appears to perpetuate itself. This quote is commonly attributed to ancient scholars such as Socrates or Plato (or both!)

The children now love luxury; they have bad manners, contempt for authority; they show disrespect for elders and love chatter in place of exercise. Children are now tyrants, not the servants of their households. They no longer rise when elders enter the room. They contradict their parents, chatter before company, gobble up dainties at the table, cross their legs, and tyrannize their teachers.

It may in fact have unknown origins, but its first reported appearance in the English language literature in 1966 indicates that this dissonance between generations is at least 50 years old (Platt, 1989), although it is likely much older.

The Conundrum: Addressing Two Problems With One Solution

Faculty must meet students somewhere. It is no longer enough to simply meet in the classroom and expect students to rise to the communication, learning and cognitive preferences of the preceding generation. Further, if the information age is accepted to be the defining historical event of Gen Z, this generation cannot be expected to fully adapt to informational sources of preceding generations. This would represent a backwards step in time, when human nature demands that the generation of initiation propels society forward, towards change. Faculty recognize this, and have adapted teaching practices to the extent that students taught in online contexts can achieve similar outcomes to face-to-face contact (Broussard & Wilson, 2018). Many faculty use online materials to various degrees (e.g., use of a learning management system to post syllabi, or a fully-online course) (Broussard & Wilson, 2018). However, the use of social media as a communication tool in the classroom remains infrequent (Broussard & Wilson, 2018). There is, therefore, significant potential for its adoption within the curriculum.

On the topic of student engagement, one key area of speech-language pathology practice is augmentative and alternative communication (AAC), which refers to any mode of communication that replaces or supplements speech, such as sign language, a text-to-speech app or a communication board (Beukelman & Mirenda, 2013). Complex communication needs (CCN) is the term used to describe individuals' use of AAC systems to supplement or replace speech to communicate. Individuals with CCN are found across genders, ages and cultural groups: however, they all require a modality to supplement or replace speech in order to communicate successfully (Beukelman & Mirenda, 2013).

Speech-language pathologists form a key part of the multidisciplinary team that matches an individual to an efficient AAC system that is appropriate to their physical, cognitive and linguistic skills (Hill & Scherer, 2008). Further, advocacy is an important part of the speech-language pathology scope of practice: the need for advocacy for individuals who use AAC and for CCN in general is clear (American Speech-Language Hearing Association (ASHA), 2016). Yet, students traditionally find AAC a difficult area to master. The experience of this author, in two countries, is that students perceive AAC to be a specialist area of clinical practice, a difficult subject and one that they prefer to avoid. This experience is consistent with the empirical research: for example, job postings for SLPs working with people with developmental disabilities are responded to less than postings for other populations (Johnson, Bloomberg, & Iacono, 2008). This is not an issue limited to practicing clinicians, however. Students express a stronger preference for working with other populations, that is, children with CCN and adults with CCN consistently rank lowest in surveys of student preferences for working with clinical populations (Johnson et al., 2008). Finally, speech-language pathologists report that they lack confidence to work with people with CCN (Johnson et al., 2008). If the so-called experts in communication are reluctant to work in this area due to perceived lack of skills and knowledge, the wider community is likely to also lack this knowledge. While the underlying reasons are unclear, it can be hypothesized that this situation contributes to the lack of normalization of AAC and CCN in the wider community.

The name of this book, "Preparing the Higher Education Space for Gen Z" reflects the shift in locus of responsibility from the incoming students to the institution. As faculty tend to be all-too-aware, "institution" generally means "faculty", particularly when it comes to classroom matters. How can faculty prepare themselves for this unprecedented change? Further, it is possible to use this opportunity to increase student engagement in course material and related social justice issues, via the use of social media in the classroom?

BACKGROUND

Teaching Context: The Importance of Education in This Speech-Language Pathology Practice Area

People with CCN form between 0.2% to 4.2% of the population, depending on the age of the study population (Beukelman & Mirenda, 2013). Yet, AAC in the general community is lacking in awareness. This poses significant barriers to participation and restricts the activities of people with CCN (World Health Organization, 2001). Further, community awareness of issues around ability is heavily weighted toward physical mobility. Whilst this is important, the lack of experience with AAC in the general community further disadvantages individuals with CCN, some of whom rely on partners to successfully communicate using their AAC systems. Augmentative and alternative communication is therefore an important area of speech-language pathology practice.

One possible barrier to normalization of augmentative and alternative modes of communication is the persistence of the so-called "deficit model" of disability, which is rooted in attitudes around "fixing" disability (Donaldson, Chabon, Lee-Wilkerson, & Kapantzoglou, 2017). The social model of disability promotes the alternative view that an individual's health condition is not handicapping per se. Rather, the attitudes and actions of society in relation to the health condition impose handicapping limitations on the individual (Donaldson et al., 2017). The social model of disability views each individual as possessing strengths that can be utilized to break down barriers to participation (Donaldson et al., 2017).

Broadly speaking, many speech-language pathology programs do not adequately prepare students to work with clients with CCN. These students lack confidence and therefore feel unprepared to work with AAC. This not only affects the client population, but also community at large, which continues to impose activity restrictions and participation limitations on people with CCN that are handicapping because of lack of understanding. It can be argued that speech-language pathologists would be stronger advocates for clients with CCN and AAC if they felt competent in this area of practice. Further, attitudes to ability in speech pathology have traditionally followed the so-called "deficit" model. This is not universal – many top-rated programs have a strong focus on AAC in the classroom, clinic and research space. Yet, the research into student and clinician attitudes and preparedness indicates that these might be in the minority. Thus, the potential for increasing student engagement in AAC via improving course content and delivery in AAC can be seen.

Faculty attitudes to learning activities are associated with their uptake by students, and with more positive student attitudes and outcomes (Rockich-Winston, Train, Rudolph, & Gillette, 2018). Therefore, faculty could, in theory, increase student engagement in AAC by introducing novel and engaging learning activities into their curricula. In the case of Gen Z, this should include the use of digital media. It can be hypothesized that increased engagement will lead to better understanding of the course content, which will be reflected in a sense of preparedness to work with people with CCN.

Goal of Courses

In Communication Sciences and Disorders graduate courses at SUNY Plattsburgh, measurement of student outcomes is achieved by externally-imposed standards. Each course must contain defined student learning outcomes (SLOs), and the instructor must certify that these are met for each student and specify the context (e.g., assessment task) under which the outcome was demonstrated. Any modification to the assessment tasks must ensure that students will have an equivalent, or better, opportunity to demonstrate mastery of the outcome/s. Changes to assessment tasks must be driven by this principle.

Whilst this may appear, at first glance, to be a very specific context, many graduate level courses lead to certification and credentialing, particularly in the fields of health, education and human services (e.g., nursing, teaching, counselling and social work, among others) (Bristol, Nelson, Sherrill, & Wangerin, 2018). Therefore, the exercise described in this chapter could easily be adapted to other courses, in other disciplines and at different instructional levels.

Traditional Practices

Many assignments in the Communication Sciences and Disorders require students to read and evaluate scientific literature relevant to the course content, in order to demonstrate an SLO. Students are generally assigned either a topic or specific readings or both, and then write an essay to demonstrate their understanding of the material. This longstanding assessment methodology is familiar to faculty.

Further, the familiarity extends to assignment submission and grading practices. For many faculty, this method of assessment is a akin to a "set and forget" strategy. By specifying assignment requirements, including delivery methods, information sources and acceptability of reference and bibliography materials in the syllabus, the course instructor experiences benefits, in terms of informal workload reduction, of repeating a known exercise. This is one way in which the volume-heavy, time-specific demands of an academic workload can be managed by faculty.

Notwithstanding, many instructors do modify the mechanics of assignments in line with developments in technology, including online databases and learning management systems (Broussard & Wilson, 2018; Peacock et al., 2018; Roblyer, McDaniel, Webb, Herman, & Witty, 2010). This demonstrates the willingness to implement change in pedagogical practices.

ISSUES, CONTROVERSIES, AND PROBLEMS

Increasing student engagement with assessments is one option for an instructor looking to modernize their curriculum. Updating delivery methods to be more in keeping with the knowledge and experiences of the digital generation is an area for exploration. For example, popular culture can be, and is, integrated into the classroom across levels of faculty experience and discipline (Peacock et al., 2018). Utilizing digital media reports, broadcast via social media, as a source of information for students is hypothesized to be more motivating and engaging than the traditional, paper-based assignment scenario described above. The requirement to appraise, and critically review the information, with reference to the scholarly literature, remains.

Use of social media in the classroom is generally encouraged as a way of connecting with the incoming generation. The term "social media" is broad, encompasses many different platforms and user interfaces, which are constantly expanding. To a digital non-native, social media may appear to be an ever-morphing entity, characterized by change: elusive, unreadable, and unpredictable. Yet, the majority of faculty (73%) report having Facebook accounts, albeit far fewer use it for communicating with students (Roblyer et al., 2010). Facebook is, therefore, one social media platform with which many faculty have at least some familiarity. Whilst it must be acknowledged that ill-judged use of Facebook may undermine faculty credibility, particularly if faculty are seen as unprofessional by students, selective use of Facebook as an information source is possible (Mazer, Murphy, & Simonds, 2007). Faculty, like other humans, relate better to familiarity and personal experience, therefore, use of Facebook as a social medium in the classroom could be considered a very good starting point for technological adoption and content change.

By contrast, students currently enrolled in college courses are comfortable with digital technology and receiving information from multiple sources. Many of these sources are seen by faculty as "non-traditional". A number of general and specialist education courses focus on teaching the skills needed to be a skilled consumer of research and intrepid detective of the accuracy and verity of scholarly sources. For example, at SUNY Plattsburgh, each undergraduate student is required to complete a library studies course, where principles and techniques of scholarship and research are taught, as a requirement of their general education. Further in the Communication Sciences and Disorders undergraduate program, seniors must complete a capstone course. The capstone is a forum for students to conduct a scoping review in an area of their choosing, thus, accurate and efficient skills in identifying and appraising relevant literature are essential. These skills are explicitly taught early in the course and refined via individualized faculty feedback throughout the semester.

Concerns regarding the accuracy and reliability of digital information arose decades ago and are still relevant today (Kleinberg, 1998). Yet, journal articles are simply another medium by which information is communicated. Therefore, students should be able to apply research appraisal skills to all informational sources, including those seen by faculty as non-traditional. If properly appraised and sited within the body of literature relevant to a course or SLO, could information transmitted via a "non-traditional" source add value to the understanding of a certain topic or issue? And, can faculty facilitate translation of critical appraisal skills taught to information on social media?

The simple changing of a delivery method, without substantially altering the requirement to appraise and digest relevant literature, is arguably a small step outside the faculty comfort zone. One endeavor around access and youth culture is the AbilityFest 2018, which took place at Melbourne's Coburg Velodrome (Ability Fest, 2018a). The event was publicized through ticketing venues, print and radio media outlets, as well as on social media, including on Facebook. In fact, the most detailed event information was found on the AbilityFest Facebook profile page, which linked to the ticketing website (Ability Fest, 2018a). Some festivalgoers may have only accessed information about the event on social media before deciding and preparing to attend (although quantifying this is beyond the scope of this chapter). It is logical, therefore, to direct students primarily to social media to investigate this event, the line-up, location, facilities and its unique contributions to accessibility and youth culture.

The aim of the AbilityFest is to "use music as a platform to normalise disability" (AbilityFest, 2018b). The festival was conceptualized by Australian Paralympian, basketball and tennis champion, Dylan Alcott. The inaugural event included multiple features to enhance access, such as the use of sign language interpreters on stage, wide access paths and raised viewing platforms. The majority of these pertained to physical accessibility. The event featured popular, local music acts, and the major sponsors were the Dylan Alcott Foundation ("Dylan Alcott Foundation I Helping young Australians with disabilities," n.d.), national youth radio broadcaster triple j ("triple j," 2018) and the Untitled Group.

Asking students to view a leisure event through the lens of normalizing disability may provide a context to shift their thinking from "fixing" disability to removing access barriers, consistent with the social model (Donaldson et al., 2017). Additionally, the use of first-person narratives challenges students to re-consider their attitudes toward ability (Hartley, Mapes, Taylor, & Bourgeois, 2016). The AbilityFest was developed based on the experiences of a young Paralympian, and the reviews of the event included many first-person narratives, albeit brief.

The risk-to-reward ratio is potentially high. Increased student engagement and enthusiasm appears to be an attractive trade-off for a temporary increase in faculty workload when trialing a new experience. To date, however, the literature contains few concrete examples of ways in which faculty in the health sciences can integrate social media into the higher education space (Peacock et al., 2018). The aim of this chapter is to describe a learning activity in which social media was used to stimulate scholarly thought, and promote its application to an authentic setting, in an area of speech-language pathology education and clinical practice.

METHOD

Assignment

Rationale

The issue of accessibility in youth culture is personally and academically relevant to graduate students enrolled in AAC courses. The academic relevance to course content is clear; discussion of accessibility in young people of a similar age to themselves introduces a powerful connection between students and the client group.

The student learning outcomes addressed by competent completion of the assignment were:

1. Examine the effects of a severe expressive communication impairment on social, psychological, educational and other developmental aspects of an individual's life.
2. Identify the characteristics of multiple diagnostic categories/etiologies that may lead to the need for AAC
3. Discuss the effects of the inability to communicate effectively on an individual's psychological and emotional status as well as educational development and development in other areas at varying stages of life.

Mastery of these SLOs is essential for students to understand the rationale for inclusion of the practice area of AAC in the speech-language pathology scope of practice. Further, consideration of people with CCN as functioning members of their community with self-actualization needs across the lifespan is consistent with the social model of disability (Donaldson et al., 2017). Typically, written assignments or examination would require students to source epidemiological studies, text books and/or outcome studies to examine these issues. It could be argued, however, that the wording of the SLOs, coupled with the requirement to search the literature base without context, may promote students to produce work that reflects an ableist perspective. However, engaging students in an endeavor to "normalize disability" is more likely to result in consideration of the issues from the perspective of integration and accommodation.

It was explained to students in class that the assignment was new to the course, designed specifically to meet the SLOs listed above and to trial something to engage students' sense of social justice, integrate their learning into practical ways to facilitate participation in community events. The social medium, Facebook, was familiar to all students. This author is the social media organizer for SUNY Plattsburgh's Speech and Hearing Center Facebook and Instagram pages. Most students had had direct contact with the author, in this context, on social media. The contact including liking posts, tagging friends and publicizing events. It was emphasized to students that the learning activity was a trial of a new methodology integrating social media and authentic assessment, and that they would not be penalized if the methodology was not as effective as more traditional styles of assignment. Students were generally positive about the endeavour during contact with the author, and did not express misgivings about their ability to demonstrate the SLOs.

The AbilityFest provided students with an authentic context under which to examine the issues relevant to achieving the learning outcomes. Many students have firsthand experience of the social and psychological benefits of being able to attend organized events such as music concerts and festivals. By considering communication accessibility, and how this could be achieved for people with various communication disorders, students were prompted to consider multiple diagnostic categories and etiologies in the area of CCN. Finally, the use of the AbilityFest as a case example leads students to consider social participation, its relationship with psychological and emotional status during young adulthood. For people who are differently abled and in particular those with CCN, young adulthood is a unique time of life where chronologically, they are considered adults, yet many are still experiencing the final few years of an extended, supported educational placement. Access to mainstream social events is an important, yet under-recognized issue in this population. It was hypothesized that, despite their year of graduate-level training in the communication sciences and disorders, the students would not have considered communication accessibility in public spaces and events. It was further hypothesized that students would be motivated by the importance of the issue, the paucity of information surrounding it and the potential for positive change in community inclusion of people with CCN.

Instructions

Students were directed to two Facebook pages: the first of which was the profile page of AbilityFest. Students were provided with Facebook links and explored the relevant pages in class time. Students were able to ask questions about any aspect of the festival, to the best of this author's knowledge. Student were encouraged to research the festival via any media available, and integrate the available information about the festival into any relevant findings from the literature.

The formal assignment instructions from the syllabus can be found below (Reynolds, 2018):

Moodle submission on communication accessibility. You will write a "Moodle post" as though you are contributing to a discussion forum, but you will submit it to me via the portal on Moodle (and not on a discussion forum). You should start your Moodle post by briefly outlining the social, psychological and developmental aspects of a severe communication impairment, to set the scene for the reader. In class, we will watch the clip about the AbilityFest, an accessible music festival for young people. Please describe the communication accessibility features of AbilityFest, and critically appraise these. You have a limit of 1,000 words (not including references – you may like to refer to your textbook or other scholarly sources to support your arguments). When you describe the features, you should list them and give a brief explanation so that a reader unfamiliar with the festival will understand the context. Your critical appraisal could include a statement about the benefits or effectiveness of the features and/or a suggestion for how they could be improved (10%). ACHIEIVING A PASSING GRADE IN THIS ASSIGNMENT WILL DEMONSTRATE ACHIEVEMENT OF THE FOLLOWING LEARNING OUTCOMES: 1, 2, 3

Results

Due to the retrospective nature of this report, the exercise was not planned for quantitative comparisons. Data were analysed while grading assignments and again after the conclusion of the relevant college term. A number of recurrent themes were identified.

Student Writing

The social model of disability was apparent in the perspective of all students. Whilst few mentioned it explicitly, many discussed the WHO ICF framework and the notion of handicap arising from societal limitations, rather than individuals' health conditions. Environmental barriers, participation restrictions and community assumptions were also discussed.

Students talked about the privilege of ability with respect to communication, although few used that term explicitly. Rather, discussions touched on taking communication skills for granted. Many students referenced the Communication Bill of Rights, a document developed to ensure that people with CCN are afforded the right to influence their existence through communication (Brady et al., 2016). Others talked about Light's purposes of communication, and of the possibility that people with CCN may be limited, by those around them, to communicating basic needs and wants (Light, 1988).

Inclusion in the community was also explored. Students considered whether invitations to participate were even extended to people with CCN in the same way, as well as whether responses to invitations could be filtered by concerns regarding access to the event. Some students considered the Social Networks Inventory (Blackstone & Hunt Berg, 2012), and, armed with the knowledge that the average size of social network in people with CCN is small, considered whether community action was required to facilitate the social participation of people with CCN. One suggestion was that, if a person with CCN had a small social network or a social network consisting mainly of caregivers, that a volunteer buddy system could match festival goers based on commonalities such as age, interests or hobbies. That way, all festivalgoers would have a companion and a readymade social support system to enjoy the festival. It was positive to see students consider a model of social participation, apply it to the assignment context, i.,e., consider potential barriers to making the decision to attend the festival at all, and propose a solution to this issue.

Each student discussed the mechanics of communication accessibility and proposed multiple ways in which this could be achieved. Suggestions were wide-ranging. For people with comprehension difficulties, using closed-captioning of song lyrics, using simplified language to convey the meaning of the song, or representing lyrics in symbol format were proposed by many students. Others discussed the need for education of venue staff. A popular idea was providing training on how to interact with people with CCN, focusing on different types of communication systems and how to use partner-assisted scanning. Other ideas for accessibility required little-to-no training: provision of photographs on menus and low-tech AAC boards included in festival tickets or social media would facilitate communication between patrons and festival staff. Students integrated learning from different courses: use of symbols to represent concepts, and the different hierarchies associated with this, was discussed in the AAC course. In the courses devoted to pediatric and adult language disorders, ways of changing information to facilitate comprehension were discussed. This demonstrated clinical application of classroom-based learning to a client population.

Many students sought information, either on the web or on social media, about inclusive facilities in their own communities. One example given was of Hershey Park, in Pennsylvania – although it was noted that the majority of accommodations also pertained to physical access. Another student considered whether the SUNY Plattsburgh Aphasia Choir could introduce any of the communication accessibility features in the biannual concerts. This demonstrated the emergence of advocacy for community inclusion.

One aspect of the assignment that faculty might find challenging to grade was referencing. Whilst the number of references cited ranged from 1 to 13 and the median was 4, the mode was 1. This may be because think-pieces, so frequent in the digital community, are rarely referenced. The wording in the assignment instructions was ambiguous ("you **may** like to refer") and the audience was not specified. Issues such as these arise from the trial and error process adopted by the author in implementing this exercise. Whilst it could be assumed that students are aware that referencing is required for all pieces of scholarly work, this format was likely new to most. Clearly, the informal style of a think-piece clashed with their ideas of scholarly writing.

The use of language that was not person-centered was infrequent, but was present. There is debate around the use of terminology when discussing ability, and whether person-first terminology is appropriate in cases where individuals view their health conditions as inherent parts of their identity. However, there is broad consensus around restricting the use of terminology that reinforces the notion that disability is a burden or by definition results in reduced quality of life (National Center on Disability and Journalism, 2018). To that end, one use of inappropriate language is one too many.

Opening the door to the use of social media did invite some pitfalls. Many students made reference to the "wrong" AbilityFest. The Seven Hills Foundation holds an annual AbilityFest, an event designed to promote physical activity in people with disabilities and their communities ("AbilityFest - Seven Hills Foundation," 2018). Given that this was an all-ages event specifically designed for people with disabilities, the focus was slightly different and this may have resulted in confusion among students – the antithesis of the intention of the learning activity. These data demonstrate that the often-bemoaned problems of "fake news" and digital information overload in the media do intrude into the higher education space.

Anecdotes

Student engagement appeared to increase when the terminology around the assignment was modified and re-named a "think piece" instead of "Moodle post". It is hypothesized that this is because students have an understanding of the cultural phenomenon that is the "think piece" and that expressing their views in this format feels authentic and meaningful (North, 2014).

Students appeared to be enthusiastic about the learning activity, making positive comments during class time. However, this was not reflected in their course evaluations, which lacked any specific comments about the assignment. Whilst these were not specifically solicited, items on the survey do relate to course assessments and space is provided for freeform comments. This is open to interpretation: it may be that students did not harbor strong feelings about the assignment, either positive or negative. The lack of negative comments may indicate that students feel the assessment was acceptable. From the perspective that assessment is a necessary evil, it can be expected that students may not feel particularly positively about assessment in general. Their baseline feelings toward the issue are likely to be skewed to the negative.

SOLUTIONS AND RECOMMENDATIONS

On reflection, the exercise ran smoothly. Despite the use of a novel medium, the requirements for the assignment were similar enough to traditional ways of reading and appraising literature for the release of assignment instructions, management of queries and grading to be in line with usual procedure. The process represented a very small change in practice but with a greater level of student engagement than anticipated, had the context been limited to the scholarly literature. The context was more authentic: authentic assessment practices help students to bridge the gap between learning space and workplace. This, too, may have increased motivation, if students imagined themselves performing a similar exercise for a future client.

Naturally, there are suggestions for refining the assignment. The issue of integrating information from a different AbilityFest into the assignment poses an interesting problem. The students did not identify this discrepancy when they appraised their information sources. It appears that the problem of verifying information from reputable sources extends from consuming the scholarly literature to social media. With this in mind, students can be counselled in advance to critique their sources carefully. Faculty, too, should be aware that students may need explicit instruction to apply their research consumption skills to less traditional sources of information in the higher education space.

In terms of referencing, potential solutions suggest themselves, and include specifying in the assignment instructions that referencing is required for arguments such as suggesting an accommodation. Well-referenced exemplars of think-pieces do exist, and could be provided to students as a guide.

Students' use of pity-evoking language in the context of ability continues to be a concern. Faculty should re-double their efforts to neutralize language use to describe client populations and community members. It could be argued that the discipline of communication sciences and disorders should lead this effort, given that its members are experts in communication.

This activity represents a minor change in practice that in itself, will not meet the needs of the incoming digital-native generation. The assignment task itself will eventually need to be modified: one possibility is that students, having read the information on social media, could seek out one of the tracks that was featured at Ability Fest and make it accessible, through the use of AAC. Students would need to think about supporting festival-goers' comprehension skills and ways in which they could participate in the experience. These ideas could be expressed in a digital medium, either via a cloudshare space or presented in class for discussion and editing, or both.

CONCLUSION

Social media reports of health and education issues are abundant, and faculty are likely to find themselves spoilt for choice when selecting content upon which to base learning activities. Selecting a platform may be a challenge, but starting with the familiar is unlikely to pose major challenges.

Students explicitly considered each of the relevant SLOs in their responses, as well as demonstrating the skills to think about ability in a different way, perhaps representing a paradigm shift for some. The proposal of multiple, potential accessibility features suggests that students are integrating the social model of disability into their world view, at least implicitly. By examining the attitudes of speech-language pathology students towards ability, and prompting them to consider communication accessibility, it can be hypothesized that students will feel more engaged with issues around the use of AAC.

In terms of changing pedagogical practices, this is but a small step. Small steps are steps, nonetheless. Selective exercises such as this, when used in a supported context, may introduce faculty to social media and its potential uses in the classroom and reinforce to faculty that newer media can be engaging, whilst retaining the opportunity for students to demonstrate learning outcomes.

ACKNOWLEDGMENT

It is essential to acknowledge the students who contributed to this learning activity. In addition, participants in Facebook discussion forums and reviews provided valuable insight into how AbilityFest was received in the community. The anonymous reviewer provided valuable feedback which resulted in improvements in this chapter. Finally, those who conceptualized, publicized and executed the event provided the context for this learning activity and inspired students to promote inclusion in local events.

REFERENCES

Ability Fest. (2018a). Ability Fest — 2018 [Facebook event]. Retrieved from https://www.facebook.com/events/153840705302082/

Ability Fest. (2018b). Ability Fest - Home [Facebook profile page]. Retrieved from https://www.facebook.com/abilityfestival/

AbilityFest - Seven Hills Foundation. (2018). Retrieved from http://www.sevenhills.org/abilityfest

American Speech-Language-Hearing Association (ASHA). (2016). Scope of Practice in Speech-Language Pathology. doi:10.1044/policy.SP2016-00343

Beukelman, D. R., & Mirenda, P. (2013). *Augmentative and alternative communication: Supporting children and adults with complex communication needs* (4th ed.). Paul H. Brookes Pub.

Blackstone, S., & Hunt Berg, M. (2012). *Social Networks: A Communication Inventory for Individuals with Complex Communication Needs and their Communication Partners*. Monterrey, CA: Attainment Company, Augmentative Communication, Inc. Retrieved from http://www.augcominc.com/index.cfm/social_networks.htm

Brady, N. C., Bruce, S., Goldman, A., Erickson, K., Mineo, B., Ogletree, B. T., ... Siegel, E. (2016). Communication services and supports for individuals with severe disabilities: Guidance for assessment and intervention. *American Journal on Intellectual and Developmental Disabilities*, *121*(2), 121–138. doi:10.1352/1944-7558-121.2.121 PMID:26914467

Bristol, T. J., Nelson, J. W., Sherrill, K. J., & Wangerin, V. S. (2018). Current State of Test Development, Administration, and Analysis: A Study of Faculty Practices. *Nurse Educator*, *43*(2), 68–72. Retrieved from https://journals.lww.com/nurseeducatoronline/Fulltext/2018/03000/Current_State_of_Test_Development,_Administration.7.aspx doi:10.1097/NNE.0000000000000425 PMID:28817472

Broussard, L., & Wilson, K. (2018). Nursing Faculty Attitudes and Practices Related to Online Teaching. *Nursing Education Perspectives*, *39*(1), 40–42. Retrieved from https://journals.lww.com/neponline/Fulltext/2018/01000/Nursing_Faculty_Attitudes_and_Practices_Related_to.12.aspx doi:10.1097/01.NEP.0000000000000208 PMID:28806277

Donaldson, A. L., Chabon, S., Lee-Wilkerson, D., & Kapantzoglou, M. (2017). Mirror, mirror on the wall: Reflections on speech-language pathologists' image as advocates, activists, and aides. *Psychology in the Schools*, *54*(10), 1285–1293. doi:10.1002/pits.22083

Dylan Alcott Foundation | Helping young Australians with disabilities. (n.d.). Retrieved from https://dylanalcottfoundation.com.au/

Hartley, M. T., Mapes, A. C., Taylor, A., & Bourgeois, P. J. (2016). Digital Media Education and Advocacy: Addressing Attitudes Toward Disability on College Campuses. *Journal of Postsecondary Education & Disability*, *29*(3), 239–247.

Hill, K., & Scherer, M. (2008). Matching persons and technology: data-driven AAC assessments. *Presented at the 23rd Annual International Conference on Technology and Persons with Disabilities*. Los Angeles, CA: CSUN.

Jansen, N. (1974). Definition of Generation and Sociological Theory. *Social Science*, *49*(2), 90–98.

Johnson, H., Bloomberg, K., & Iacono, T. (2008). Student and professional attitudes and interests in working with people with complex communication needs. *International Journal of Speech-Language Pathology*, *10*(5), 286–296. doi:10.1080/14417040701689329 PMID:20840028

Kleinberg, J. M. (1998). Authoritative sources in a hyperlinked environment. In *Proceedings of the ACM-SIAM Symposium on Discrete Algorithms*.

Light, J. (1988). Interaction involving individuals using augmentative and alternative communication systems: State of the art and future directions. *Augmentative and Alternative Communication*, *4*(2), 66–82. doi:10.1080/07434618812331274657

Macquarie Dictionary Online. (2016). Generation Z. *Macquarie Dictionary Online*. Macquarie Dictionary Publishers, an imprint of Pan Macmillan Australia Pty Ltd. Retrieved from https://www.macquariedictionary.com.au/

Mazer, J. P., Murphy, R. E., & Simonds, C. J. (2007). I'll See You On "Facebook": The Effects of Computer-Mediated Teacher Self-Disclosure on Student Motivation, Affective Learning, and Classroom Climate. *Communication Education*, *56*(1), 1–17. doi:10.1080/03634520601009710

Merriam-Webster.com. (n.d.). generation Z. Retrieved from https://www.merriam-webster.com

National Center on Disability and Journalism. (2018). Disability Language Style Guide. Retrieved from https://ncdj.org/style-guide/

North, A. (2014, November 13). Think Pieces Were Made for Millennials Who Majored in English. NY Times. Retrieved from https://op-talk.blogs.nytimes.com/2014/11/13/think-pieces-were-made-for-millennials-who-majored-in-english/

Oxford English Dictionary. (n.d.). Generation Z. Retrieved from http://www.oed.com/viewdictionaryentry/Entry/11125

Peacock, J., Covino, R., Auchter, J., Boyd, J., Klug, H., Laing, C., & Irvin, L. (2018). University faculty perceptions and utilization of popular culture in the classroom. *Studies in Higher Education*, *43*(4), 601–613. doi:10.1080/03075079.2016.1180673

Platt, S. (Ed.). (1989). *Respectfully Quoted: A Dictionary of Quotations Requested from the Congressional Research Service*. Washington, DC: Library of Congress. Retrieved from https://www.bartleby.com/73/195.html

Reynolds, V. (2018). CSD537A Augmentative and Alternative Communication Systems Summer 2018 Syllabus.

Roblyer, M. D., McDaniel, M., Webb, M., Herman, J., & Witty, J. V. (2010). Findings on Facebook in higher education: A comparison of college faculty and student uses and perceptions of social networking sites. *The Internet and Higher Education*, *13*(3), 134–140. doi:10.1016/j.iheduc.2010.03.002

Rockich-Winston, N., Train, B. C., Rudolph, M. J., & Gillette, C. (2018). Faculty motivations to use active learning among pharmacy educators. *Currents in Pharmacy Teaching and Learning*, *10*(3), 277–284. doi:10.1016/j.cptl.2017.11.015 PMID:29764630

triple j. (2018). [Collection]. Retrieved from https://www.abc.net.au/triplej/

World Health Organization. (2001). International Classification of Functioning, Disability and Health (ICF). Retrieved from http://www.who.int/classifications/icf/en/

Chapter 9
Texting With Students:
Facilitating Learning in Higher Education

A. S. CohenMiller
https://orcid.org/0000-0001-6871-6898
Nazarbayev University, Kazakhstan

ABSTRACT

Text messaging has become a standard form of communication between students. However, how texting can be used in higher education as a pedagogical practice has not been fully explored or articulated. This chapter provides critical insight into the value of text messaging as formal and informal communication both between faculty and students and also messaging led by students. Juxtaposing literature on the use of texting in educational environments with practical examples of university teaching in the United States and post-Soviet Kazakhstan, the chapter outlines challenges, benefits, and suggested methods of texting with students in higher education. Framed within concepts of 21st-century learning, multilingualism, and multiliteracies, the author suggests clear benefits for utilizing technology that students commonly use, while also creating an environment valuing students' changing modes of communication which puts less pressure on the traditional academic discussion, and gives a voice to the individual.

DOI: 10.4018/978-1-5225-7763-8.ch009

INTRODUCTION

When I first started teaching at the university level, I had a colleague tell me they gave their cell phone number to their students. I was shocked. I couldn't imagine passing along such a personal piece of information to students. I assumed students contacted the faculty member nonstop, creating obstacles for getting other work done and for any separation of work and family life. Jump ahead eleven years and add an international move from the US to Kazakhstan, and my view on handing out my phone number has changed drastically. One of the first things I do with my graduate students is to give them my cell phone number and create a texting group with the students. More specifically, I have one of them volunteer to form the group, guiding them to take ownership of course-related dialogue both in and outside the formal class environment.

Are there times when students text in the middle of the night? Yes. Does it bother me? No. Because I adjust my telephone preferences accordingly. I inform the students of this too, noting an open policy for texting, with the caveat that I will not always respond (i.e., if I need quiet, my phone will be off or on silent). These practical conversations have helped to lay the groundwork for a cooperative and engaged class. But does this present a problem of work and family life conflict? Mostly no, as I find it simpler to check a group text thread rather than logging it to several email sites (e.g., Moodle and University). In practice, texting with students has facilitated my workflow as I can spend a few minutes checking texts on my computer in between other work. In these in-between times, I respond to questions, clarify topics, encourage conversation, and remind students of any upcoming deadlines. Only occasionally have I found students will write in the late evening, typically occurring when there is a burning question, concern, or an update on the health of someone in the group. And in most of these cases, another student will respond with an answer, encouraging, or with a comment about how they are also confused. The ability to write back in a text format and say something simple, such as, "I don't understand" or "can you explain this?" or "will we still meet at 10 am?" while referring to a specific text. Overall, using text messages as formal and informal communication with students has helped guide them through their coursework in a way that values students' changing modes of communication, puts less pressure on traditional academic communication, and gives voice to the individual.

BACKGROUND AND MAIN FOCUS OF THE CHAPTER

Setting the Global Stage in a Move to Kazakhstan

To back up a bit, let me provide a bit more context for where I am currently working. Since 2015, I have been working in Kazakhstan at a research-intensive university. We moved to the country with our two young children when they were about five months old and four years old. The University enrolls over 4000 students across undergraduate to graduate level, employs faculty from over 50 countries ("NU at a glance," 2018) and partners with universities around the world to help guide its development. My department, the Graduate School of Education, has a partnership with the University of Pennsylvania and Cambridge University, both of whom provide advice and guidance in the development of our programs and support for dissertation students. In these last few years, we have graduated two sets of Ph.D. students and over 100 MSc and MA students. Historically, the universities in the region followed a Soviet style of teaching which centers on a teacher-centered, hierarchical approach. However, with independence in 1991, pedagogy has been rapidly changing with immense educational reforms to advance teaching practices (Bridges, 2014). The top-down educational reforms require for teachers at public schools to learn new professional knowledge (Yakavets, Bridges, & Shamatov, 2017), such as teaching in three languages (i.e., trilingual reform) and new teaching approaches. At the university level, teachers are often required to follow standard practices set by the State (Prilipko, 2017) with little encouragement or freedom to be innovative (Sarinzhipov, 2013, vi) to address student needs. While the country is moving towards trilingual education, the University itself is an English as a medium of instruction institution.

Pedagogical Changes

When I look back, it isn't surprising to see this change in my pedagogical practices. The use of texting with my students has been the next logical sequence in the evolution of my teaching. Stemming from a Montessori educational background to now actively seeking to incorporate experiential research activities within a course framework emphasizing feedback and self-reflection. Texting has helped to achieve these outcomes in multiple ways, such as allowing for data collection on personal phones and shared through texting groups. Likewise, I have found myself in the last couple of years strongly affected by the "going gradeless" movement (Blackwelder

& Hazeu, 2018). Those from around the world, in particular in US middle and high schools, are harnessing research about problematic effects of grades on student learning, and are substituting intensive feedback and student reflection (Chiaravalli, 2017). Texting can then be seen as an opportunity for immediate, reflective, and quality feedback between faculty and student and also as a form of peer learning. As Hilsdon (2014) notes, peer learning can provide a context for facilitating informal learning:

Such comments fit well with the notion of a potential 'third space' for learning, albeit one directed by students rather than a teacher, where the discourses of informal contexts and peer-networks can be used to reflect on, and to find ways to make sense of, and then take ownership of academic discourse and practice. (p. 249)

With these tenants, the graduate seminar moves from a hierarchical environment to one where we sit together collectively, figuratively and literally. On the first day of class, I have students look around at the tables, chairs, and where they are sitting. I ask them if the arrangement allows everyone to talk with one another easily or if any changes could be made to facilitate discussion and learning. Every class, the students make changes. Sometimes the classroom has permanently affixed tables and chairs in which case, the students move to a different location, or I bring a small table closer to them to bring us on more equal footing. At other times, they can rearrange the desks and often first try a semi-circle positioning me as the professor at the head of the classroom. It takes some work to undo this type of hierarchical thinking; I am not the center of the learning, the students need to be, for them to truly internalize their thinking and learning. The idea is to move from thinking of the teacher as the center of knowledge to the students as essential contributors who offer exceptional insight. In seeing students as "Funds of Knowledge" (Moll, Amanti, Neff, & Gonzalez, 1992), teachers recognize the contribution of students in particular to cultural, linguistic, and societal practices. For example, Debolina Maitra (2017) provides a clear synopsis, connecting funds of knowledge to the academic world in general:

FOK [Funds of Knowledge] is crucial in academics because when teachers look beyond their role as an authority figure and accept a role as a co-learner with students, they can get to know their students and the students' families with a new perspective. (p. 95)

Students in my classes primarily come from throughout Kazakhstan and have a variety of ethnic and linguistic practices. The Ministry of Education recognizes the country to have over 130 ethnicities and 47 languages (Ministry of Education and Science of the Republic of Kazakhstan JSC "Information-Analytic Center," 2017), with Russian being the primary language for business, Kazakh the primary language for social interaction in particular in Southern regions, and English quickly becoming a third language of instruction/communication within schools. At home, however, students have often been raised in multilingual and plurilingual environments, growing up understanding, speaking, and moving between two, three, or more languages. While in the US, the term bilingual education is commonly used to refer to teaching two or more languages within formal schooling, plurilingual is recognized as a key concept in other contexts. As defined by the Council of Europe (2001), plurilingualism is:

the ability to use languages for the purposes of communication and to take part in intercultural interaction, where a person, viewed as a social agent, has proficiency of varying degrees, in several languages, and experience of several cultures. This is not seen as the superposition or juxtaposition of distinct competencies, but rather as the existence of a complex or even composite competence on which the user may draw. (p. 168)

In other words, plurilingual individuals typically grow up within an intersection of languages and culture and have the ability to move seamlessly between them. As such, plurilingual students inherently communicate not just linguistically but in a more multimodal manner to overcome any linguistic difficulty.

Where I teach, students must pass a high stakes English exam to gain admission. Students then take the majority of their courses in English, which means they are often in learning environments where the language of instruction and communication is commonly their third, fourth, or fifth language. Within the Kazakhstani context, and our changing global environment, it becomes increasingly important to consider how we interact with our students, in the choice of language, as well as the manner and mode in which we engage.

ISSUES, CONTROVERSIES, PROBLEMS: LEARNING AND TEACHING IN AN INTERCONNECTED WORLD

With a growing awareness of the varied linguistic and cultural backgrounds of our students, meaning-making are essential concepts to consider. As Hämäläinen,

Kiili, and Smith (2017) explain as a central tenet of their article on 21st century learning in higher education, "The use of technology offers novel possibilities to take into account the voices of students" (p. 1107). In an age of social media, one such way to enhance communication with students is through texting (McKnight et al., 2016). Texting can be framed within the concepts of 21st-century learning, multiliteracies, and competencies, which address technology affecting higher education and multimodality in learning. The phrase, 21st-century learning (Burnett, Davies, Merchant, & Rowsell, 2014), is commonly used to explain the dynamic changes in student learning styles and needs in our evolving times. It became widely used in the context of multiliteracies over two decades ago as described by Kalantzis, Cope, and Harvey (2003), it "is considered as micro-cosmic of the broader notion of a new basics, in which both the traditional content of, and the traditional orientations to, knowledge have been substantially revised" (p. 17). In other words, multiliteracy is a term which can help us understand how knowledge is evolving, requiring multiple types of input and comprehension both in and outside the home. Furthermore, multiliteracies can be considered a salient concept of 21st-century learning, such as focusing on how knowledge is reconstructed and co-constructed within and across contexts (Pahl, 2016). As such, multiliteracies provides a means to understand new learning students engage in with the use of mobile devices (Boivin & CohenMiller, 2018).

The terminology used for the contemporary and future needs and skills suggested for students varies depending on the cultural context. For example, as a result of reforms in East Asia, the phrase 21st century competencies developed to "identify the characteristics of a successful young person in the 21st century, and therefore define the expected competencies that would be required and link them to the core values of the society" (Cheng et al., 2017, p. iii). Communication skills in and outside the classroom could relate to the growing use of technology, including texting. In Singapore, 21st-century competencies emphasize three concentric circles (see Image 1), addressing: Civic Literacy, Global Awareness, and Cross-Cultural Skills; Critical and Inventive Thinking; and Communication, Collaboration and Information Skills (Ministry of Education Singapore, 2015). Typical common threads are technological ability and interaction. As the OECD (2017) report on work and education notes, there is great potential for "technology to improve educational outcomes" (p. 19).

As higher education is changing, how we teach and interact with students are also bound to change. In some cases, we can see these changes occurring through flipped classrooms (Al-Zahrani, 2015; Altemueller & Lindquist, 2017) and blended learning environments (Dias & Diniz, 2014; Kirkwood, 2014; Pombo, Loureiro, & Moreira, 2010). These topics were discussed at the recent Eurasian Higher Education

Leadership Forum, where scholars from around the world discussed innovativeness and future changes needed to address globalization (Smat et al., 2018). A common focus has been on "flipping" the classroom, which broadly describes using class time for hands-on, experiential learning (Kuk & Holst, 2018; Seaman, Brown, & Quay, 2017), and time at home for reading and recorded lectures.

These changes occurring in higher education can also be felt in lower grades as well. In Kazakhstan, we have seen how text messaging has become a principal mode of interaction for students, even as early as 8th and 9th grade. From an intensive practical internship, two graduate students demonstrated how text groups between students and instructors could improve language comprehension, reducing students' affective filter (their stress level in having to perform in a new language), and apparently increasing student eagerness to engage in speaking English as a foreign language (Gimranova, Nurmanova, & CohenMiller, 2017). Similarly, other studies have shown how texting can support student learning, in particular for foreign language (Minalla, 2018). In bilingual, multilingual and plurilingual contexts, texting can create a less pressured educational environment versus the more formal expectations with academic email.

One way to address technology is through being aware of the technological applications devices, and activities, with which our students engage. The practice of texting in class is not unique to the Kazakhstani context. More than ten years ago, Livingston (2009) noted the near universal use of phones by students, "Mobile phone usage among our students has become virtually universal. Isn't it time for us to stop ignoring and start taking advantage of this fact?" (para 2). As Swartzwelder (2014) found in using texting within an online nursing class, students appreciated it as an interactive tool for learning. Likewise, Alshammari, Parkes, and Adlington (2017) found positive feelings by students when texting was used as supplementary communication within in an English as a Foreign Language learning classroom in Saudi Arabia. Similarly, Voss (2013) used texting as a means to "facilitate greater engagement" in teaching engineering ethics.

Specifics of how to use texts have been addressed recently by Rust (2018). She explains the use of various technologies to support texting with students as a form of "nudging" and reminder for class, mirroring earlier research on the topic. She provides example technological platforms for texting, such as by using a separate phone number through Google Voice, arranging small groups on GroupMe and applications, as well as describing the formal method in which she communicates with students. Further, Rust (2018) addresses an important aspect of teaching and texting as communication for those who are less familiar with the process and applications. The ability to leave voice messages could be a useful method for sharing information with students, such as reminders and encouragements about classwork and assignments, shown over a decade ago to encourage social support in transitioning to college (Harley et al., 2007). In a recent book, Castleman (2015) addresses the utility of texting to improve education, such as providing "nudges" to improve educational outcomes across the educational spectrum.

However, some concerns have also arisen from the potential detrimental aspect of texting as related to academic language writing. For example, Korros and Kosgei Kipkenda (2016) note a reduction in Kenyan students' academic English as shown across different types of courses while also explaining an opposite viewpoint,

Those who stated that it does not affect student writing skills were confident that students use different formats of writing at different scenarios and this comes up like a register and the students tend to know that official work calls for official language and they rarely break the rules. (p. 160)

However, Hyler and Hicks found different results, noting how texting with students can be used to teach grammar (2017). While there is more to understand the academic outcomes of texting, the use of texting as a form of communication to support teaching, learning and overall interaction continues to show importance.

SOLUTIONS AND RECOMMENDATIONS

Texting: A Hands-On Approach

In my courses, as the class unfolds, the students are both taught about the particular content of the course and also about new pedagogical practices. Likewise, I learn both about the students themselves, their experiences, and also about new ways in which to support engagement in learning. In my first semester in Kazakhstan, I used Moodle and email. The second semester I started moving to create class websites and online discussion chat groups. Then, starting last year, I found one more technique for interaction that worked better than them all – texting.

I have taught in the US, and the idea of giving out a personal phone number never sounded like a useful idea. I did not want late night texts or phone calls. I did not want my home life blended with work life. However, at my current university and with the changing nature of texting, it is more commonly understood that texts can be received and not answered right away, that everyone has a cell phone and is not charged exorbitantly for text messages sent or received. The nature of communication has changed for this new generation of students. Even without encouragement, students create class group chats to share information and problems. However, it took a few semesters before I felt comfortable trying this style of communication with my students, even though I had heard from other faculty members that they found texting with students much more effective than email for actually getting students to respond. In this way, I ended up, almost by accident, to happen upon a way to interact that seems to facilitate communication during and, at times even, after the culmination of the course. In contrast to email, text messages (at least in this particular context in an English medium university in Kazakhstan with primarily Kazakhstani students), have allowed students to more easily communicate, helping them to have a voice, while also allowing me as the faculty to better assess their struggles and level of engagement.

I have found since I started using texting as formal and informal communication with my graduate students, it is simpler and more effective to evaluate how students are managing within the course. Being able to have additional insight into working with students in blended learning or intensive modes through texting groups have been particularly useful. The students who take those courses are often balancing full-time work with also raising young children, being in a graduate program full time, and often have to travel long distances to come to class for the intensive one-month session. The stress these students feel they have previously described as if they were a "bomb in a box," with so much going on that they weren't sure if they were going to explode. These feelings will come out in parts within texting groups, yet have never emerged in an email thread. At times, I will write to students to check on them, especially those taking a course in a blended learning model, working from their home cities around the country while working full time, and I will ask them to "write one emoji to show how you are feeling about your thesis progress." Their responses provide valuable insight to their peers and me about their sense of where they are academically and emotionally in the class context and often leads to longer explanations. Texting informally allows students to demonstrate their concerns in a safer way than regular email, also allowing for mentioning struggles without being overly vulnerable. In other words, texting with and between students can provide an immediacy and simplicity which can connect to a more connected feeling of communication and learning.

Considerations in Texting for Teaching and Learning

While it is useful to highlight the utility of texting with students, there are also drawbacks. Texting with students presents possible problems ranging from practical to more broad issues. On the practical side, the following are the primary potential issues with text messaging with students: maintaining records of texts, messages sent at inconvenient times, cultural challenges of misinterpretation, and general technological comfort with the technology. Keeping records of texts requires multiple steps, irrespective of the type of texting program or app used. Unlike messages on email, which are kept indefinitely, or those on Moodle, which are maintained through a central server and fairly easily searchable and retrievable, text messages have varied levels of accessibility after being sent. For instance, in WhatsApp, while there is a search feature across all texts, it is not solely focused on one text thread and does not consistently locate information well. However, WhatsApp's search feature is more advanced than those of Apple Messaging and Facebook Messenger, which both have a search feature but with the primary ability in locating a person who sent a message. For example, when searching for a person's name, these message apps bring up all the message threads where that person sent or received a message, but *not* the text threads where the person's name was mentioned.

The problem with all communication is the potential for misinterpretations and varied understandings of the same message, which is reduced in face-to-face conversation. Across languages, the challenge is heightened however between different cultures, or for a second or third language learner who may interpret words, expressions or behaviors differently than intended in the first language. With online communication, the potential for misinterpretation abounds. At times, this is because of a difference in the cultural understanding, and at other times this can be attributed to being more or less familiar with being in an online world. For some, this divide is considered a "digital native" versus a "digital immigrant" with those who were born after the mid-1980s being regarded as native to the digital technology, growing up with it around them (such as Generation Z), and those born prior to that time frame having to develop the capabilities in technology. For classroom communication, Riordan, Kreuz, and Blair (2018) demonstrate a difference between younger and older generations in a Western context, or for those who grew up with technology and those without it. They show how the use of a period or a line break in a text message can affect the way a digital native and digital immigrant understands the text message (Riordan, Kreuz, & Blair, 2018).

Considering that universities often enroll students from varied academic, ethnic, and linguistic backgrounds, text messaging can be situated within the multilingual education literature as a form of reducing the affective filter—the invisible barrier often discussed as hindering language learning. Within the classroom, practices such as utilizing authentic materials and total physical response help students by-pass some concerns in producing the needed language. Therefore, if faculty are comfortable with using texts, they can allow their teaching to be a conduit providing a means towards simplifying content knowledge by reducing the stress on language production. However, the choice of a texting platform is an important one. While some learning platforms, like Moodle, offer a texting option within the system, it does so in a way unnatural to many students. Students most frequently use their phones for texting through typical apps, such as iMessage, Messenger (Facebook), and WhatsApp (a particularly common platform in international contexts or with students who have family outside of the US). Therefore, it is reasonable to consider going to a different platform, would create an obstacle to accessing information. Until Moodle (and other learning platforms such as Blackboard and Canvas) integrates their texting as part of daily used texting formats, teaching and learning through the discussion pages is still problematic for teaching and learning. With varied linguistic backgrounds of our students, there can be challenges in interpretation and written communication ability, but texting can provide for an understanding of meaning, allowing for quickly asking questions and reframing as needed.

FUTURE RESEARCH AND PRACTICAL DIRECTIONS

Future Studies

The potential of texting for (in)formal means should be further studied. There is a burgeoning set of studies examining this type of communication. As educators, we know the more we can support our students in feeling comfortable in their learning environment, the better students will learn. While some faculty members are integrating this type of communication on a more regular basis, it is still unclear as to whether this will become *the* future of student communication. Will texting overcome email and soon develop potential avenues for record keeping for instance? Currently, there is texting available through course management systems such as Moodle and Blackboard. However, course management systems are designed for an institutional application rather than immediate feedback and are often cumbersome and fairly clunky as compared to more intuitive texting apps. Perhaps studies in the future will help uncover ways in which to integrate texting through apps such as WhatsApp or Messenger to disseminate to Moodle, Blackboard or the Google suite. Should studies also be conducted to examine the ability of texting to support varied styles/personalities of students? For instance, it appears faculty texting helps students who are more introverted or shy within class contexts to share in another format, however, this has yet to be examined.

Future research could examine how students experience voice messages sent in the text format—do they feel the same nudges as in regular text format? Do students still perceive encouragement and less concern about saying the "right" thing linguistically or academically? What differences do students from different generations experience as a result of texting chats? The potential for texting as support for all students provides an exciting new step in our increasingly globalized educational world, playing a significant role in the growing blended and online educational landscape.

Practical Steps

Although finding a solution to maintain records of texts presents a challenge, I have identified two ways to save text messages of course communication, (1) copy and paste each message into another document or (2) take screenshots of discussion. As I tend to use WhatsApp (as that is most commonly used in the Kazakhstani context and allows for ease of replying to an individual comment), I can either copy and paste messages from the desktop version of the app, or take screenshots from my phone. The advantage of copying and pasting messages is that the resultant document is searchable. However, by taking screenshots, it is easier to indicate when there are a set of embedded question and answers.

To address texts that could be sent and received at inconvenient times, there are two standard ways to confront this issue. Either faculty can be direct with students in terms of when texts are permitted/encouraged (e.g., 9am-6pm), or the texting thread could agree upon an open time frame for any messages. I have found that allowing texts throughout the day or night, encourages student communication and questions, with the caveat being, I do not always respond at all times. I explain to students they are allowed to text at any time (including during the night), but my phone will be off or on silent at times I am not available. For those native to texting threads, on most apps, it is possible to set a message thread to "silent" mode, while other threads may continue to indicate texts received. As a mother of young children, I find I am often up sporadically throughout the night and might be able (and willing) to answer a short text to answer a question, or I get a chance to can see the encouragement and support provided by other students for each other. An unexpected outcome of the texting group has been observing students collaborate and support one another. Students can even use this as evidence for their class participation.

In general, within my courses there seem to be few misunderstandings of text messages; however, I have seen differences in who texts more frequently and who replies the most frequently. Although it is possible to misinterpret a text message,

I would argue these misinterpretations are less of an issue than via email, due to the informal nature of texting which has allowed for more students to ask questions and clarifications in this mode of communication. Likewise, there is also evidence for the utility and positive outcomes of using such means of interaction. For Gimranova, Nurmanova, and CohenMiller (2017), the use of texting allowed for engaged discussion across a large group of students. In particular, they showed how the use of the texting program, WhatsApp, helped increase interaction and support for middle-school students in learning English. The non-threatening environment of a text chat allowed for students to be less concerned with their responses and questions; freely interact and share words, pictures, and videos. Likewise, Minella (2018) found that a WhatsApp group similarly supported English language learners' acquisition. Both sets of researchers discussed how texting allowed for an extension of the classroom into the lives of students in authentic manners.

Other benefits of texting I have seen include: seeing when/who has seen a message, responding quickly to an individual question within a long thread, reducing the affective filter for students struggling linguistically, sending simple class reminders/updates to a full class (e.g., room changes, reminder to bring a computer), and facilitating sending photos/videos/audio (e.g., class projects). In particular, the ease of sharing photos and videos have been particularly useful for courses where experiential learning takes students outside of the classroom. For example, within most graduate courses, I have students collect data for in-class or external analysis and texting has allowed for sharing of imagery faster and more accessible than via email, which does not allow large attachments. These images and videos can then be saved in a cloud-based educational program (e.g., Google drive) for all student access. This type of data collection can be used across courses, whether taking photos as part of an observational activity, to document imagery around campus, or to highlight a particular concept. Within my courses, for instance, I have had students collect imagery on their phones and text them to the group for photovoice project in a research methods course and have had students text our group photos they took around campus to document the gender balance of posters and pictures for a class on cultural contexts of education.

CONCLUSION

For institutions seeking to support the dynamic needs of students in the 21st-century learning environment, it is essential to consider how our teaching needs to adjust. One such technological advancement, now regularly used by students from middle school throughout graduate school, is text messages on the phone and computer. While texting is often considered an unofficial means of communication, curt phrases and emojis sent at all time of day and night, text messages should also be harnessed for formal and informal teaching and learning in higher education.

Text messaging with students and as peer learning can be used as an avenue for communication, in a formal manner using "academic English" and a signature line, or it can be a path towards more informal discussion and support. Both ways encourage student learning using technology students use regularly. For my work with graduate students in an international context, the more informal method of writing texts has led to many classes of students easily asking questions, responding to prompts, and engaging eagerly in learning. As universities seek to become more diverse and inclusive, the more critical it becomes to consider the range of students entering our rooms, such as first-generation university students and those learning in their non-native language. Despite the potential challenges, there are significant benefits and potential for texting with students as formal--and informal--communication in higher education. As such, text messaging with students when used appropriately can provide an essential outlet to support student voice, communication, and learning.

ACKNOWLEDGMENT

I would like to thank Dr. Heidi Schnackenberg for the encouragement to write this chapter. Thank you to Dr. Bridget Goodman and Dr. Sulusash Kerimkulova who assisted in defining key terms related to multilingual education. The insightful comments and clarifications from Dr. Nettie Boivin enhanced the final version of this article.

REFERENCES

Al-Zahrani, A. (2015). From passive to active: The impact of the flipped classroom through social learning platforms on higher education students' creative thinking. *British Journal of Educational Technology*, *46*(6), 1133–1148. doi:10.1111/bjet.12353

Alshammari, R., Parkes, M., & Adlington, R. (2017). Using WhatsApp in EFL instruction with Saudi Arabian university students. Arab World English Journal, 8, 68–84.

Altemueller, L., & Lindquist, C. (2017). Flipped classroom instruction for inclusive learning. *British Journal of Special Education*, *44*(3), 341–358. doi:10.1111/1467-8578.12177

Blackwelder, A., & Hazeu, S. (2018). *Teachers going gradeless: Grow beyond grades*. Retrieved from https://teachersgoinggradeless.com

Boivin, N., & CohenMiller, A. S. (2018). Breaking the "Fourth Wall" in Qualitative Research: Participant-Led Digital Data Construction. *Qualitative Report*, *23*(3), 581–592.

Bridges, D. (Ed.). (2014). *Educational Reform and Internationalisation: The case of school reform in Kazakhstan*. Cambridge: Cambridge University Press.

Castleman, B. L. (2015). *The 160-Character Solution: How Text Messaging and Other Behavioral Strategies Can Improve Education*. Baltimore, MD: Johns Hopkins University Press.

Cheng, B. K., Jackson, L. & Lee, W. (2017). Advancing 21st Century Competencies in Hong Kong Advancing 21st Century Competencies in Hong Kong. Center for Global Education.

Chiaravalli, A. (2017, April 8). Teachers Going Gradeless: Toward a Future of Growth Not Grades. *Medium*. Retrieved from https://medium.com/teachers-going-gradeless/teachers-going-gradeless-50d621c14cad

Dias, S. B., & Diniz, J. A. (2014). Towards an Enhanced Learning Management System for Blended Learning in High. *Journal of Educational Technology & Society*, *17*, 307–319.

Gimranova, A., Nurmanova, M., & CohenMiller, A. S. (2017). Texting to Motivate Language Learning: WhatsApp Group Chats and Near Peer Role Modeling (NPRM). *LEARNing Landscapes, 11*(1), 121–136.

Hämäläinen, R., Kiili, C., & Smith, B. E. (2017). Orchestrating 21st century learning in higher education: A perspective on student voice. *British Journal of Educational Technology, 48*(5), 1106–1118. doi:10.1111/bjet.12533

Harley, D., Winn, S., Pemberton, S., & Wilcox, P. (2007). Using texting to support students' transition to university. *Innovations in Education and Teaching International, 44*(3), 229–241. doi:10.1080/14703290701486506

Hilsdon, J. (2014). Peer learning for change in higher education. *Innovations in Education and Teaching International, 51*(3), 244–254. Retrieved from https://www.tandfonline.com/doi/full/10.1080/14703297.2013.796709 doi:10.1080/14703297.2013.796709

Kalantzis, M., Cope, B., & Harvey, A. (2003). Assessing Multiliteracies and the New Basics. *Assessment in Education: Principles, Policy & Practice, 10*(1), 15–26. doi:10.1080/09695940301692

Kirkwood, A. (2014). Teaching and learning with technology in higher education: Blended and distance education needs 'joined-up thinking' rather than technological determinism. *Open Learning, 29*(3), 206–221. doi:10.1080/02680513.2015.1009884

Koross, R., & Kosgei Kipkenda, P. (2016). The Short Message Service (SMS) Texting Style of Communication and Its impact on Kenyan University Students. *Written Communication Skills, 3*(6), 151–162.

Kuk, H.-S., & Holst, J. D. (2018). A Dissection of Experiential Learning Theory: Alternative Approaches to Reflection. *Adult Learning*. doi:10.1177/1045159518779138

Livingston, A. (2009). The Revolution No One Noticed: Mobile Phones and Multimobile Services in Higher Education. Retrieved from https://er.educause.edu/articles/2009/3/the-revolution-no-one-noticed-mobile-phones-and-multimobile-services-in-higher-education

Maitra, D. (2017). Funds of Knowledge: An Underrated Tool for School Literacy and Student Engagement. *International Journal of Society, Culture & Language, 5*(1), 94-102. Retrieved from http://search.proquest.com/openview/0895f8abb03009cc2165dd4a987203ab/1?pq-origsite=gscholar&cbl=2045594

McKnight, K., O'Malley, K., Ruzic, R., Horsley, M., Franey, J. J., & Bassett, K. (2016). Teaching in a digital age: How educators use technology to improve student learning. *Journal of Research on Technology in Education, 48*(3), 194–211. doi:10.1080/15391523.2016.1175856

Minalla, A. A. (2018). The Effect of WhatsApp Chat Group in Enhancing EFL Learners' Verbal Interaction outside Classroom Contexts. *English Language Teaching, 11*(3), 1–7. doi:10.5539/elt.v11n3p1

Ministry of Education and Science of the Republic of Kazakhstan JSC Information-Analytic Center. (2017). *Teaching in three languages: International experience and recommendations for Kazakhstan.*

Ministry of Education. Singapore. (2015). Framework for 21st Century Competencies and Student Outcomes. Retrieved from https://www.moe.gov.sg/education/education-system/21st-century-competencies

Moll, L. C., Amanti, C., Neff, D., & Gonzalez, N. (1992). Funds of knowledge for teaching: Using a qualitative approach to connect homes and classrooms. *Theory into Practice, 31*(2), 132–141. doi:10.1080/00405849209543534

Nazarbayev University. (2018). NU at a glance. Retrieved from https://nu.edu.kz/about-nazarbayev-university/nu-at-a-glance

OECD. (2017). OECD work on education. Retrieved from http://www.oecd.org/education/Directorate-for-education-and-skills-brochure.pdf

Pombo, L., Loureiro, M. J., & Moreira, A. (2010). Assessing collaborative work in a higher education blended learning context: Strategies and students' perceptions. *Educational Media International, 47*(3), 217–229. doi:10.1080/09523987.2010.518814

Prilipko, A. (2017). *Managing Implementation of English Medium of Instruction in Higher Education in Kazakhstan: Practices and Challenges.* Nazarbayev University.

Riordan, M. A., Kreuz, R. J., & Blair, A. N. (2018). The digital divide: Conveying subtlety in online communication. *Journal of Computers in Education*, *5*(1), 49–66. doi:10.100740692-018-0100-6

Rust, D. Z. (2018). Using Text Messaging Systems as a Class Communication Tool. *College Teaching, 29–31*. doi:10.1080/87567555.2018.1509292

Sarinzhipov, A. (2013). *Opportunities for faculty to influence academic matters at Kazakh National University and Eurasian National University*. University of Pennsylvania.

Seaman, J., Brown, M., & Quay, J. (2017). The Evolution of Experiential Learning Theory. *Journal of Experiential Education, 105382591668926*. doi:10.1177/1053825916689268

Smat, N., Aikenova, A., Yelibay, M., Filipova, L., Rakisheva, A., Kavashev, Z., & CohenMiller, A. S. (2018). Thinking "outside the box" in innovating higher education in the Age of Disruption: A review of the Eurasian Higher Education Leaders Forum (EHELF) 2018. *Information and Analytical Magazine, Bologna Process, 23*(3), 56–61.

Swartzwelder, K. (2014). Examining the Effect of Texting on Students' Perceptions of Learning. *Nursing Education Perspectives*, *35*(6), 405–407. doi:10.5480/12-1012.1

Yakavets, N., Bridges, D., & Shamatov, D. (2017). On constructs and the construction of teachers' professional knowledge in a post-Soviet context. *Journal of Education for Teaching*, *43*(5), 594–615. doi:10.1080/02607476.2017.1355086

ADDITIONAL READING

Benade, L. (2015). Bits, Bytes and Dinosaurs: Using Levinas and Freire to address the concept of "twenty-first century learning.". *Educational Philosophy and Theory*, *47*(9), 935–948. doi:10.1080/00131857.2015.1035159

Bühmann, D., & Trudell, B. (2018). *Mother Tongue Matters: A Key to Effective Learning*.

Cenos, J., & Gorter, D. (Eds.). (2015). *Multilingual Education: Between Language Learning and Translanguaging*. Cambridge: Cambridge University Press.

Darling-Hammond, L. (Ed.). (2014). *Next Generation Assessment: Moving beyond the Bubble Test to Support 21st Century Learning*. San Francisco, CA: Jossey-Bass.

Hämäläinen, R., Kiili, C., & Smith, B. E. (2017). Orchestrating 21st century learning in higher education: A perspective on student voice. *British Journal of Educational Technology*, *48*(5), 1106–1118. doi:10.1111/bjet.12533

King, L. (2003). Education in a multilingual world. *UNESCO*. Retrieved from http://unesdoc.unesco.org/images/0012/001297/129728e.pdf

Merriam, S. B. (2007). Non-Western Perspectives On Learning and Knowing: Perspectives from Around the World.

Moll, L. C., Amanti, C., Neff, D., & Gonzalez, N. (1992). Funds of knowledge for teaching: Using a qualitative approach to connect homes and classrooms. *Theory into Practice*, *31*(2), 132–141. doi:10.1080/00405849209543534

Maitra, D. (2017). Funds of Knowledge: An Underrated Tool for School Literacy and Student Engagement. *International Journal of Society, Culture & Language*, *5*(1), 94–102.

Seaman, J., Brown, M., & Quay, J. (2017). The Evolution of Experiential Learning Theory. *Journal of Experiential Education*. doi:10.1177/1053825916689268

KEY TERMS AND DEFINITIONS

21st Century Learning, 21st Century Skills, 21st Century Capacities: Commonly used in educational reform referring to the set of skills and/or capabilities students need to be successful as they move from the educational to work sphere.

Bilingual Education: The use of two languages used formally within an educational context.

Experiential Learning: A teaching and learning approach developed within adult education, emphasizing the use of hands-on practical work within/outside the classroom.

Funds of Knowledge: The knowledge students embody that can directly or indirectly connect to formal classroom learning.

iMessage: The proprietary app developed and run by Apple, available for use on computers and smartphones.

Messenger: The proprietary app developed and operated by Facebook, available for use on computers and smartphones.

Multilingual Education: The use of two or more languages used formally within the educational context.

Multiliteracies: An approach to learning that situates knowledge as mediated through various multimodal sources such as oral, visual, auditory, tactile, taste.

Plurilingual Individual: The term refers to those who typically grow up within an intersection of languages and culture and have the ability to move seamlessly between them.

WhatsApp: A standalone app commonly used within international contexts that encourages group communication and individualized responses to texts; available for use on computers and smartphones.

Glossary

21st Century Learning, 21st Century Skills, 21st Century Capacities: Commonly used in educational reform referring to the set of skills and/or capabilities students need to be successful as they move from the educational to work sphere.

Bilingual Education: The use of two languages used formally within an educational context.

Connectivism Theory: Learning theory for the digital age that explains how complex and constantly changing the social digital world is.

Constructivism Learning: Learning through experience, one develops their own understanding and knowledge.

Digital Immigrant: A person born or brought up prior to the proliferation of digital technology.

Digital Native: A person born or brought up during or into the age of digital technology.

Educational Technology: The field of study that facilitates learning through the effective and appropriate/ethical use of technological resources.

Experiential Learning: A teaching and learning approach developed within adult education, emphasizing the use of hands-on practical work within/outside the classroom.

Formal Learning: Structured learning with planned objectives.

Funds of Knowledge: The knowledge students embody that can directly or indirectly connect to formal classroom learning.

Generation: A collective group of people born during the same span of years, influenced by world and geopolitical events, and shared/common experiences and cultural elements.

Generation X: A generation born between the years 1964 and 1982.

Generation Z: People born from the mid-1990s to early 2000s; the generation after Millennials.

Google: (For the purposes of this chapter) an internet search engine.

Higher Education Professional: Professional-level staff at a postsecondary educational institution whose primary responsibilities are not connected to formal teaching/research roles.

iMessage: The proprietary app developed and run by Apple, available for use on computers and smartphones.

Informal Learning: Learning through participation (unorganized, unstructured).

Instagram: An online social networking service where users can share photos and videos.

Learning Management System (LMS): A system for educational courses to be delivered, documented, and overseen.

Messenger: The proprietary app developed and operated by Facebook, available for use on computers and smartphones.

Millennial Generation: A generation born between the years 1982 and 1994.

Multilingual Education: The use of two or more languages used formally within the educational context.

Multiliteracies: An approach to learning that situates knowledge as mediated through various multimodal sources such as oral, visual, auditory, tactile, taste.

Personal Social Media Use: Social media use unrelated to higher education.

Plurilingual Individual: The term refers to those who typically grow up within an intersection of languages and culture and have the ability to move seamlessly between them.

Problem-Based Learning (PBL): Given a challenging situation, or complex problem, students are given extended time to investigate and work.

Professional Social Media Use: Social media use for higher education, but not teaching or class.

Social Learning: Learning from one another through social situations that can include observing, imitating, or modeling.

Social Media: World Wide Web-based applications designed to facilitate interpersonal connections among users.

Teaching Social Media Use: Social media use specifically for teaching or class.

Technology: (For the purposes of this chapter) machinery and equipment developed from scientific knowledge.

Twitter: An online social networking and news service where users post 140 character messages called "tweets."

WhatsApp: A standalone app commonly used within international contexts that encourages group communication and individualized responses to texts; available for use on computers and smartphones.

Compilation of References

Aaron, L. S., & Roche, C. M. (2011). Teaching learning, and collaborating in the cloud: Applications of cloud computing for educators in post-secondary institutions. *Journal of Educational Technology Systems*, *40*(2), 95–111. doi:10.2190/ET.40.2.b

Abdul-Alim, J. (2015). Saudi Arabian women receive online learning techniques from U.S. *Diverse Education*. Retrieved from http://diverseeducation.com/article/76935/

AbdulHafeez. M., Asadullah, S., Rosydi, M., & Farooq, A. (2013, March). Inculcating ethical values in the students through e-learning platform. In *2013 5th International Conference on Information and Communication Technology for the Muslim World (ICT4M)* (pp. 1-6). IEEE.

Ability Fest. (2018a). Ability Fest — 2018 [Facebook event]. Retrieved from https://www.facebook.com/events/153840705302082/

Ability Fest. (2018b). Ability Fest - Home [Facebook profile page]. Retrieved from https://www.facebook.com/abilityfestival/

AbilityFest - Seven Hills Foundation. (2018). Retrieved from http://www.sevenhills.org/abilityfest

Acharya, J. P., Acharya, I., & Waghrey, D. (2013). A study on some psychological health effects of cell-phone usage amongst college going students. *International Journal of Medical Research & Health Sciences*, *2*(3), 388. doi:10.5958/j.2319-5886.2.3.068

Ahlquist, J. (2014). Trending now: Digital leadership education using social media and the social change model. *The Journal of Leadership Studies*, *8*(2), 57–60. doi:10.1002/jls.21332

Ahlquist, J. (2015). *Developing digital student leaders: A mixed methods study of student leadership, identity, and decision making on social media.* California Lutheran University.

Ahlquist, J. (2016). The digital identity of student affairs professionals. *New Directions for Student Services, 2016*(155), 29–46. doi:10.1002s.20181

Ahlquist, J. (2017). Digital Student Leadership Development. *New Directions for Student Leadership, 2017*(153), 47–62. doi:10.1002/yd.20229 PMID:28199059

Ahmed, A. (2018). Perceptions of using assistive technology for students with disabilities in the classroom. *International Journal of Special Education, 33*(1), 129–139.

Airini, S., Conner, L., McPherson, K., Midson, B., & Wilson, C. (2011). Learning to be leaders in higher education: What helps or hinders women's advancement as leaders in universities. *Educational Management Administration & Leadership, 39*(1), 44–62. doi:10.1177/1741143210383896

Al Alhareth, Y., McBride, N., Prior, M., Leigh, M., & Flick, C. (2013). Saudi women and e-learning. *Paper presented at the Pixel International Conference: The Future of Education,* Florence, Italy, June 13–14. Retrieved from http://conference.pixel-online.net/foe2013/common/download/Paper_pdf/142-ELE15-FP-Alhareth-FOE2013.pdf

Al-Ahmadi, H. (2011). Challenges facing women leaders in Saudi Arabia. *Human Resource Development International, 14*(2), 149–166. doi:10.1080/13678868.2011.558311

Al-Asmari, A. & Khan, S. (2014). E-learning in Saudi Arabia: Past, present and future. *Near and Middle Eastern Journal of Research in Education, 2*(1), 2-11.

Al-Bahrani, A., & Patel, D. (2015). Incorporating Twitter, Instagram, and Facebook in economics classrooms. *The Journal of Economic Education, 46*(1), 56-67. from http://reddog.rmu.edu:2061/eds/pdfviewer/pdfviewer?vid=3&sid=650d2878-c8d1-4897-8cd7-b53af0f42def@sessionmgr4008

Aldridge, P. R., Jeffrey, P., Taylor, G., & Barringer-Brown, C. H. (2017). Social skills training for students of color with disabilities through the use of social networking. *Multicultural Education, 24*(2), 34–38.

Aldubais, F. (2017, May 5). تمكين المرأة السعودية من الخدمات دون موافقة ولي الأمر. Retrieved from https://www.okaz.com.sa/article/1544591/

AlGhamdi, R., Drew, S., & AbuGabah, A. (2011). Designing government strategies to facilitate diffusion of online commerce: A focus on KSA. *Journal of Information & System Management*, *1*(3), 97–106.

Aljabre, A. (2012). An exploration of distance learning in Saudi Arabian universities: Current practices and future possibilities. *International Journal of Instructional Technology and Distance Learning*, *2*(9), 21–28.

Al-Khalifa, H. (2010). E-learning and ICT integration in colleges and universities in Saudi Arabia. Retrieved from http://elearnmag.acm.org/featured.cfm?aid=1735849

AlMegren, A., & Yassin, S. Z. (2013). Learning object repositories in e-learning: Challenges for learners in Saudi Arabia. *European Journal of Open. Distance and E-Learning*, *16*(1), 115–130.

Al-Munajjed, M. (2009). *Women's education in Saudi Arabia: The way forward.* Retrieved from http://arabdevelopmentportal.com/sites/default/files/publication/211.womens_education_in_saudi_arabia_the_way_forward.pdf

Al-Rasheed, M. (2013). *A most masculine state: Gender, politics and religion in Saudi Arabia.* Cambridge: Cambridge University Press. doi:10.1017/CBO9781139015363

Alrashidi, A. (2014). E-learning in Saudi Arabia: A review of the literature. *British Journal of Education, Society &. Behavioral Science*, *4*(5), 656–672.

Alsaqqaf, A. (2015). Toward open educational resources: Opportunities and challenges. In N. Sultan & H. J. Al-Lail (Eds.), *Creative learning and MOOCs: Harnessing the technology for a 21st century education* (pp. 110–127). Newcastle upon Tyne: Cambridge Scholars Publishing.

Alshahrani, K., & Ally, M. (2017). MOOC in the Arab world: A case study. In K. Alshahrani & M. Ally (Eds.), *Transforming education in the Gulf region: Emerging learning technologies and innovative pedagogy for the 21st century* (pp. 178–187). New York: Routledge.

Alshammari, R., Parkes, M., & Adlington, R. (2017). Using WhatsApp in EFL instruction with Saudi Arabian university students. Arab World English Journal, 8, 68–84.

AlShaya, H., & Oyaid, A. (2017). Mobile learning in Gulf Cooperation Council countries: theory and practice. In K. Alshahrani & M. Ally (Eds.), *Transforming education in the Gulf region: Emerging learning technologies and innovative pedagogy for the 21st century* (pp. 83–97). New York: Routledge.

Al-Shehri, S. (2017). Technology-enhanced language instruction: are we in the loop? In K. Alshahrani & M. Ally (Eds.), *Transforming education in the Gulf region: Emerging learning technologies and innovative pedagogy for the 21st century* (pp. 36–50). New York: Routledge.

Altemueller, L., & Lindquist, C. (2017). Flipped classroom instruction for inclusive learning. *British Journal of Special Education*, *44*(3), 341–358. doi:10.1111/1467-8578.12177

Alturki, U. (2014). The development of online distance education in Saudi Arabia. *Elearnmag*. Retrieved from http://elearnmag.acm.org/archive.cfm?aid=2673861

Alwasal, S., & Alhadlaq, S. (2012). Preparing Middle Eastern students for the future: Saudi Arabia as a case study. In J. Groccia, M. Alsudairi, & W. Buskist (Eds.), *Handbook of college and university teaching: A global perspective* (pp. 77–90). Thousand Oaks, CA: SAGE Publications, Inc. doi:10.4135/9781412996891.n6

Al-Zahrani, A. (2015). From passive to active: The impact of the flipped classroom through social learning platforms on higher education students' creative thinking. *British Journal of Educational Technology*, *46*(6), 1133–1148. doi:10.1111/bjet.12353

American College of Pediatricians. (2016). *The impact of pornography on children*. Retrieved from https://www.acpeds.org/the-college-speaks/position-statements/the-impact-of-pornography-on-children

American Psychological Association. (2013, June). College students' mental health is a growing concern, survey finds. *Monitor on Psychology*, *44*, 6. Retrieved from https://www.apa.org/monitor/2013/06/college-students.aspx

American Speech-Language-Hearing Association (ASHA). (2016). Scope of Practice in Speech-Language Pathology. doi:10.1044/policy.SP2016-00343

An Educator's Guide to the "Four Cs". (n.d.). *NEA*. Retrieved from http://www.nea.org/tools/52217.htm

Anderson, M., & Perrin, A. (2017, April 07). Disabled Americans less likely to use technology. *Pew Research Center*. Retrieved from http://www.pewresearch.org/fact-tank/2017/04/07/disabled-americans-are-less-likely-to-use-technology/

Ariel, K. (2013). Effects of the great recession on child development. *The Annals of the American Academy of Political and Social Science*, *232*. Retrieved from http://search.ebscohost.com.webdb.plattsburgh.edu:2048/login.aspx?direct=true&db=edsjsr&AN=edsjsr.24541684&site=eds-live&scope=site

Arnett, J. J. (2007). Emerging adulthood: What is it, and what is it good for? *Child Development Perspectives*, *1*(2), 68–73. doi:10.1111/j.1750-8606.2007.00016.x

Arokiasamy, A. R. (2017). A systematic review approach of mobile technology adoption in higher education. *Economics, Management and Sustainability, 2*(2), 48-55. Retrieved from https://zenodo.org/record/1145854/files/05_Anantha_01.pdf

Ashtari, S., & Eydgahi, A. (2016). Student perceptions of cloud applications effectiveness in higher education. *Journal of Computational Science*, *23*, 173–180. doi:10.1016/j.jocs.2016.12.007

Asiri, M., Mahmud, R. B., Abu Bakar, K., & Mohd Ayub, A. F. B. (2012). Factors influencing the use of learning management system in Saudi Arabian higher education: A theoretical framework. *Higher Education Studies*, *2*(2), 125–137. doi:10.5539/hes.v2n2p125

Asmar, M. (2018, February 26). Why this Denver elementary school replaced detention with yoga. *Chalkbeat.* Retrieved from https://www.chalkbeat.org/posts/co/2018/02/26/why-this-denver-elementary-school-has-replaced-detention-with-yoga/

Awuah, L. J. (2015). Supporting 21st-century teaching and learning: The role of google apps for education (GAFE). *Journal of Instructional Research, 4*, 12-22.

Aydin, S. (2012). A review of research on Facebook as an educational environment. *Educational Technology Research and Development*, *60*(6), 1093–1106. doi:10.100711423-012-9260-7

Banks, J., Au, K., Ball, A. F., Bell, P., Gordon, E., Gutiérrez, K., ... & Valdes, G. (2007). Learning in and out of school in diverse environments. Retrieved from http://life-slc.org/docs/Banks_etal-LIFE-Diversity-Report.pdf

Bates, T. (2009). *A personal view of e-learning in Saudi Arabia.* Retrieved from http://www.tonybates.ca/2009/11/05/a-personal-view-of-e-learning-in-saudi-arabia/

Behrend, T. S., Wiebe, E. N., London, J. E., & Johnson, E. C. (2011). Cloud computing adoption and usage in community colleges. *Behaviour & Information Technology, 30*(2), 231–240. doi:10.1080/0144929X.2010.489118

Benson, S. (2011). Social media and the classroom. *AACE Review*. Retrieved from https://www.aace.org/social-media-and-the-classroom/

Berk, R. A. (2009). Teaching strategies for the net generation. *Transformative Dialogues. Teaching & Learning Journal, 3*(2), 1–23.

Bers, M. U. (2010). Beyond computer literacy: Supporting youth's positive development through technology. *New Directions for Student Leadership*, (128), 13–23. PMID:21240949

Beukelman, D. R., & Mirenda, P. (2013). *Augmentative and alternative communication: Supporting children and adults with complex communication needs* (4th ed.). Paul H. Brookes Pub.

Bhise, A., Ghatule, A., & Ghatule, A. (2014). Study of mobile addiction among students. *Indian Journal of Research in Management, Business and Social Sciences, 21*(1A), 17-21. Retrieved from http://www.ijrmbss.com/assets/pdf/Vol2Iss1a/5.pdf

Bialy, S.E. & Jalali, A. (2015). Go where the students are: A comparison of the use of social networking sites between medical students and medical educators. *JMIR Medical Education, 1*(2). Retrieved from http://mededu.jmir.org/2015/2/e7/

Bill & Melinda Gates Foundation. (2012b). Primary sources 2012: America's teachers on the teaching profession, a project of Scholastic and the Bill & Melinda Gates Foundation. Retrieved from http://www.scholastic.com/primarysources/pdfs/Gates2012_full.pdf

Blackstone, S., & Hunt Berg, M. (2012). *Social Networks: A Communication Inventory for Individuals with Complex Communication Needs and their Communication Partners*. Monterrey, CA: Attainment Company, Augmentative Communication, Inc. Retrieved from http://www.augcominc.com/index.cfm/social_networks.htm

Blackwelder, A., & Hazeu, S. (2018). *Teachers going gradeless: Grow beyond grades*. Retrieved from https://teachersgoinggradeless.com

Blattner, G., & Fiori, M. (2009). Facebook in the language classroom: Promises and possibilities. *International Journal of Instructional Technology and Distance Learning*, *6*(1), 17–28.

Boivin, N., & CohenMiller, A. S. (2018). Breaking the "Fourth Wall" in Qualitative Research: Participant-Led Digital Data Construction. *Qualitative Report*, *23*(3), 581–592.

Bonilla, Y., & Rosa, J. (2015). # Ferguson: Digital protest, hashtag ethnography, and the racial politics of social media in the United States. *American Ethnologist*, *42*(1), 4–17. doi:10.1111/amet.12112

Bosch, T. (2009). Using online social networking for teaching and learning: Facebook use at the University of Cape Town. *Communicatio: South African Journal for Communication Theory and Research*, *35*(2), 185–200.

Bourke, B. (2014). Adult Millennials: Conceptualizing a student subpopulation with implications for online teaching and learning. In J. Keengwe & K. Kungu (Eds.), *Cross-cultural online learning in higher education and corporate training* (pp. 62–78). Hershey, PA: IGI Global Publishing. doi:10.4018/978-1-4666-5023-7.ch003

Boyd, D. M., & Ellison, N. B. (2007). Social network sites: Definition, history, and scholarship. *Journal of Computer-Mediated Communication*, *13*(1), 11. doi:10.1111/j.1083-6101.2007.00393.x

Brady, N. C., Bruce, S., Goldman, A., Erickson, K., Mineo, B., Ogletree, B. T., ... Siegel, E. (2016). Communication services and supports for individuals with severe disabilities: Guidance for assessment and intervention. *American Journal on Intellectual and Developmental Disabilities*, *121*(2), 121–138. doi:10.1352/1944-7558-121.2.121 PMID:26914467

Bridges, D. (Ed.). (2014). *Educational Reform and Internationalisation: The case of school reform in Kazakhstan*. Cambridge: Cambridge University Press.

Bristol, T. J., Nelson, J. W., Sherrill, K. J., & Wangerin, V. S. (2018). Current State of Test Development, Administration, and Analysis: A Study of Faculty Practices. *Nurse Educator*, *43*(2), 68–72. Retrieved from https://journals.lww.com/nurseeducatoronline/Fulltext/2018/03000/Current_State_of_Test_Development,_Administration.7.aspx doi:10.1097/NNE.0000000000000425 PMID:28817472

Brotheim, H. (2014). Introducing generation Z. *American Jails*, 15-20.

Broussard, L., & Wilson, K. (2018). Nursing Faculty Attitudes and Practices Related to Online Teaching. *Nursing Education Perspectives*, *39*(1), 40–42. Retrieved from https://journals.lww.com/neponline/Fulltext/2018/01000/Nursing_Faculty_Attitudes_and_Practices_Related_to.12.aspx doi:10.1097/01.NEP.0000000000000208 PMID:28806277

Brown, J. S., & Adler, R. P. (2008). Minds on fire: open education, the long tail, and learning 2.0. *Educause Review,* 16-32. Retrieved from http://www.oss.net/dynamaster/file_archive/080618/bdb5129a636e9ffbe734351363466c23/Minds%20on%20Fire.%20Open%20Education,%20the%20Long%20Tail,%20and%20Learning%202. 0%20-%20Brown,%20Adler%20(2008).pdf

Brown, M. E., & Hocutt, D. L. (2015). Learning to use, useful for learning: A usability study of Google apps for education. *Journal of Usability Studies*, *10*(4), 160–181.

Buelens, H., Totte, N., Deketelaere, A., & Dierickx, K. (2007). Electronic discussion forums in medical ethics education: The impact of didactic guidelines and netiquette. *Medical Education*, *41*(7), 711–717. doi:10.1111/j.1365-2923.2007.02793.x PMID:17614893

Burns, K., & Polman, J. (2006). The impact of ubiquitous computing in the internet age: How middle school teachers integrated wireless laptops in the initial stages of implementation. *Journal of Technology and Teacher Education, 14*(2), 363-385. Retrieved from https://www.learntechlib.org/p/5777/

Cameron, E. A., & Pagnattaro, M. A. (2017). Beyond millennials: Engaging generation Z in business law classes. *Journal of Legal Studies Education*, *34*(2), 317–324. doi:10.1111/jlse.12064

Carli, L., & Eagly, A. (2017). Leadership and gender. In J. Antonakis & D. David (Eds.), *The nature of leadership* (pp. 244–271). Sage publications, Inc.

Carter, T. (2018). Preparing Generation Z for the teaching profession. *SRATE Journal*, *27*(1), 1–8.

Carter, T. (2018). Preparing Generation Z for the Teaching Profession. *SRATE Journal*, *27*(1), 1–8.

Casey, G. (2013). Social media in the classroom: A simple yet complex hybrid environment for students. *Journal of Educational Multimedia and Hypermedia, 22*(1), 5-24. Retrieved from https://www.learntechlib.org/p/41333/

Casey, G. (2013). Interdisciplinary literacy through social media in the mathematics classroom: An action research study. *Journal of Adolescent & Adult Literacy*, *57*(1), 60–71. doi:10.1002/jaal.216

Castleman, B. L. (2015). *The 160-Character Solution: How Text Messaging and Other Behavioral Strategies Can Improve Education*. Baltimore, MD: Johns Hopkins University Press.

Centers for Disease Control and Prevention. (2015). *Trends in the Prevalence of Sexual Behaviors and HIV Testing National YRBS: 1991—2015*. Retrieved from https://www.cdc.gov/healthyyouth/data/yrbs/pdf/trends/2015_us_sexual_trend_yrbs.pdf

Centers for Disease Control and Prevention. (2018). *U.S. drug overdose deaths continue to rise; increase fueled by synthetic opioids* [Press Release]. Retrieved from https://www.cdc.gov/media/releases/2018/p0329-drug-overdose-deaths.html

Charmaz, K. (2006). *Constructing grounded theory: A practical guide through qualitative analysis*. Los Angeles, CA: SAGE Publications.

Chen, B., & Bryer, T. (2012). Investigating instructional strategies for using social media in formal and informal learning. *The International Review of Research in Open and Distributed Learning, 13*(1). Retrieved from http://www.irrodl.org/index.php/irrodl/article/view/1027/2073?utm_campaign=elearningindustry.com&utm_source=/10-tips-to-effectively-use-social-media-in-formal-learning&utm_medium=link

Cheng, B. K., Jackson, L. & Lee, W. (2017). Advancing 21st Century Competencies in Hong Kong Advancing 21st Century Competencies in Hong Kong. Center for Global Education.

Chester, Andrea & Gwynne, Gillian. (1998). Online teaching: Encouraging collaboration through anonymity. *Journal of Computer-Mediated Communication, 4*(2).

Chiaravalli, A. (2017, April 8). Teachers Going Gradeless: Toward a Future of Growth Not Grades. *Medium*. Retrieved from https://medium.com/teachers-going-gradeless/teachers-going-gradeless-50d621c14cad

Chickering, A. W., & Gamson, Z. F. (1987). Seven principles for good practice in undergraduate education. *AAHE Bulletin, 3*, 2–6.

Chiu, M. H. P., & Juang, M. J. (2013). A Content Analysis of Facebook Pages for Children with Disability. *Journal of Educational Media & Library Sciences, 50*(3), 383–392.

Chou, W. S., Hunt, Y. M., Beckjord, E. B., Moser, R. P., & Hesse, B. W. (2009). Social media use in the United States: Implications for health communication. *Journal of Medical Internet Research, 11*(4), e48. doi:10.2196/jmir.1249 PMID:19945947

Cilliers, E. J. (2017). The challenge of teaching generation Z. *PEOPLE. The International Journal of Social Sciences (Islamabad), 3*(1), 188–198.

Ciullo, S., & Dimino, J. A. (2017). The Strategic Use of Scaffolded Instruction in Social Studies Interventions for Students with Learning Disabilities. *Learning Disabilities Research & Practice, 32*(3), 155–165.

Coleman-Jensen, A., Nord, M., Andrews, M., & Carlson, S. (2012). Household food security in the United States in 2011. Economic Research Report Number 141. Washington, DC: United States Department of Agriculture. Retrieved from https://www.ers.usda.gov/webdocs/publications/45020/30967_err141.pdf?v=41165

Community College Research Center. (2017). Community college enrollment and completion. Retrieved from https://www.ccidinc.org/single-post/2017/05/04/Community-College-Enrollment-and-Completion

Conefrey, T. (2016). Technology in the college classroom: Crisis and opportunity. *Educational Technology, 56*(4), 37–40.

Cox, J. W., & Rich, S. (2018, March 25). Scarred by school shootings. *The Washington Post.* Retrieved from www.washingtonpost.com/graphics/2018/local/us-school-shootings-history/?utm_term=.fe7ba70c0eaf

Coyne, J., Lane, M., Nickson, L., Hollas, T., & Potter, J. P. (2017). Assessing Pre-Service Teachers' Attitudes and Self-Efficacy in Using Technology in the Classroom. *Teacher Education and Practice, 30*(4), 637–651.

Daly, U., & Young, L. (2016). *Saudi eLearning pioneers transform teaching and learning through open education consortium collaboration.* Retrieved from https://conference.oeconsortium.org/2016/presentation/saudi-elearning-pioneers-transform-teaching-and-learning-through-open-education-consortium-collaboration/

Darling-Hammond, L., Kammerness, K., Grossman, P., Rust, F., & Shulman, L. (2005). The design of teacher education programs. In L. Darling-Hammond & J. Bransford (Eds.), *Preparing teachers for a changing world: What teachers should learn and be able to do*. San Francisco, CA: Jossey-Bass.

Datnow, A. (2012). Teacher agency in educational reform: Lessons from social networks research. *American Journal of Education, 119*(1), 193–201. doi:10.1086/667708

David, M. (2017). Women and gender equality in higher education? In H. Eggins (Ed.), *The changing role of women in higher education: Academic and leadership issues* (pp. 209–225). Switzerland: Springer International Publishing. doi:10.1007/978-3-319-42436-1_11

Davidson, M., & Burke, R. (2004). Women in management worldwide: Facts, figures and analysis–An overview. In M. Davidson & R. Burke (Eds.), *Women in management worldwide: Facts, figures and analysis* (pp. 1–18). Aldershot: Ashgate.

Davidson, M., & Burke, R. (2011). Women in management worldwide: Progress and prospects–An overview. In M. Davidson & R. Burke (Eds.), *Women in management worldwide: Progress and prospects* (pp. 1–20). New York: Routledge.

Davidson, N., & Major, C. H. (2014). Boundary crossing: Cooperative learning, collaborative learning, and problem-based learning. *Journal on Excellence in College Teaching, 25*(3&4), 7–55.

Davis, C. H. III, Deil-Amen, R., Rios-Aguilar, C., & González Canché, M. S. (2015). Social media, higher education, and community colleges: A research synthesis and implications for the study of two-year institutions. *Community College Journal of Research and Practice, 39*(5), 409–422. doi:10.1080/10668926.2013.828665

DeAndrea, D. C., Ellison, N. B., LaRose, R., Steinfield, C., & Fiore, A. (2012). Serious social media: On the use of social media for improving students' adjustment to college. *The Internet and Higher Education, 15*(1), 15–23. doi:10.1016/j.iheduc.2011.05.009

DeLay, D., Zhang, L., Hanish, L. D., Miller, C. F., Fabes, R. A., Martin, C. L., ... Updegraff, K. A. (2016). Peer Influence on Academic Performance: A Social Network Analysis of Social-Emotional Intervention Effects. *Prevention Science: The Official Journal Of The Society For Prevention Research, 17*(8), 903–913. doi:10.100711121-016-0678-8 PMID:27436291

Denton, D. (2012). Enhancing instruction through constructivism, cooperative learning, and cloud computing. *TechTrends*, *56*(4), 34–41. doi:10.100711528-012-0585-1

Department of Education. (January, 2017). *Reimagining the role of technology in education: 2017 national education technology plan update.* Retrieved from https://tech.ed.gov/files/2017/01/NETP17.pdf

Desai, S. P., & Lele, V. (2017). Correlating Internet, Social Networks and Workplace – a Case of Generation Z Students. *Journal of Commerce and Management Thought*, (4), 802-815.

Dias, S. B., & Diniz, J. A. (2014). Towards an Enhanced Learning Management System for Blended Learning in High. *Journal of Educational Technology & Society*, *17*, 307–319.

Digital Citizenship Curriculum. (2018, October 24). Retrieved from https://www.commonsense.org/education/digital-citizenship/curriculum?topic=privacy--security

Donaldson, A. L., Chabon, S., Lee-Wilkerson, D., & Kapantzoglou, M. (2017). Mirror, mirror on the wall: Reflections on speech-language pathologists' image as advocates, activists, and aides. *Psychology in the Schools*, *54*(10), 1285–1293. doi:10.1002/pits.22083

Duverge, G. (2016, June 15). Web Accessibility Standards for People with Disabilities. Retrieved from https://online.pointpark.edu/information-technology/web-accessibility-people-with-disabilities/

Dwyer, L. (2014, October 3). When anxiety hits at schools. *The Atlantic*. Retrieved from https://www.theatlantic.com/health/archive/2014/10/when-anxiety-hits-at-school/380622/

Dylan Alcott Foundation | Helping young Australians with disabilities. (n.d.). Retrieved from https://dylanalcottfoundation.com.au/

Ellahi, A. (2018). Social Networking Sites as Formal Learning Environments in Business Education. *Journal of Educational Technology & Society*, *21*(4), 64–75.

Evans, C. (n.d.). 5 Ways to Help Students with Special Needs. *Special Needs*. Retrieved from http://www.specialneeds.com/activities/general-special-needs/five-ways-help-students-special-needs

Fernández-Cruz, F. J., & Fernández-Díaz, M. J. (2016). Generation Z's Teachers and their Digital Skills. *Comunicar, 24*(46), 97–105. doi:10.3916/C46-2016-10

Field, A. (2013). *Discovering statistics using IBM SPSS statistics* (4th ed.). Los Angeles, CA: Sage.

Forkosh-Baruch, A., & Hershkovitz, A. (2012). A case study of Israeli higher education institutes sharing scholarly information with the community via social networks. *The Internet and Higher Education, 15*(1), 58–68. doi:10.1016/j.iheduc.2011.08.003

Foulger, T. S., Buss, R. R., Wetzel, K., & Lindsey, L. (2012). Preservice teacher education benchmarking a standalone ed tech course in preparation for change. *Journal of Digital Learning in Teacher Education, 29*(2), 48–58. doi:10.1080/21532974.2012.10784704

Friedman, L. (2014, April 22). 5 Benefits of Using Social Media. Retrieved from https://www.linkedin.com/pulse/20140422162738-44670464-5-benefits-of-using-social-media

Fulton, A. (2018). Teens sleeping too much, or not enough? Parents can help. *NPR*. Retrieved from https://www.npr.org/sections/health-shots/2018/09/23/650452971/teens-sleeping-too-much-or-not-enough-parents-can-help

Gay, G. (2014). *Accessibility in e-learning: What you need to know*. Retrieved from https://www.uwo.ca/tsc/resources/pdf/accessibility-in-e-learning.pdf

Gearhart, D. (2001). Ethics in distance education: Developing ethical policies. *Online Journal of Distance Learning Administration, 4*(1), 1–4.

Gearhart, D. (2014). Ethics for eLearning: Two sides of the ethical coin. In R. Luppicini (Ed.), *Evolving issues surrounding technoethics and society in the digital age* (pp. 232–244). Hershey, PA: IGI Global. doi:10.4018/978-1-4666-6122-6.ch015

Geck, C. (2007). The generation Z connection: Teaching information literacy to the newest net generation. *Toward a 21st-Century School Library Media Program, 235*-241.

Ghamdi, A., Barakati, S., Adal, K., Jumaiah, S., & Soman, A. (2011). *Students outside the walls of higher education*. Retrieved from http://www.okaz.com.sa/new/Issues/20110702/Con20110702430523.htm

Gikas, J., & Grant, M. M. (2013). Mobile computing devices in higher education: Student perspectives on learning with cellphones, smartphones & social media. *The Internet and Higher Education, 19*, 18–26. doi:10.1016/j.iheduc.2013.06.002

Gilbert, E., & Karahalios, K. (2009). Predicting tie strength with social media. In *Proceedings of the International Conference on Human Factors in Computing Systems* (pp. 211-220).

Gimranova, A., Nurmanova, M., & CohenMiller, A. S. (2017). Texting to Motivate Language Learning: WhatsApp Group Chats and Near Peer Role Modeling (NPRM). *LEARNing Landscapes, 11*(1), 121–136.

Gin, K. J., Martínez-Alemán, A. M., Rowan-Kenyon, H. T., & Hottell, D. (2017). Racialized aggressions and social media on campus. *Journal of College Student Development, 58*(2), 159–174. doi:10.1353/csd.2017.0013

Golding, P., Raeymaeckers, K., & Sousa, H. (2017). Social media – New challenges and approaches for communications research. *European Journal of Communication, 32*(1), 3–5. doi:10.1177/0267323116682801

Goodsell, A.S., Maher, M.R., Tinto, V., Smith, B.L., & MacGregor, J. (1992). *Collaborative learning: A sourcebook for higher education.* National Center on Postsecondary Teaching, Learning, and Assessment.

Gopnik, A. (2016). *The Carpenter and the Gardener: What the New Science of Child Development Tells Us About the Relationship Between Parents and Children.* New York, NY: Farrar, Straus & Giroux.

Greenhow, C., & Robelia, B. (2009). Informal learning and identity formation in online social networks. *Learning, Media and Technology, 34*(2), 119–140. doi:10.1080/17439880902923580

Greenwood, S., Perrin, A., & Duggan, M. (2016). Social media update 2016. Pew Research Center. Retrieved from http://assets.pewresearch.org/wp-content/uploads/sites/14/2016/11/10132827/PI_2016.11.11_Social-Media-Update_FINAL.pdf

Griffin, R. (2015, July 21). Social media is changing how college students deal with mental health, for better or worse. *Huffington Post.* Retrieved from https://www.huffingtonpost.com/entry/social-media-college-mental-health_us_55ae6649e4b08f57d5d28845

Gütl, C., Cheong, C., Cheong, F., Chang, V., Nau, S. Z., & Pirker, J. (2015). Expectations of the generation NeXt in higher education: Learning engagement approaches in information sciences subjects. In *Proceedings of the Annual Meeting of the International Conference on Interactive Collaborative Learning (ICL)* (pp. 205-214). 10.1109/ICL.2015.7318027

Hämäläinen, R., Kiili, C., & Smith, B. E. (2017). Orchestrating 21st century learning in higher education: A perspective on student voice. *British Journal of Educational Technology*, *48*(5), 1106–1118. doi:10.1111/bjet.12533

Hamdan, A. (2005). Women and education in Saudi Arabia: Challenges and achievements. *International Education Journal*, *6*(1), 42–64.

Hamdan, A. (2014). The reciprocal and correlative relationship between learning culture and online education: A case from Saudi Arabia. *International Review of Research in Open and Distance Learning*, *15*(1), 309–336. doi:10.19173/irrodl.v15i1.1408

Hamdan, A. (2015). The interaction between online learning and educational culture: A Saudi Arabian experience. In N. Sultan & H. J. Al-Lail (Eds.), *Creative learning and MOOCs: Harnessing the technology for a 21st century education* (pp. 197–204). Newcastle upon Tyne, UK: Cambridge Scholars Publishing.

Hamdan, A., Alexander, N., & Al-Hattami, A. (2016). Saudi female students' perceptions of leadership: *An overview. Advancing Women in Leadership*, *36*(1), 36–48.

Hao, S., Cui, M., Dennen, V. P., Türel, Y. K., & Mei, L. (2017). Analysis of mobile learning as an innovation in higher education: A comparative study of three countries. *International Journal of Mobile Learning and Organization*, *11*(4), 314. Retrieved from http://www.inderscience.com/info/inarticle.php?artid=87080 doi:10.1504/IJMLO.2017.087080

Hargrave, C., & Hsu, Y.-S. (2000). Survey of instructional technology courses for preservice teachers. *Journal of Technology and Teacher Education*, *8*(4), 303–314.

Harley, D., Winn, S., Pemberton, S., & Wilcox, P. (2007). Using texting to support students' transition to university. *Innovations in Education and Teaching International*, *44*(3), 229–241. doi:10.1080/14703290701486506

Hartley, M. T., Mapes, A. C., Taylor, A., & Bourgeois, P. J. (2016). Digital Media Education and Advocacy: Addressing Attitudes Toward Disability on College Campuses. *Journal of Postsecondary Education & Disability, 29*(3), 239–247.

Hashim, K. F., Rashid, A., & Atalla, S. (2018). Social Media for Teaching and Learning within Higher Education Institution: A Bibliometric Analysis of the Literature (2008-2018). *International Journal of Interactive Mobile Technologies, 12*(7), 4–19. doi:10.3991/ijim.v12i7.9634

Hawkins, D. (2015). *Here comes generation Z. What makes them tick*. NEA Today.

Hemsley, B., Balandin, S., Palmer, S., & Dann, S. (2017). A call for innovative social media research in the field of augmentative and alternative communication. *AAC: Augmentative & Alternative Communication, 33*(1), 14–22. PMID:28121173

Hew, K. F., & Brush, T. (2006). Integrating technology into K-12 teaching and learning: current knowledge gaps and recommendations for future research. *Educational Technology Research and Development, 55*(3), 223-252. Retrieved from https://www.researchgate.net/publication/225668789_Integrating_technology_into_K-12_teaching_and_learning_Current_knowledge_gaps_and_recommendations_for_future_research

Hill, K., & Scherer, M. (2008). Matching persons and technology: data-driven AAC assessments. *Presented at the 23rd Annual International Conference on Technology and Persons with Disabilities*. Los Angeles, CA: CSUN.

Hilsdon, J. (2014). Peer learning for change in higher education. *Innovations in Education and Teaching International, 51*(3), 244–254. Retrieved from https://www.tandfonline.com/doi/full/10.1080/14703297.2013.796709 doi:10.1080/14703297.2013.796709

Hodges, J. (2017). Cracking the walls of leadership: Women in Saudi Arabia. *Gender in Management, 32*(1), 34–46. doi:10.1108/GM-11-2015-0106

Hofer, M. (2005). Technology and teacher preparation in exemplary institutions: 1994-2003. *Journal of Computing in Teacher Education, 22*(1), 5–11.

Hoffmann, M. M., & Ramirez, A. Y. (2018). Students' Attitudes Toward Teacher Use of Technology in Classrooms. *Multicultural Education, 25*(2), 51–56.

Hoge, E., Bickham, D., & Cantor, J. (2017). Digital media, anxiety, and depression in children. *Pediatrics*, *140*(Supplement 2), S76–S80. doi:10.1542/peds.2016-1758G PMID:29093037

Hope, J. (2016). Get your campus ready for Generation Z. *Dean & Provost: Practical Advice and Strategies for Academic Leaders*, *17*(8), 5–7. doi:10.1002/dap.30177

Horovitz, B. (2012). After Gen X, Millennials, what should next generation be? *USA Today*. Retrieve May 9, 2018 from http://usatoday30.usatoday.com/money/advertising/story/2012-05-03/naming-the-next-generation/54737518/1

House, K. (2012). *On Saudi Arabia: Its people, past, religion, fault lines--and future*. New York: Alfred A. Knopf.

Hsu, P.-S. (2012, June). Examining the impact of educational technology courses on preservice teachers' technological pedagogical content knowledge. *Teaching Education*, *23*(2), 195–213. doi:10.1080/10476210.2011.622041

Hutt, R. (2017). The world's most popular social networks, mapped. *World Economic Forum*. Retrieved from https://www.weforum.org/agenda/2017/03/most-popular-social-networks-mapped/

Igel, C., & Urquahart, V. (2012). Generation Z, meet cooperative learning. *Middle School Journal*, *43*(4), 16–21. doi:10.1080/00940771.2012.11461816

International Society for Technology in Education. (2018). ISTE Standards for Educators. *ISTE*. Retrieved from https://www.iste.org/standards/for-educators

Ismail, N. S., Harun, J., Salleh, S. M., & Zakaria, M. A. (2016). Supporting students' critical thinking with a mobile learning environment: A meta-analysis. In *INTED2016 Proceedings*. Retrieved from https://www.researchgate.net/publication/312940527_SUPPORTING_STUDENTS'_CRITICAL_THINKING_WITH_A_MOBILE_LEARNING_ENVIRONMENT_A_META-ANALYSIS

Issa, T., & Isaias, P. (2016). Internet factors influencing generations Y and Z in Australia and Portugal: A practical study. *Information Processing & Management*, *52*(4), 592–617. doi:10.1016/j.ipm.2015.12.006

Jacquemin, S. J., Smelser, L. K., & Bernot, M. J. (2014). Twitter in the higher education classroom: A student and faculty assessment of use and perception. *Journal of College Science Teaching, 43*(6), 22-27. Retrieved from http://reddog.rmu.edu:2061/eds/pdfviewer/pdfviewer?vid=10&sid=df38a0c7-71a8-446d-a62a-587a3d7c43c6%40sessionmgr4010

Jamjoom, F., & Kelly, P. (2013). Higher education for women in the Kingdom of Saudi Arabia. In L. Smith & A. Abouammoh (Eds.), *Higher Education in Saudi Arabia Achievements, Challenges and Opportunities* (pp. 117–125). Dordrecht: Springer. doi:10.1007/978-94-007-6321-0_11

Jansen, N. (1974). Definition of Generation and Sociological Theory. *Social Science, 49*(2), 90–98.

Januszewski, A., & Molenda, M. (2007). *Educational technology: A definition with commentary* (2nd ed.). New York, NY: Routledge.

Jenkins, R. (2017). Who is Generation Z? This timeline reveals it all. *Inc.* Retrieved from https://www.inc.com/ryan-jenkins/complete-guide-to-who-is-generation-z.html

Johnson, H., Bloomberg, K., & Iacono, T. (2008). Student and professional attitudes and interests in working with people with complex communication needs. *International Journal of Speech-Language Pathology, 10*(5), 286–296. doi:10.1080/14417040701689329 PMID:20840028

Jonathon, R., & Victoria, Z. (2011). Social Networking in an Intensive English Program Classroom: A Language Socialization Perspective. *CALICO Journal*, (2), 326.

Jones, K.A. & Jones, J.L. (2008). Making cooperative learning work in the college classroom: An application of the 'five pillars' of cooperative learning to post-secondary instruction. *The Journal of Effective Teaching, 8*(2), 61-76.

Kabilan, M. K., Ahmad, N. A., & Abidin, M. J. Z. (2010). Facebook: An online environment for learning of English in institutions of higher education. *The Internet and Higher Education, 13*(4), 179–187. doi:10.1016/j.iheduc.2010.07.003

Kalantzis, M., Cope, B., & Harvey, A. (2003). Assessing Multiliteracies and the New Basics. *Assessment in Education: Principles, Policy & Practice, 10*(1), 15–26. doi:10.1080/09695940301692

Kaplan, A. M., & Haenlein, M. (2010). Users of the world, unite! The challenges and opportunities of Social Media. *Business Horizons*, *53*(1), 59–68. Retrieved from http://michaelhaenlein.eu/Publications/Kaplan,%20Andreas%20-%20Users%20 of%20the%20wor ld,%20unite.pdf doi:10.1016/j.bushor.2009.09.003

Kelly, S. M., & Smith, T. J. (2008). The Digital Social Interactions of Students with Visual Impairments: Findings from Two National Surveys. *Journal of Visual Impairment & Blindness*, *102*(9), 528–539. doi:10.1177/0145482X0810200903

Khan, B. (2010, March 20). *Girls' education in Saudi Arabia and the Middle East with e-learning* [YouTube video]. Retrieved from https://www.youtube.com/ watch?v=A-HtbStHQoY

Kim, E., & Drumwright, M. (2016). Full length article: Engaging consumers and building relationships in social media: How social relatedness influences intrinsic vs. extrinsic consumer motivation. *Computers in Human Behavior*, *63*, 970–979. doi:10.1016/j.chb.2016.06.025

Kind, T., & Evans, Y. (2015). Social media for lifelong learning. *International Review of Psychiatry (Abingdon, England)*, *27*(2), 124–132. doi:10.3109/0954026 1.2014.990421 PMID:25906988

Kirkwood, A. (2014). Teaching and learning with technology in higher education: Blended and distance education needs 'joined-up thinking' rather than technological determinism. *Open Learning*, *29*(3), 206–221. doi:10.1080/02680513.2015.1009884

Kirschner, P. A., & De Bruyckere, P. (2017). The myths of the digital native and the multitasker. *Teaching and Teacher Education*, *67*, 135–142. doi:10.1016/j. tate.2017.06.001

Kleinberg, J. M. (1998). Authoritative sources in a hyperlinked environment. In *Proceedings of the ACM-SIAM Symposium on Discrete Algorithms*.

Knowledge is Power Program (KIPP) (2018). Focus on Character. *KIPP*. Retrieved from http://www.kipp.org/approach/character

Koross, R., & Kosgei Kipkenda, P. (2016). The Short Message Service (SMS) Texting Style of Communication and Its impact on Kenyan University Students. *Written Communication Skills*, *3*(6), 151–162.

Koulopoulos, T., & Keldsen, D. (2014). *The Gen Z Effect: The six forces shaping the future business*. Brookline, MA: Bibliomotion Inc.

Kuk, H.-S., & Holst, J. D. (2018). A Dissection of Experiential Learning Theory: Alternative Approaches to Reflection. *Adult Learning*. doi:10.1177/1045159518779138

Lester, D., Tudor, R. K., Loyd, D. D., & Mitchell, T. (2012). Marketing mavens' fusion with social media. *Atlantic Marketing Journal*, *1*(1), 79–94.

Lewis-Beck, M. S., Bryman, A., & Liao, F. T. (2004). The SAGE encyclopedia of social science research methods. Thousand Oaks, CA: SAGE Publications. doi:10.4135/9781412950589

Liao, H. (2014). Examining the role of collaborative learning in a public speaking course. *College Teaching*, *62*(2), 47–54. doi:10.1080/87567555.2013.855891

Light, J. (1988). Interaction involving individuals using augmentative and alternative communication systems: State of the art and future directions. *Augmentative and Alternative Communication*, *4*(2), 66–82. doi:10.1080/07434618812331274657

Li, J., Snow, C., & White, C. (2015). Urban adolescent students and technology: Access, use and interest in learning language and literacy. *Innovation in Language Learning and Teaching*, *9*(2), 143–162. doi:10.1080/17501229.2014.882929

Lin, L. Y., Sidani, J. E., Shensa, A., Radovic, A., Miller, E., & Colditz, J. …Primack, B. A. (2016). Association between social media use and depression among U.S. young adults. *Depression and Anxiety, 33*(4), 323-331. Retrieved from https://www.ncbi.nlm.nih.gov/pmc/articles/PMC4853817/pdf/nihms749957.pdf

Linder, K. E., Bruenjes, L. S., & Smith, S. A. (2017). Hybrid platforms, tools, and resources. *New Directions for Teaching and Learning*, *2017*(149), 27–36. doi:10.1002/tl.20224

Lipka, S. (2018). 'I didn't know how to ask for help': Stories of students with anxiety. *The Chronicle of Higher Education*, *64*(22), 14. Retrieved from https://www.chronicle.com/article/I-Didn-t-Know-How-to-Ask/242412

Livingston, A. (2009). The Revolution No One Noticed: Mobile Phones and Multimobile Services in Higher Education. Retrieved from https://er.educause.edu/articles/2009/3/the-revolution-no-one-noticed-mobile-phones-and-multimobile-services-in-higher-education

Loader, B. D., Vromen, A., Xenos, M. A., Steel, H., & Burgum, S. (2015). Campus politics, student societies and social media. *The Sociological Review*, *63*(4), 820–839. doi:10.1111/1467-954X.12220

Lough, E., & Fisher, M. H. (2016). Internet use and online safety in adults with Williams syndrome. *Journal of Intellectual Disability Research*, *60*(10), 1020–1030. doi:10.1111/jir.12281 PMID:27174494

Loveland, E. (2017). Instant Generation. *Journal of College Admission*, (234): 34–38.

Luppicini, R. (2010). Educational and professional technoethics. In R. Luppicini (Ed.), *Technoethics and the Evolving Knowledge Society: Ethical Issues in Technological Design, Research, Development, and Innovation* (pp. 163–179). Hershey, PA: IGI Global. doi:10.4018/978-1-60566-952-6

Luppicini, R., & Saleh, R. (2017). The role of online social networks for divorced Saudi women in the face of social, psychological, economic, and legal challenges. *Technology in Society*, *51*, 142–152. doi:10.1016/j.techsoc.2017.07.008

Macquarie Dictionary Online. (2016). Generation Z. *Macquarie Dictionary Online*. Macquarie Dictionary Publishers, an imprint of Pan Macmillan Australia Pty Ltd. Retrieved from https://www.macquariedictionary.com.au/

Macy, B. (2018). *Dopesick: Dealers, Doctors, and the Drug Company that Addicted America*. New York, NY: Little Brown & Company.

Madge, C., Meek, J., Wellens, J., & Hooley, T. (2009). Facebook, social integration and informal learning at university: 'It is more for socializing and talking to friends about work than for actually doing work.' *Learning, Media and Technology*, *34*(2), 141–155. doi:10.1080/17439880902923606

Maitra, D. (2017). Funds of Knowledge: An Underrated Tool for School Literacy and Student Engagement. *International Journal of Society, Culture & Language*, *5*(1), 94-102. Retrieved from http://search.proquest.com/openview/0895f8abb030 09cc2165dd4a987203ab/1?pq-origsite=gscholar&cbl=2045594

Making decisions: Suggestions for schools and early childhood services. (n.d.). *Kids Matter*. Retrieved from https://www.kidsmatter.edu.au/mental-health-matters/social-and-emotional-learning/making-decisions/suggestions-schools-and-early

Maslow, A. (1971). *The farther reaches of human nature*. New York, NY: The Viking Press.

Masters in Special Education Degree Program Guide. (2018). *Is There a Role for Social Media in Special Education*. Retrieved from https://www.masters-in-special-education.com/faq/is-there-a-role-for-social-media-in-special-education

Mazer, J. P., Murphy, R. E., & Simonds, C. J. (2007). I'll See You On "Facebook": The Effects of Computer-Mediated Teacher Self-Disclosure on Student Motivation, Affective Learning, and Classroom Climate. *Communication Education*, *56*(1), 1–17. doi:10.1080/03634520601009710

McCoy, B. (2016). Digital distractions in the classroom phase II: Student classroom use of digital devices for non-class related purposes. *Journal of Media Education* (7) 5-32. Retrieved on 20 January 2018 from https://digitalcommons.unl.edu/cgi/viewcontent.cgi?referer=https://www.google.com/&httpsredir=1&article=1091&context=journalismfacpub

McKnight, K., O'Malley, K., Ruzic, R., Horsley, M., Franey, J. J., & Bassett, K. (2016). Teaching in a digital age: How educators use technology to improve student learning. *Journal of Research on Technology in Education*, *48*(3), 194–211. doi:10.1080/15391523.2016.1175856

Media, H. H. (2018). Meet Gen Z: The social generation. Retrieved from http://thinking.hhcc.com/?utm_campaign=ThoughtLeadership—GenZ&utm_source=ppc&gclid=Cj0KCQiA8f_eBRDcARIsAEKwRGcKjpjl6Gw8rvoQfZD7_gmts7FmfvzHxrbvc0cgdzRDT2y1RJb5igwaAlNbEALw_wcB

MediaS. (2004). Retrieved from https://www.merriam-webster.com/dictionary/social-media

Merriam-Webster.com. (n.d.). generation Z. Retrieved from https://www.merriam-webster.com

Miller, R. A. (2017). "My voice is definitely strongest in online communities": Students using social media for queer and disability identity-making. *Journal of College Student Development*, *58*(4), 509–525.

Minalla, A. A. (2018). The Effect of WhatsApp Chat Group in Enhancing EFL Learners' Verbal Interaction outside Classroom Contexts. *English Language Teaching*, *11*(3), 1–7. doi:10.5539/elt.v11n3p1

Ministry of Education and Science of the Republic of Kazakhstan JSC Information-Analytic Center. (2017). *Teaching in three languages: International experience and recommendations for Kazakhstan*.

Ministry of Education. Singapore. (2015). Framework for 21st Century Competencies and Student Outcomes. Retrieved from https://www.moe.gov.sg/education/education-system/21st-century-competencies

Mirza, A., & Al-Abdulkareem, M. (2011). Models of e-learning adopted in the Middle East. *Applied Computing and Informatics*, *9*(2), 83–93. doi:10.1016/j.aci.2011.05.001

Moll, L. C., Amanti, C., Neff, D., & Gonzalez, N. (1992). Funds of knowledge for teaching: Using a qualitative approach to connect homes and classrooms. *Theory into Practice*, *31*(2), 132–141. doi:10.1080/00405849209543534

Moran, M., Seaman, J., & Tinti-Kane, H. (2011). Teaching, learning, and sharing: How today's higher education faculty use social media. Pearson. Retrieved from https://files.eric.ed.gov/fulltext/ED535130.pdf

Moran, M., Seaman, J., & Tinti-Kane, H. (2012). *Blogs, wikis, podcasts And Facebook. Pearson Learning Solutions: how today's higher education faculty use social media*. Pearson. Retrieved from https://www.onlinelearningsurvey.com/reports/blogswikispodcasts.pdf

Muhammad, A. H., Wahsheh, H. A., Shah, A., & Ahmad, F. (2014, November). Ethical perspective of learning management system a model to support moral character of online learner. In *The 5th International Conference on Information and Communication Technology for The Muslim World (ICT4M)* (pp. 1-6). IEEE.

Muhammad, A., Ghalib, M. F. M. D., Ahmad, F., Naveed, Q. N., & Shah, A. (2016). A study to investigate state of ethical development in e-learning. *J. Adv. Comput. Sci. Appl*, *7*(4), 284–290.

Musbahtiti, K., Saady, M. R., & Muhammad, A. (2013). Comprehensive e-learning system based on Islamic principles. In *2013 5th International Conference on Information and Communication Technology for the Muslim World (ICT4M)* (pp. 1-5). IEEE.

Muzamil, M., & Shah, G. (2016). Cyberbullying and self-perceptions of students associated with their academic performance. *International Journal of Education and Development Using Information and Communication Technology*, *12*(3), 79–92.

National Center on Disability and Journalism. (2018). Disability Language Style Guide. Retrieved from https://ncdj.org/style-guide/

Nazarbayev University. (2018). NU at a glance. Retrieved from https://nu.edu.kz/about-nazarbayev-university/nu-at-a-glance

Nichols, T., & Wright, M. (2018). Generational differences: Understanding and exploring generation z. In *Proceedings of the Annual Meeting of the Southwest Academy of Management* (pp. 177-185).

North, A. (2014, November 13). Think Pieces Were Made for Millennials Who Majored in English. NY Times. Retrieved from https://op-talk.blogs.nytimes.com/2014/11/13/think-pieces-were-made-for-millennials-who-majored-in-english/

O'Keeffe, G. S., & Clarke-Pearson, K. (2011). The impact of social media on children, adolescents, and families. *American Academy of Pediatrics, 127*(4). Retrieved from http://research3.fit.edu/sealevelriselibrary/documents/doc_mgr/1006/O'Keeffe_and_Pearson._2011._The_Impact_of_Social_Media_on_Children,_Adolescents,_and_Families.pdf

OECD. (2017). OECD work on education. Retrieved from http://www.oecd.org/education/Directorate-for-education-and-skills-brochure.pdf

Omair, K. (2008). Women in management in the Arab context. *Education, Business and Society*, *1*(2), 107–123. doi:10.1108/17537980810890293

Oriji, A., & Efebo, P. I. (2013). New technology, new methodology: The "digital natives" and "digital immigrants" debate. *Journal of Educational Review*, *6*(2).

Orphus, J. D., & Abbitt, J. T. (2009). Exploring the potential perceptions of social networking systems in university courses. *MERLOT Journal of Online Learning and Teaching*, *5*(4). Retrieved from http://jolt.merlot.org/vol5no4/ophus_1209.htm

Oxford English Dictionary. (n.d.). Generation Z. Retrieved from http://www.oed.com/viewdictionaryentry/Entry/11125

Palacio, R. J. (2012). *Wonder*. New York, NY: Alfred A. Knopf Inc.

Pantic, I., Damjanovic, A., Todorovic, J., Topalovic, D., Bojovic-Jovic, D., Ristic, S., & Pantic, S. (2012). Association between online social networking and depression in high school students: Behavioral physiology viewpoint. *Psychiatria Danubina, 24*(1), 90–93. Retrieved on 20 January 2018 from http://www.hdbp.org/psychiatria_danubina/pdf/dnb_vol24_no1/dnb_vol24_no1_90.pdf PMID:22447092

Park, H., & Lee, H. (2013). Show us you are real: The effect of human-versus-organizational presence on online relationship building through social networking sites. *Cyberpsychology, Behavior, and Social Networking, 16*(4), 265–271. doi:10.1089/cyber.2012.0051 PMID:23363228

Patel, D. (2017a, April 8). 10 tips for marketing to Gen Z on social media. *Forbes Magazine*. Retrieved from https://www.forbes.com/sites/deeppatel/2017/08/08/10-tips-for-marketing-to-gen-z-on-social-media/#765056a32718

Patel, D. (2017b, September 21). 8 ways Generation Z will differ from Millennials in the workplace. *Forbes Magazine*. Retrieved from https://www.forbes.com/sites/deeppatel/2017/09/21/8-ways-generation-z-will-differ-from-millennials-in-the-workplace/#7527d56b76e5

Peacock, J., Covino, R., Auchter, J., Boyd, J., Klug, H., Laing, C., & Irvin, L. (2018). University faculty perceptions and utilization of popular culture in the classroom. *Studies in Higher Education, 43*(4), 601–613. doi:10.1080/03075079.2016.1180673

Piwek, L., & Joinson, A. (2016). "What do they snapchat about?" Patterns of use in time-limited instant messaging service. *Computers in Human Behavior, 54*, 358–367. doi:10.1016/j.chb.2015.08.026

Platt, S. (Ed.). (1989). *Respectfully Quoted: A Dictionary of Quotations Requested from the Congressional Research Service*. Washington, DC: Library of Congress. Retrieved from https://www.bartleby.com/73/195.html

Pombo, L., Loureiro, M. J., & Moreira, A. (2010). Assessing collaborative work in a higher education blended learning context: Strategies and students' perceptions. *Educational Media International, 47*(3), 217–229. doi:10.1080/09523987.2010.518814

Prensky, M. (2001). Digital natives, digital immigrants. *On the Horizon, 9*(5), 1–6. doi:10.1108/10748120110424816

Prensky, M. (2001a). *Digital game-based learning*. New York: McGraw-Hill.

Prensky, M. (2001c). Immigrants part 2: Do they. *On the Horizon, 9*, 2–6.

Prilipko, A. (2017). *Managing Implementation of English Medium of Instruction in Higher Education in Kazakhstan: Practices and Challenges*. Nazarbayev University.

Probst, D. (2017). Social Media Literacy as an IEP Intervention for Social and Emotional Learning. *The Journal of Media Literacy Education, 9*(2), 45–57. doi:10.23860/JMLE-2019-09-02-04

Puiu, S. (2017). Generation Z -- an Educational and Managerial Perspective. *Revista Tinerilor Economisti [Young Economists Journal], 14*(29), 62–72.

Quraishi, A. (2012). More Saudi universities boarding e-learning bandwagon. *Arab News*. Retrieved from http://www.arabnews.com/more-saudi-universities-boarding-e-learning-bandwagon

Ranaldo, M. (2013). Communicating with 21st Century Bulletin Boards. *Exceptional Parent, 43*(2), 30–32.

Read, J. P., Ouimette, P., White, J., Colder, C., & Farrow, S. (2011). Rates of DSM-IV-TR trauma exposure and posttraumatic stress disorder among newly matriculated college students. *Psychological Trauma: Theory, Research, Practice, and Policy, 3*(3), 148–156. doi:10.1037/a0021260 PMID:25621098

Reynolds, V. (2018). CSD537A Augmentative and Alternative Communication Systems Summer 2018 Syllabus.

Rickes, P. C. (2016). Generations in flux: How gen Z will continue to transform higher education space. *Planning for Higher Education, 44*(4), 21.

Riordan, M. A., Kreuz, R. J., & Blair, A. N. (2018). The digital divide: Conveying subtlety in online communication. *Journal of Computers in Education*, *5*(1), 49–66. doi:10.100740692-018-0100-6

Rivera, C. J., Hudson, M. E., Weiss, S. L., & Zambone, A. (2017). Using a Multicomponent Multimedia Shared Story Intervention with an iPad to Teach Content Picture Vocabulary to Students with Developmental Disabilities. *Education & Treatment of Children*, *40*(3), 327–352. doi:10.1353/etc.2017.0014

Roblyer, M. D., McDaniel, M., Webb, M., Herman, J., & Witty, J. V. (2010). Findings on Facebook in higher education: A comparison of college faculty and student uses and perceptions of social networking sites. *The Internet and Higher Education*, *13*(3), 134–140. doi:10.1016/j.iheduc.2010.03.002

Rockich-Winston, N., Train, B. C., Rudolph, M. J., & Gillette, C. (2018). Faculty motivations to use active learning among pharmacy educators. *Currents in Pharmacy Teaching and Learning*, *10*(3), 277–284. doi:10.1016/j.cptl.2017.11.015 PMID:29764630

Rodriguez, J. E. (2011). Social Media Use in Higher Education: Key Areas to Consider for Educators. *MERLOT Journal of Online Learning and Teaching*, *7*(4), 539–550.

Ross, H. M., Banow, R., & Yu, S. (2015). The use of Twitter in large lecture courses: Do the students see a benefit? *Contemporary Educational Technology*, *6*(2), 126-139. Retrieved from http://reddog.rmu.edu:2061/eds/pdfviewer/pdfviewer?vid=11&sid=df38a0c7-71a8-446d-a62a-587a3d7c43c6%40sessionmgr4010

Rothman, D. (2016). A Tsunami of learners called Generation Z. Retrieved from http://www.mdle.net/JoumaFA_Tsunami_of_Learners_Called_Generation_Z.pdf

Round, K. (2011). E-Learning 2.0: Cloud computing and the online learner. *Journal of Applied Learning Technology*, *1*(4), 24–27.

Rowan-Kenyon, H. T., Alemán, A. M., Gin, K., Blakeley, B., Gismondi, A., & Lewis, J. … Knight, S. (2016). Social media in higher education. *ASHE Higher Education Report*, *42*(5), 7-128. Retrieved from http://onlinelibrary.wiley.com/doi/10.1002/aehe.20088/epdf

Rugh, W. (2002). Education in Saudi Arabia: Choices and constraints. *Middle East Policy*, *9*(2), 40–55. doi:10.1111/1475-4967.00056

Rust, D. Z. (2018). Using Text Messaging Systems as a Class Communication Tool. *College Teaching*, *29–31*. doi:10.1080/87567555.2018.1509292

Saleh, R., & Luppicini, R. (2017). Exploring the challenges of divorce on Saudi women. *Journal of Family History*, *2*(42), 1–15.

Salubi, O. G., Ondari-Okemwa, E., & Nekhwevha, F. (2018). Utilisation of Library Information Resources among Generation Z Students: Facts and Fiction. *Publications*, *6*(2), 16. doi:10.3390/publications6020016

Sampasa-Kanyinga, H., & Lewis, R. F. (2015). Frequent use of social networking sites is associated with poor psychological functioning among children and adolescents. *Cyberpsychology, Behavior, and Social Networking*, *18*(7), 380–385. doi:10.1089/cyber.2015.0055 PMID:26167836

Sarinzhipov, A. (2013). *Opportunities for faculty to influence academic matters at Kazakh National University and Eurasian National University*. University of Pennsylvania.

Satsangi, R., Hammer, R., & Hogan, C. D. (2018). Studying virtual manipulatives paired with explicit instruction to teach algebraic equations to students with learning disabilities. *Learning Disability Quarterly*, *41*(4), 227–242. doi:10.1177/0731948718769248

Scheuermann, L., & Taylor, G. (1997). Netiquette. *Internet Research*, *7*(4), 269–273. doi:10.1108/10662249710187268

Schlagwein, D., & Hu, M. (2017). How and why organizations use social media: Five use types and their relation to absorptive capacity. *Journal of Information Technology*, *32*(2), 194–209. doi:10.1057/jit.2016.7

Schlee, R. P., & Harich, K. R. (2013). Teaching Students How to Integrate and Assess Social Networking Tools in Marketing Communications. *Marketing Education Review*, *23*(3), 209–224. doi:10.2753/MER1052-8008230301

Schnackenberg, H. L., & Still, G. III. (2014). Teacher preparation programs and technology integration: Best practices for curriculum design. *International Journal of Education and Practice*, *2*(7), 147–158. Retrieved from http://www.pakinsight.com/?ic=archive&journal=61&month=07-2014&issue=7 doi:10.18488/journal.61/2014.2.7/61.7.147.158

Schwieger, D., & Ladwig, C. (2018). Reaching and Retaining the Next Generation: Adapting to the Expectations of Gen Z in the Classroom. *Information Systems Education Journal*, *16*(3), 45–54.

Seale, J. (2014). *E-learning and disability in higher education: Accessibility theory and practice*. London, New York: Routledge.

Seaman, J., & Tinti-Kane, H. (2013). *Social media for teaching and learning*. Pearson. Retrieved from http://www.pearsonlearningsolutions.com/assets/downloads/reports/social-media-for-teaching-and-learning-2013-report.pdf#view=FitH,0

Seaman, J., Brown, M., & Quay, J. (2017). The Evolution of Experiential Learning Theory. *Journal of Experiential Education*, *105382591668926*. doi:10.1177/1053825916689268

Seemiller, C., & Grace, M. (2016). *Generation Z goes to college*. San Francisco, CA: Jossey-Bass.

Seemiller, C., & Grace, M. (2017). Generation Z: Educating and Engaging the Next Generation of Students. *About Campus: Enriching the Student Learning Experience*, *22*(3), 21–26. doi:10.1002/abc.21293

Shea, V. (1994). *Netiquette*. San Francisco, CA: Albion Books.

Shepley, C., Lane, J. D., & Gast, D. L. (2016). Using SMART board technology to teach young students with disabilities and limited group learning experience to read environmental text. *Education and Training in Autism and Developmental Disabilities*, *51*(4), 404–420.

Siemens, G. (2005). Connectivism: A learning theory for the digital age. *International Journal of Instructional Technology and Distance Learning (ITDL)*. Retrieved from http://www.itdl.org/journal/jan_05/article01.htm

Simard, D. A., & Schnackenberg, H. L. (2006). Online Course Creation and Facilitation: The New Classroom Management. Department of Special Education SUNY Plattsburgh, New York. Retrieved from http://citeseerx.ist.psu.edu/viewdoc/download?doi=10.1.1.627.422&rep=rep1&type=pdf

Simard, D. A., & Schnackenberg, H. L. (2012). Student and faculty preferences toward the use of social networks for academic purposes. In Q. Lin (Ed.), *Advancement in Online Education: Exploring the Best Practices* (Vol. 1). New York, NY: Nova Science Publishers.

Singh, A. (July. (2014). Challenges of Issues of Generation Z. *IOSR Journal of Business and Management*, *16*(7), 59–63.

Slavin, R. E. (2018). *Educational Psychology: theory and practice*. NY, NY: Pearson.

Smart Technologies and Teachers Complete Their First Global Collaboration Project. (2016). eParent.com.

Smat, N., Aikenova, A., Yelibay, M., Filipova, L., Rakisheva, A., Kavashev, Z., & CohenMiller, A. S. (2018). Thinking "outside the box" in innovating higher education in the Age of Disruption: A review of the Eurasian Higher Education Leaders Forum (EHELF) 2018. *Information and Analytical Magazine, Bologna Process, 23*(3), 56–61.

Smith, A. A. (2015, March 26). Community college to bachelor's. *Inside Higher Ed*. Retrieved from https://www.insidehighered.com/news/2015/03/26/nearly-half-four-year-college-graduates-attended-two-year-college

Smith, S.D. & Caruso, J.B. (2010, October). *The ECAR Study of Undergraduate Students and Information Technology*. Boulder, CO: EDUCAUSE Center for Applied Research.

Smith, B. G., & Gallicano, T. D. (2015). Terms of engagement: Analyzing public engagement with organizations through social media. *Computers in Human Behavior*, *53*, 82–90. doi:10.1016/j.chb.2015.05.060

Statista. (2018). *Most popular social networks of teenagers in the United States from fall 2012 to fall 2017*. Retrieved from https://www.statista.com/statistics/250172/social-network-usage-of-us-teens-and-young-adults/

Steers, M. N., Wickham, R. E., & Acitelli, L. K. (2014). Seeing everyone else's highlight reels: How Facebook usage is linked to depressive symptoms. *Journal of Social and Clinical Psychology*, *33*(8), 701–731. doi:10.1521/jscp.2014.33.8.701

Stevens, L. B. (2105, June 25). 5 Dangers of Social Media to Discuss With Your Kids. *Care*. Retrieved from https://www.care.com/c/stories/4275/5-dangers-of-social-media-to-discuss-with-you/

Stewart, Georgina. (2016). Reviewing and ethics in the online academy. *Educational philosophy, 48*(5), 437-442.

Substance Abuse and Mental Health Services Administration. (2017). *Key substance use and mental health indicators in the United States: Results from the 2016 National Survey on Drug Use and Health* (HHS Publication No. SMA 17-5044, NSDUH Series H-52). Rockville, MD: Center for Behavioral Health Statistics and Quality, Substance Abuse and Mental Health Services Administration. Retrieved from https://www. samhsa.gov/data/

Summers, J. J., Bertetvas, S. N., Svinicki, M. D., & Gorin, J. S. (2005). Evaluating collaborative learning and community. *Journal of Experimental Education*, *73*(3), 165–188. doi:10.3200/JEXE.73.3.165-188

Swartzwelder, K. (2014). Examining the Effect of Texting on Students' Perceptions of Learning. *Nursing Education Perspectives*, *35*(6), 405–407. doi:10.5480/12-1012.1

Swett, D. (2016). Online student orientation: Guerrilla style. *Change: The Magazine of Higher Learning*, *48*(5), 26–35. doi:10.1080/00091383.2016.1227673

Tam, K. (2015). *Saudi Arabia prepares female faculty members for online education* [Press Release]. Retrieved from https://www.prnewswire.com/news-releases/saudi-arabia-prepares-female-faculty-members-for-online-education-300115711.html

Teaching Students with Disabilities about Online Safety. (2014). *Power up what works*. Retrieved from https://powerupwhatworks.org/technology/teaching-students-disabilities-about-online-safety

Thompson, M. (2015). Saudi women leaders: Challenges and opportunities. *Journal of Arabian Studies*, *5*(1), 15–36. doi:10.1080/21534764.2015.1050880

Thompson, P. (2015). How digital native learners describe themselves. *Education and Information Technologies*, *20*(3), 467–484. doi:10.100710639-013-9295-3

Tinti-Kane, H., Seaman, J., & Levy, J. (2010). *Social media in higher education: The survey*. Pearson. Retrieved from https://www.babson.edu/Academics/Documents/babson-survey-research-group/social-media-in-hi gher-education.pdf

Traxler, J. (2008). Mobile learning in a social, ethical, and legal environment. In T. Hansson (Ed.), *Handbook of research on digital information technologies: Innovations, methods, and ethical issues* (pp. 520–532). Hershey, PA: IGI Global. doi:10.4018/978-1-59904-970-0.ch033

triple j. (2018). [Collection]. Retrieved from https://www.abc.net.au/triplej/

Tufford, L., & Newman, P. (2012). Bracketing in qualitative research. *Qualitative Social Work: Research and Practice*, *11*(1), 80–96. doi:10.1177/1473325010368316

Turner, A. (2015). Generation Z: Technology and social interest. *Journal of Individual Psychology*, *71*(2), 103–113. doi:10.1353/jip.2015.0021

Twenge, J. M. (2017, September). Have smart-phones destroyed a generation? *The Atlantic*. Retrieved from https://www.theatlantic.com/magazine/archive/2017/09/has-the-smartphone-destroyed-a-generation/534198/

Twenge, J. M. (2017). *IGEN: Why today's super-connected kids are growing up less rebellious, more tolerant, less happy-- and completely unprepared for adulthood and (what this means for the rest of us)*. New York, NY: Atria.

Twenge, J. M., Joiner, T. E., Rogers, M. L., & Martin, G. N. (2017). Increases in depressive symptoms, suicide-related outcomes, and suicide rates among U.S. adolescents after 2010 and links to increased new media screen time. *Clinical Psychological Science*, *6*(1), 3–17. doi:10.1177/2167702617723376

U.S. population with a social media profile 2018. (2018). *Statista*. Retrieved from https://www.statista.com/statistics/273476/percentage-of-us-population-with-a-social-network-profile/

Umbach, P. D., & Wawrzynski, M. R. (2005). Faculty do matter: The role of college faculty in student learning and engagement. *Research in Higher Education*, *46*(2), 153–184. doi:10.100711162-004-1598-1

Ventimiglia, L.M. (1993). Cooperative learning at the college level. *The NEA Higher Education Journal*, 5-30.

Vogel, F., Wecker, C., Kollar, I., & Fischer, F. (2017). Socio-cognitive scaffolding with computer-supported collaboration scripts: A meta-analysis. *Educational Psychology Review*, *29*(3), 477–511. doi:10.100710648-016-9361-7

VoiceThread. (n.d.). VoiceThread fills the social presence gap found in online learning interactions. Retrieved from https://voicethread.com/products/highered/

Vu, P., & Gaskill, M. (2018). Can pre-service teachers create digital game-based activities without coding knowledge? In Gamification in education: Breakthroughs in education and practice (pp. 159-173). Hershey, PA: IGI Global. doi:10.4018/978-1-5225-5198-0.ch009

Wang, K., Lv, Y., & Zhang, Z. (2018). Relationship between Extroversion and Social Use of Social Networking Sites. *Social Behavior and Personality*, *46*(10), 1597–1609. doi:10.2224bp.7210

Wang, Z., & Tchernev, J. M. (2012). The "myth" of media multitasking: Reciprocal dynamics of media multitasking, personal needs, and gratifications. *Journal of Communication*, *62*(3), 493–513. doi:10.1111/j.1460-2466.2012.01641.x

What is Kahoot! (2017). Kahoot. Retrieved from https://kahoot.com/what-is-kahoot/

What is Social Media. (n.d.). Educational Council of New Zealand. Retrieved from https://www.teachersandsocialmedia.co.nz/what-social-media

Williams, F. (2017). *The Nature Fix: Why Nature Makes Us Happier, Healthier, and More Creative*. New York, NY: W.W. Norton & Company.

Witmer, M. M. (2005). The fourth R in education – relationships. *The Clearing House: A Journal of Educational Strategies, Issues and Ideas*, *78*(5), 224–228. doi:10.3200/TCHS.78.5.224-228

Wollak, B. A., & Koppenhaver, D. A. (2011). Developing technology-supported, evidence-based writing instruction for adolescents with significant writing disabilities. *Assistive Technology Outcomes And Benefits*, *7*(1), 1–23.

World Health Organization. (2001). International Classification of Functioning, Disability and Health (ICF). Retrieved from http://www.who.int/classifications/icf/en/

World Health Organization. (2018). *Gaming disorder. Online Q & A*. Retrieved from https://www.who.int/features/qa/gaming-disorder/en/

Xiaoqing, G., Yuankun, Z., & Xiaofeng, G. (2013). Meeting the "digital natives": Understanding the acceptance of technology in classrooms. *Journal of Educational Technology & Society*, *16*(1), 392–402.

Yakavets, N., Bridges, D., & Shamatov, D. (2017). On constructs and the construction of teachers' professional knowledge in a post-Soviet context. *Journal of Education for Teaching*, *43*(5), 594–615. doi:10.1080/02607476.2017.1355086

Yamin, M. (2013). A socio-cultural overview of e-learning in Saudi Arabia. *International Journal of Emerging Technology and Advanced Engineering*, *3*(12), 57–59.

Yildirim, C. (2014). Exploring the dimensions of nomophobia: Developing and validating a questionnaire using mixed methods research. Retrieved from https://lib.dr.iastate.edu/cgi/viewcontent.cgi?article=5012&context=etd

Young Health Movement. (n.d.). Retrieved from http://www.yhm.org.uk/

Yu, A. Y., Tian, S. W., Vogel, D., & Kwok, R. C.-W. (2010). Can learning be virtually boosted? An investigation of online social networking impacts. *Computers & Education*, *55*(4), 1494–1503. doi:10.1016/j.compedu.2010.06.015

Zaremohzzabieh, Z., Samah, B. A., Omar, S. Z., Bolong, J., & Kamarudin, N. A. (2014). Addictive Facebook use among university students. *Asian Social Science*, *10*(6), 107–117. doi:10.5539/ass.v10n6p107

Zorn, R. (2017). Coming in 2017: A new generation of graduate students – The generation Z. *College and University*, *92*(1), 61–63.

Zorn, R. L. (2016). Coming in 2017: A new generation of graduate students - The z generation. *College and University*, *92*(1), 61–63.

Zorn, R. L. (2017). Coming in 2017: A new generation of graduate students – the Z generation. *College and University*, *92*(1), 61–63.

Zuhur, S. (2011). *Saudi Arabia*. Santa Barbara, CA: ABC-CLIO.

Related References

To continue our tradition of advancing academic research, we have compiled a list of recommended IGI Global readings. These references will provide additional information and guidance to further enrich your knowledge and assist you with your own research and future publications.

Aburezeq, I. M., & Dweikat, F. F. (2017). Cloud Applications in Language Teaching: Examining Pre-Service Teachers' Expertise, Perceptions and Integration. *International Journal of Distance Education Technologies, 15*(4), 39–60. doi:10.4018/IJDET.2017100103

Adera, B. (2017). Supporting Language and Literacy Development for English Language Learners. In J. Keengwe (Ed.), *Handbook of Research on Promoting Cross-Cultural Competence and Social Justice in Teacher Education* (pp. 339–354). Hershey, PA: IGI Global. doi:10.4018/978-1-5225-0897-7.ch018

Ahamer, G. (2011). How Technologies Can Localize Learners in Multicultural Space: A Newly Developed "Global Studies" Curriculum. *International Journal of Technology and Educational Marketing, 1*(2), 1–24. doi:10.4018/ijtem.2011070101

Ahamer, G. (2015). Conclusions from Social Dynamics in Collaborative Environmental Didactics. *International Journal of Technology and Educational Marketing, 5*(2), 68–92. doi:10.4018/IJTEM.2015070105

Ahamer, G. (2015). Designing and Analyzing Social Dynamics for Collaborative: Environmental Didactics. *International Journal of Technology and Educational Marketing, 5*(2), 46–67. doi:10.4018/IJTEM.2015070104

Ahamer, G. (2017). Quality Assurance for a Developmental "Global Studies" (GS) Curriculum. In I. Management Association (Ed.), Educational Leadership and Administration: Concepts, Methodologies, Tools, and Applications (pp. 438-477). Hershey, PA: IGI Global. doi:10.4018/978-1-5225-1624-8.ch023

Ahamer, G. (2017). Quality Assurance for a Developmental "Global Studies" (GS) Curriculum. In I. Management Association (Ed.), Educational Leadership and Administration: Concepts, Methodologies, Tools, and Applications (pp. 438-477). Hershey, PA: IGI Global. doi:10.4018/978-1-5225-1624-8.ch023

Alegre de la Rosa, O. M., & Angulo, L. M. (2017). Social Inclusion and Intercultural Values in a School of Education. In S. Mukerji & P. Tripathi (Eds.), *Handbook of Research on Administration, Policy, and Leadership in Higher Education* (pp. 518–531). Hershey, PA: IGI Global. doi:10.4018/978-1-5225-0672-0.ch020

Ambikairajah, E., Sethu, V., Eaton, R., & Sheng, M. (2014). Evolving Use of Educational Technologies: Enhancing Lectures. In F. Alam (Ed.), *Using Technology Tools to Innovate Assessment, Reporting, and Teaching Practices in Engineering Education* (pp. 241–258). Hershey, PA: IGI Global. doi:10.4018/978-1-4666-5011-4.ch018

Anderson, K. M. (2017). Preparing Teachers in the Age of Equity and Inclusion. In I. Management Association (Ed.), Medical Education and Ethics: Concepts, Methodologies, Tools, and Applications (pp. 1532-1554). Hershey, PA: IGI Global. doi:10.4018/978-1-5225-0978-3.ch069

Awdziej, M. (2017). Case Study as a Teaching Method in Marketing. In D. Latusek (Ed.), *Case Studies as a Teaching Tool in Management Education* (pp. 244–263). Hershey, PA: IGI Global. doi:10.4018/978-1-5225-0770-3.ch013

Bain, B. (2014). Exploring Assessment of Critical Thinking Learning Outcomes in Online Higher Education. In V. Wang (Ed.), *Handbook of Research on Education and Technology in a Changing Society* (pp. 1191–1202). Hershey, PA: IGI Global. doi:10.4018/978-1-4666-6046-5.ch089

Banas, J. R., & York, C. S. (2017). Pre-Service Teachers' Motivation to Use Technology and the Impact of Authentic Learning Exercises. In L. Tomei (Ed.), *Exploring the New Era of Technology-Infused Education* (pp. 121–140). Hershey, PA: IGI Global. doi:10.4018/978-1-5225-1709-2.ch008

Bariso, E. U. (2015). Educational Policy Analysis Debates and New Learning Technologies in England. In M. Khosrow-Pour (Ed.), *Encyclopedia of Information Science and Technology* (3rd ed.; pp. 2371–2378). Hershey, PA: IGI Global. doi:10.4018/978-1-4666-5888-2.ch230

Beycioglu, K., & Wildy, H. (2015). Principal Preparation: The Case of Novice Principals in Turkey. In K. Beycioglu & P. Pashiardis (Eds.), *Multidimensional Perspectives on Principal Leadership Effectiveness* (pp. 1–17). Hershey, PA: IGI Global. doi:10.4018/978-1-4666-6591-0.ch001

Beycioglu, K., & Wildy, H. (2017). Principal Preparation: The Case of Novice Principals in Turkey. In I. Management Association (Ed.), Educational Leadership and Administration: Concepts, Methodologies, Tools, and Applications (pp. 1152-1169). Hershey, PA: IGI Global. doi:10.4018/978-1-5225-1624-8.ch054

Bharwani, S., & Musunuri, D. (2018). Reflection as a Process From Theory to Practice. In M. Khosrow-Pour, D.B.A. (Ed.), Encyclopedia of Information Science and Technology, Fourth Edition (pp. 1529-1539). Hershey, PA: IGI Global. doi:10.4018/978-1-5225-2255-3.ch132

Bisschoff, T., & Rhodes, C. (2011). Transformation through Marketing: A Case of a Secondary School in South Africa. In P. Tripathi & S. Mukerji (Eds.), *Cases on Innovations in Educational Marketing: Transnational and Technological Strategies* (pp. 263–272). Hershey, PA: IGI Global. doi:10.4018/978-1-60960-599-5.ch016

Bodomo, A. B. (2010). Educational Technologies (WebCT): Creating Constructivist and Interactive Learning Communities. In A. Bodomo (Ed.), *Computer-Mediated Communication for Linguistics and Literacy: Technology and Natural Language Education* (pp. 252–290). Hershey, PA: IGI Global. doi:10.4018/978-1-60566-868-0.ch010

Bohjanen, S. L., Cameron-Standerford, A., & Meidl, T. D. (2018). Capacity Building Pedagogy for Diverse Learners. In J. Keengwe (Ed.), *Handbook of Research on Pedagogical Models for Next-Generation Teaching and Learning* (pp. 195–212). Hershey, PA: IGI Global. doi:10.4018/978-1-5225-3873-8.ch011

Brewer, J. C. (2018). Measuring Text Readability Using Reading Level. In M. Khosrow-Pour, D.B.A. (Ed.), Encyclopedia of Information Science and Technology, Fourth Edition (pp. 1499-1507). Hershey, PA: IGI Global. doi:10.4018/978-1-5225-2255-3.ch129

Brown, S. L. (2017). A Case Study of Strategic Leadership and Research in Practice: Principal Preparation Programs that Work – An Educational Administration Perspective of Best Practices for Master's Degree Programs for Principal Preparation. In V. Wang (Ed.), *Encyclopedia of Strategic Leadership and Management* (pp. 1226–1244). Hershey, PA: IGI Global. doi:10.4018/978-1-5225-1049-9.ch086

Brzozowski, M., & Ferster, I. (2017). Educational Management Leadership: High School Principal's Management Style and Parental Involvement in School Management in Israel. In V. Potocan, M. Üngan, & Z. Nedelko (Eds.), *Handbook of Research on Managerial Solutions in Non-Profit Organizations* (pp. 55–74). Hershey, PA: IGI Global. doi:10.4018/978-1-5225-0731-4.ch003

Cannaday, J. (2017). The Masking Effect: Hidden Gifts and Disabilities of 2e Students. In P. Dickenson, P. Keough, & J. Courduff (Eds.), *Preparing Pre-Service Teachers for the Inclusive Classroom* (pp. 220–231). Hershey, PA: IGI Global. doi:10.4018/978-1-5225-1753-5.ch011

Capobianco, B. M., & Lehman, J. D. (2010). Fostering Educational Technology Integration in Science Teacher Education: Issues of Teacher Identity Development. In J. Yamamoto, J. Kush, R. Lombard, & C. Hertzog (Eds.), *Technology Implementation and Teacher Education: Reflective Models* (pp. 245–257). Hershey, PA: IGI Global. doi:10.4018/978-1-61520-897-5.ch014

Chao, G. H., Hsu, M. K., & Scovotti, C. (2013). Predicting Donations from a Cohort Group of Donors to Charities: A Direct Marketing Case Study. In J. Wang (Ed.), *Optimizing, Innovating, and Capitalizing on Information Systems for Operations* (pp. 196–214). Hershey, PA: IGI Global. doi:10.4018/978-1-4666-2925-7.ch010

Chauhan, A. (2015). Beyond the Phenomenon: Assessment in Massive Open Online Courses (MOOCs). In E. McKay & J. Lenarcic (Eds.), *Macro-Level Learning through Massive Open Online Courses (MOOCs): Strategies and Predictions for the Future* (pp. 119–140). Hershey, PA: IGI Global. doi:10.4018/978-1-4666-8324-2.ch007

Coffman, T. L., & Klinger, M. B. (2013). Managing Quality in Online Education. In G. Kurubacak & T. Yuzer (Eds.), *Project Management Approaches for Online Learning Design* (pp. 220–233). Hershey, PA: IGI Global. doi:10.4018/978-1-4666-2830-4.ch011

Contreras, E. C., & Contreras, I. I. (2018). Development of Communication Skills through Auditory Training Software in Special Education. In M. Khosrow-Pour, D.B.A. (Ed.), Encyclopedia of Information Science and Technology, Fourth Edition (pp. 2431-2441). Hershey, PA: IGI Global. doi:10.4018/978-1-5225-2255-3.ch212

Cook, R. G. (2011). Educational Marketing: Coming Down from the Cloud Using Landing Gear. In U. Demiray & S. Sever (Eds.), *Marketing Online Education Programs: Frameworks for Promotion and Communication* (pp. 26–31). Hershey, PA: IGI Global. doi:10.4018/978-1-60960-074-7.ch003

Cook, R. G., & Ley, K. (2015). Past, Future and Presents: Meeting New Online Challenges with Primal Marketing Solutions. *International Journal of Technology and Educational Marketing*, *5*(2), 19–33. doi:10.4018/IJTEM.2015070102

Cooley, D., & Whitten, E. (2017). Special Education Leadership and the Implementation of Response to Intervention. In F. Topor (Ed.), *Handbook of Research on Individualism and Identity in the Globalized Digital Age* (pp. 265–286). Hershey, PA: IGI Global. doi:10.4018/978-1-5225-0522-8.ch012

Cosner, S., Tozer, S., & Zavitkovsky, P. (2017). Enacting a Cycle of Inquiry Capstone Research Project in Doctoral-Level Leadership Preparation. In I. Management Association (Ed.), Educational Leadership and Administration: Concepts, Methodologies, Tools, and Applications (pp. 1460-1481). Hershey, PA: IGI Global. doi:10.4018/978-1-5225-1624-8.ch067

Crawford, C. M. (2018). Instructional Real World Community Engagement. In M. Khosrow-Pour, D.B.A. (Ed.), Encyclopedia of Information Science and Technology, Fourth Edition (pp. 1474-1486). Hershey, PA: IGI Global. doi:10.4018/978-1-5225-2255-3.ch127

Crosby-Cooper, T., & Pacis, D. (2017). Implementing Effective Student Support Teams. In P. Dickenson, P. Keough, & J. Courduff (Eds.), *Preparing Pre-Service Teachers for the Inclusive Classroom* (pp. 248–262). Hershey, PA: IGI Global. doi:10.4018/978-1-5225-1753-5.ch013

Curran, C. M., & Hawbaker, B. W. (2017). Cultivating Communities of Inclusive Practice: Professional Development for Educators – Research and Practice. In C. Curran & A. Petersen (Eds.), *Handbook of Research on Classroom Diversity and Inclusive Education Practice* (pp. 120–153). Hershey, PA: IGI Global. doi:10.4018/978-1-5225-2520-2.ch006

Dass, S., & Dabbagh, N. (2018). Faculty Adoption of 3D Avatar-Based Virtual World Learning Environments: An Exploratory Case Study. In I. Management Association (Ed.), Technology Adoption and Social Issues: Concepts, Methodologies, Tools, and Applications (pp. 1000-1033). Hershey, PA: IGI Global. doi:10.4018/978-1-5225-5201-7.ch045

Davison, A. M., & Scholl, K. G. (2017). Inclusive Recreation as Part of the IEP Process. In C. Curran & A. Petersen (Eds.), *Handbook of Research on Classroom Diversity and Inclusive Education Practice* (pp. 311–330). Hershey, PA: IGI Global. doi:10.4018/978-1-5225-2520-2.ch013

DeCoito, I. (2018). Addressing Digital Competencies, Curriculum Development, and Instructional Design in Science Teacher Education. In M. Khosrow-Pour, D.B.A. (Ed.), Encyclopedia of Information Science and Technology, Fourth Edition (pp. 1420-1431). Hershey, PA: IGI Global. doi:10.4018/978-1-5225-2255-3.ch122

DeCoito, I., & Richardson, T. (2017). Beyond Angry Birds™: Using Web-Based Tools to Engage Learners and Promote Inquiry in STEM Learning. In I. Levin & D. Tsybulsky (Eds.), *Digital Tools and Solutions for Inquiry-Based STEM Learning* (pp. 166–196). Hershey, PA: IGI Global. doi:10.4018/978-1-5225-2525-7.ch007

Delmas, P. M. (2017). Research-Based Leadership for Next-Generation Leaders. In R. Styron Jr & J. Styron (Eds.), *Comprehensive Problem-Solving and Skill Development for Next-Generation Leaders* (pp. 1–39). Hershey, PA: IGI Global. doi:10.4018/978-1-5225-1968-3.ch001

Demiray, U., & Ekren, G. (2018). Administrative-Related Evaluation for Distance Education Institutions in Turkey. In K. Buyuk, S. Kocdar, & A. Bozkurt (Eds.), *Administrative Leadership in Open and Distance Learning Programs* (pp. 263–288). Hershey, PA: IGI Global. doi:10.4018/978-1-5225-2645-2.ch011

Dickenson, P. (2017). What do we Know and Where Can We Grow?: Teachers Preparation for the Inclusive Classroom. In P. Dickenson, P. Keough, & J. Courduff (Eds.), *Preparing Pre-Service Teachers for the Inclusive Classroom* (pp. 1–22). Hershey, PA: IGI Global. doi:10.4018/978-1-5225-1753-5.ch001

Dickerson, J., & Coleman, H. V. (2012). Technology, E-Leadership and Educational Administration in Schools: Integrating Standards with Context and Guiding Questions. In V. Wang (Ed.), *Encyclopedia of E-Leadership, Counseling and Training* (pp. 408–422). Hershey, PA: IGI Global. doi:10.4018/978-1-61350-068-2.ch030

Dickerson, J., Coleman, H. V., & Geer, G. (2012). Thinking like a School Technology Leader. In V. Wang (Ed.), *Technology and Its Impact on Educational Leadership: Innovation and Change* (pp. 53–63). Hershey, PA: IGI Global. doi:10.4018/978-1-4666-0062-1.ch005

Donne, V., & Hansen, M. (2017). Teachers' Use of Assistive Technologies in Education. In L. Tomei (Ed.), *Exploring the New Era of Technology-Infused Education* (pp. 86–101). Hershey, PA: IGI Global. doi:10.4018/978-1-5225-1709-2.ch006

Donne, V., & Hansen, M. A. (2018). Business and Technology Educators: Practices for Inclusion. In I. Management Association (Ed.), Business Education and Ethics: Concepts, Methodologies, Tools, and Applications (pp. 471-484). Hershey, PA: IGI Global. doi:10.4018/978-1-5225-3153-1.ch026

Dreon, O., Shettel, J., & Bower, K. M. (2017). Preparing Next Generation Elementary Teachers for the Tools of Tomorrow. In M. Grassetti & S. Brookby (Eds.), *Advancing Next-Generation Teacher Education through Digital Tools and Applications* (pp. 143–159). Hershey, PA: IGI Global. doi:10.4018/978-1-5225-0965-3.ch008

Drinka, D., Voge, K., & Yen, M. Y. (2005). From Principles to Practice: Analyzing a Student Learning Outcomes Assessment System. *Journal of Cases on Information Technology*, *7*(3), 37–56. doi:10.4018/jcit.2005070103

Durak, H. Y., & Güyer, T. (2018). Design and Development of an Instructional Program for Teaching Programming Processes to Gifted Students Using Scratch. In J. Cannaday (Ed.), *Curriculum Development for Gifted Education Programs* (pp. 61–99). Hershey, PA: IGI Global. doi:10.4018/978-1-5225-3041-1.ch004

Egorkina, E., Ivanov, M., & Valyavskiy, A. Y. (2018). Students' Research Competence Formation of the Quality of Open and Distance Learning. In V. Mkrttchian & L. Belyanina (Eds.), *Handbook of Research on Students' Research Competence in Modern Educational Contexts* (pp. 364–384). Hershey, PA: IGI Global. doi:10.4018/978-1-5225-3485-3.ch019

Ekren, G., Karataş, S., & Demiray, U. (2017). Understanding of Leadership in Distance Education Management. In I. Management Association (Ed.), Educational Leadership and Administration: Concepts, Methodologies, Tools, and Applications (pp. 34-50). Hershey, PA: IGI Global. doi:10.4018/978-1-5225-1624-8.ch003

Elmore, W. M., Young, J. K., Harris, S., & Mason, D. (2017). The Relationship between Individual Student Attributes and Online Course Completion. In K. Shelton & K. Pedersen (Eds.), *Handbook of Research on Building, Growing, and Sustaining Quality E-Learning Programs* (pp. 151–173). Hershey, PA: IGI Global. doi:10.4018/978-1-5225-0877-9.ch008

Ercegovac, I. R., Alfirević, N., & Koludrović, M. (2017). School Principals' Communication and Co-Operation Assessment: The Croatian Experience. In I. Management Association (Ed.), Educational Leadership and Administration: Concepts, Methodologies, Tools, and Applications (pp. 1568-1589). Hershey, PA: IGI Global. doi:10.4018/978-1-5225-1624-8.ch072

Everhart, D., & Seymour, D. M. (2017). Challenges and Opportunities in the Currency of Higher Education. In K. Rasmussen, P. Northrup, & R. Colson (Eds.), *Handbook of Research on Competency-Based Education in University Settings* (pp. 41–65). Hershey, PA: IGI Global. doi:10.4018/978-1-5225-0932-5.ch003

Farmer, L. S. (2017). Managing Portable Technologies for Special Education. In V. Wang (Ed.), *Encyclopedia of Strategic Leadership and Management* (pp. 977–987). Hershey, PA: IGI Global. doi:10.4018/978-1-5225-1049-9.ch068

Farmer, L. S. (2018). Optimizing OERs for Optimal ICT Literacy in Higher Education. In J. Keengwe (Ed.), *Handbook of Research on Mobile Technology, Constructivism, and Meaningful Learning* (pp. 366–390). Hershey, PA: IGI Global. doi:10.4018/978-1-5225-3949-0.ch020

Fındık, L. Y. (2017). Self-Assessment of Principals Based on Leadership in Complexity. In I. Management Association (Ed.), Educational Leadership and Administration: Concepts, Methodologies, Tools, and Applications (pp. 978-991). Hershey, PA: IGI Global. doi:10.4018/978-1-5225-1624-8.ch047

Flor, A. G., & Gonzalez-Flor, B. (2018). Dysfunctional Digital Demeanors: Tales From (and Policy Implications of) eLearning's Dark Side. In I. Management Association (Ed.), The Dark Web: Breakthroughs in Research and Practice (pp. 37-50). Hershey, PA: IGI Global. doi:10.4018/978-1-5225-3163-0.ch003

Floyd, K. K., & Shambaugh, N. (2017). Instructional Design for Simulations in Special Education Virtual Learning Spaces. In T. Kidd & L. Morris Jr., (Eds.), *Handbook of Research on Instructional Systems and Educational Technology* (pp. 202–215). Hershey, PA: IGI Global. doi:10.4018/978-1-5225-2399-4.ch018

Giovannini, J. M. (2017). Technology Integration in Preservice Teacher Education Programs: Research-based Recommendations. In M. Grassetti & S. Brookby (Eds.), *Advancing Next-Generation Teacher Education through Digital Tools and Applications* (pp. 82–102). Hershey, PA: IGI Global. doi:10.4018/978-1-5225-0965-3.ch005

Good, S., & Clarke, V. B. (2017). An Integral Analysis of One Urban School System's Efforts to Support Student-Centered Teaching. In J. Keengwe & G. Onchwari (Eds.), *Handbook of Research on Learner-Centered Pedagogy in Teacher Education and Professional Development* (pp. 45–68). Hershey, PA: IGI Global. doi:10.4018/978-1-5225-0892-2.ch003

Grobler, B. (2015). The Relationship between Emotional Competence and Instructional Leadership and Their Association with Learner Achievement. In K. Beycioglu & P. Pashiardis (Eds.), *Multidimensional Perspectives on Principal Leadership Effectiveness* (pp. 373–407). Hershey, PA: IGI Global. doi:10.4018/978-1-4666-6591-0.ch017

Hamidi, F., Owuor, P. M., Hynie, M., Baljko, M., & McGrath, S. (2017). Potentials of Digital Assistive Technology and Special Education in Kenya. In C. Ayo & V. Mbarika (Eds.), *Sustainable ICT Adoption and Integration for Socio-Economic Development* (pp. 125–151). Hershey, PA: IGI Global. doi:10.4018/978-1-5225-2565-3.ch006

Heavin, C., & Neville, K. (2015). Addressing the Learning Needs of Future IS Security Professionals through Social Media Technology. In M. Khosrow-Pour (Ed.), *Encyclopedia of Information Science and Technology* (3rd ed.; pp. 4766–4775). Hershey, PA: IGI Global. doi:10.4018/978-1-4666-5888-2.ch468

Henderson, L. K. (2017). Meltdown at Fukushima: Global Catastrophic Events, Visual Literacy, and Art Education. In R. Shin (Ed.), *Convergence of Contemporary Art, Visual Culture, and Global Civic Engagement* (pp. 80–99). Hershey, PA: IGI Global. doi:10.4018/978-1-5225-1665-1.ch005

Hismanoglu, M. (2012). Important Issues in Online Education: E-Pedagogy and Marketing. In I. Management Association (Ed.), E-Marketing: Concepts, Methodologies, Tools, and Applications (pp. 676-701). Hershey, PA: IGI Global. doi:10.4018/978-1-4666-1598-4.ch041

Howard, B. C. (2008). Common Features and Design Principles Found in Exemplary Educational Technologies. *International Journal of Information and Communication Technology Education*, *4*(4), 31–52. doi:10.4018/jicte.2008100104

Howard, B. C., & Tomei, L. A. (2008). The Classroom of the Future and Emerging Educational Technologies: Introduction to the Special Issue. *International Journal of Information and Communication Technology Education*, *4*(4), 1–8. doi:10.4018/jicte.2008100101

Hudgins, T., & Holland, J. L. (2018). Digital Badges: Tracking Knowledge Acquisition Within an Innovation Framework. In I. Management Association (Ed.), Wearable Technologies: Concepts, Methodologies, Tools, and Applications (pp. 1118-1132). Hershey, PA: IGI Global. doi:10.4018/978-1-5225-5484-4.ch051

Ion, G., Tomàs, M., Castro, D., & Salat, E. (2015). Analysis of the Tasks of School Principals in Secondary Education in Catalonia: Case Study. In K. Beycioglu & P. Pashiardis (Eds.), *Multidimensional Perspectives on Principal Leadership Effectiveness* (pp. 39–58). Hershey, PA: IGI Global. doi:10.4018/978-1-4666-6591-0.ch003

Janus, M., & Siddiqua, A. (2018). Challenges for Children With Special Health Needs at the Time of Transition to School. In I. Management Association (Ed.), Autism Spectrum Disorders: Breakthroughs in Research and Practice (pp. 339-371). Hershey, PA: IGI Global. doi:10.4018/978-1-5225-3827-1.ch018

Jesus, R. A. (2018). Screencasts and Learning Styles. In M. Khosrow-Pour, D.B.A. (Ed.), Encyclopedia of Information Science and Technology, Fourth Edition (pp. 1548-1558). Hershey, PA: IGI Global. doi:10.4018/978-1-5225-2255-3.ch134

Kaplan-Rakowski, R., & Rakowski, D. (2011). Educational Technologies for the Neomillennial Generation. In E. Dunkels, G. Franberg, & C. Hallgren (Eds.), *Interactive Media Use and Youth: Learning, Knowledge Exchange and Behavior* (pp. 12–31). Hershey, PA: IGI Global. doi:10.4018/978-1-60960-206-2.ch002

Karpinski, A. C., D'Agostino, J. V., Williams, A. K., Highland, S. A., & Mellott, J. A. (2018). The Relationship Between Online Formative Assessment and State Test Scores Using Multilevel Modeling. In M. Khosrow-Pour, D.B.A. (Ed.), Encyclopedia of Information Science and Technology, Fourth Edition (pp. 5183-5192). Hershey, PA: IGI Global. doi:10.4018/978-1-5225-2255-3.ch450

Kats, Y. (2017). Educational Leadership and Integrated Support for Students with Autism Spectrum Disorders. In I. Management Association (Ed.), Educational Leadership and Administration: Concepts, Methodologies, Tools, and Applications (pp. 101-114). Hershey, PA: IGI Global. doi:10.4018/978-1-5225-1624-8.ch007

Kaya, G., & Altun, A. (2018). Educational Ontology Development. In M. Khosrow-Pour, D.B.A. (Ed.), Encyclopedia of Information Science and Technology, Fourth Edition (pp. 1441-1450). Hershey, PA: IGI Global. doi:10.4018/978-1-5225-2255-3.ch124

Keough, P. D., & Pacis, D. (2017). Best Practices Implementing Special Education Curriculum and Common Core State Standards using UDL. In P. Dickenson, P. Keough, & J. Courduff (Eds.), *Preparing Pre-Service Teachers for the Inclusive Classroom* (pp. 107–123). Hershey, PA: IGI Global. doi:10.4018/978-1-5225-1753-5.ch006

Kilburn, M., Henckell, M., & Starrett, D. (2018). Factors Contributing to the Effectiveness of Online Students and Instructors. In M. Khosrow-Pour, D.B.A. (Ed.), Encyclopedia of Information Science and Technology, Fourth Edition (pp. 1451-1462). Hershey, PA: IGI Global. doi:10.4018/978-1-5225-2255-3.ch125

Konecny, L. T. (2017). Hybrid, Online, and Flipped Classrooms in Health Science: Enhanced Learning Environments. In I. Management Association (Ed.), Flipped Instruction: Breakthroughs in Research and Practice (pp. 355-370). Hershey, PA: IGI Global. doi:10.4018/978-1-5225-1803-7.ch020

Kowch, E. G. (2013). Towards Leading Diverse, Smarter and More Adaptable Organizations that Learn. In J. Lewis, A. Green, & D. Surry (Eds.), *Technology as a Tool for Diversity Leadership: Implementation and Future Implications* (pp. 11–34). Hershey, PA: IGI Global. doi:10.4018/978-1-4666-2668-3.ch002

Krezmien, M., Powell, W., Bosch, C., Hall, T., & Nieswandt, M. (2017). The Use of Tablet Technology to Support Inquiry Science for Students Incarcerated in Juvenile Justice Settings. In I. Levin & D. Tsybulsky (Eds.), *Optimizing STEM Education With Advanced ICTs and Simulations* (pp. 267–295). Hershey, PA: IGI Global. doi:10.4018/978-1-5225-2528-8.ch011

Leach, L. F., Winn, P., Erwin, S., & Benedict, L. P. (2015). What 21st Century Students Want: Factors that Influence Student Selection of Educational Leadership Graduate Programs. *International Journal of Technology and Educational Marketing*, *5*(1), 15–28. doi:10.4018/ijtem.2015010102

Leng, H. K. (2014). An Update on the Use of Facebook as a Marketing Tool by Private Educational Institutions in Singapore. In I. Lee (Ed.), *Trends in E-Business, E-Services, and E-Commerce: Impact of Technology on Goods, Services, and Business Transactions* (pp. 191–205). Hershey, PA: IGI Global. doi:10.4018/978-1-4666-4510-3.ch011

Leone, S. (2018). An Open Learning Format for Lifelong Learners' Empowerment. In M. Khosrow-Pour, D.B.A. (Ed.), Encyclopedia of Information Science and Technology, Fourth Edition (pp. 1517-1528). Hershey, PA: IGI Global. doi:10.4018/978-1-5225-2255-3.ch131

Ley, K., & Gannon-Cook, R. (2010). Marketing a Blended University Program: An Action Research Case Study. In S. Mukerji & P. Tripathi (Eds.), *Cases on Technology Enhanced Learning through Collaborative Opportunities* (pp. 73–90). Hershey, PA: IGI Global. doi:10.4018/978-1-61520-751-0.ch005

Loose, W., & Marcos, T. (2016). Instructional Design for Millennials: Instructor Efficiency in Streamlining Content, Assignments, and Assessments. In P. Dickenson & J. Jaurez (Eds.), *Increasing Productivity and Efficiency in Online Teaching* (pp. 1–25). Hershey, PA: IGI Global. doi:10.4018/978-1-5225-0347-7.ch001

Lovell, K. L. (2017). Development and Evaluation of Neuroscience Computer-Based Modules for Medical Students: Instructional Design Principles and Effectiveness. In J. Stefaniak (Ed.), *Advancing Medical Education Through Strategic Instructional Design* (pp. 262–276). Hershey, PA: IGI Global. doi:10.4018/978-1-5225-2098-6.ch013

Manuel, N. N. (2016). Angolan Higher Education, Policy, and Leadership: Towards Transformative Leadership for Social Justice. In N. Ololube (Ed.), *Handbook of Research on Organizational Justice and Culture in Higher Education Institutions* (pp. 164–188). Hershey, PA: IGI Global. doi:10.4018/978-1-4666-9850-5.ch007

Marouchou, D. V. (2015). The Impact of Academic Beliefs on Student Learning. In M. Khosrow-Pour (Ed.), *Encyclopedia of Information Science and Technology* (3rd ed.; pp. 4796–4804). Hershey, PA: IGI Global. doi:10.4018/978-1-4666-5888-2.ch471

McCormack, V. F., Stauffer, M., Fishley, K., Hohenbrink, J., Mascazine, J. R., & Zigler, T. (2018). Designing a Dual Licensure Path for Middle Childhood and Special Education Teacher Candidates. In D. Polly, M. Putman, T. Petty, & A. Good (Eds.), *Innovative Practices in Teacher Preparation and Graduate-Level Teacher Education Programs* (pp. 21–36). Hershey, PA: IGI Global. doi:10.4018/978-1-5225-3068-8.ch002

McDaniel, R. (2017). Strategic Leadership in Instructional Design: Applying the Principles of Instructional Design through the Lens of Strategic Leadership to Distance Education. In V. Wang (Ed.), *Encyclopedia of Strategic Leadership and Management* (pp. 1570–1584). Hershey, PA: IGI Global. doi:10.4018/978-1-5225-1049-9.ch109

Memon, R. N., Ahmad, R., & Salim, S. S. (2018). Critical Issues in Requirements Engineering Education. In I. Management Association (Ed.), Computer Systems and Software Engineering: Concepts, Methodologies, Tools, and Applications (pp. 1953-1976). Hershey, PA: IGI Global. doi:10.4018/978-1-5225-3923-0.ch081

Mendenhall, R. (2017). Western Governors University: CBE Innovator and National Model. In K. Rasmussen, P. Northrup, & R. Colson (Eds.), *Handbook of Research on Competency-Based Education in University Settings* (pp. 379–400). Hershey, PA: IGI Global. doi:10.4018/978-1-5225-0932-5.ch019

Mense, E. G., Griggs, D. M., & Shanks, J. N. (2018). School Leaders in a Time of Accountability and Data Use: Preparing Our Future School Leaders in Leadership Preparation Programs. In E. Mense & M. Crain-Dorough (Eds.), *Data Leadership for K-12 Schools in a Time of Accountability* (pp. 235–259). Hershey, PA: IGI Global. doi:10.4018/978-1-5225-3188-3.ch012

Mense, E. G., Griggs, D. M., & Shanks, J. N. (2018). School Leaders in a Time of Accountability and Data Use: Preparing Our Future School Leaders in Leadership Preparation Programs. In E. Mense & M. Crain-Dorough (Eds.), *Data Leadership for K-12 Schools in a Time of Accountability* (pp. 235–259). Hershey, PA: IGI Global. doi:10.4018/978-1-5225-3188-3.ch012

Mestry, R., & Naicker, S. R. (2017). Exploring Distributive Leadership in South African Public Primary Schools in the Soweto Region. In I. Management Association (Ed.), Educational Leadership and Administration: Concepts, Methodologies, Tools, and Applications (pp. 1041-1064). Hershey, PA: IGI Global. doi:10.4018/978-1-5225-1624-8.ch050

Monaghan, C. H., & Boboc, M. (2017). (Re) Defining Leadership in Higher Education in the U.S. In V. Wang (Ed.), *Encyclopedia of Strategic Leadership and Management* (pp. 567–579). Hershey, PA: IGI Global. doi:10.4018/978-1-5225-1049-9.ch040

Muthee, J. M., & Murungi, C. G. (2018). Relationship Among Intelligence, Achievement Motivation, Type of School, and Academic Performance of Kenyan Urban Primary School Pupils. In M. Khosrow-Pour, D.B.A. (Ed.), Encyclopedia of Information Science and Technology, Fourth Edition (pp. 1540-1547). Hershey, PA: IGI Global. doi:10.4018/978-1-5225-2255-3.ch133

Naranjo, J. (2018). Meeting the Need for Inclusive Educators Online: Teacher Education in Inclusive Special Education and Dual-Certification. In D. Polly, M. Putman, T. Petty, & A. Good (Eds.), *Innovative Practices in Teacher Preparation and Graduate-Level Teacher Education Programs* (pp. 106–122). Hershey, PA: IGI Global. doi:10.4018/978-1-5225-3068-8.ch007

Nkabinde, Z. P. (2017). Multiculturalism in Special Education: Perspectives of Minority Children in Urban Schools. In J. Keengwe (Ed.), *Handbook of Research on Promoting Cross-Cultural Competence and Social Justice in Teacher Education* (pp. 382–397). Hershey, PA: IGI Global. doi:10.4018/978-1-5225-0897-7.ch020

Nkabinde, Z. P. (2018). Online Instruction: Is the Quality the Same as Face-to-Face Instruction? In J. Keengwe (Ed.), *Handbook of Research on Digital Content, Mobile Learning, and Technology Integration Models in Teacher Education* (pp. 300–314). Hershey, PA: IGI Global. doi:10.4018/978-1-5225-2953-8.ch016

O'Connor, J. R. Jr, & Jackson, K. N. (2017). The Use of iPad® Devices and "Apps" for ASD Students in Special Education and Speech Therapy. In Y. Kats (Ed.), *Supporting the Education of Children with Autism Spectrum Disorders* (pp. 267–283). Hershey, PA: IGI Global. doi:10.4018/978-1-5225-0816-8.ch014

Okolie, U. C., & Yasin, A. M. (2017). TVET in Developing Nations and Human Development. In U. Okolie & A. Yasin (Eds.), *Technical Education and Vocational Training in Developing Nations* (pp. 1–25). Hershey, PA: IGI Global. doi:10.4018/978-1-5225-1811-2.ch001

Paciga, K. A., & Hoffman, J. L. (2015). Realizing the Potential of e-Books in Early Education. In M. Khosrow-Pour (Ed.), *Encyclopedia of Information Science and Technology* (3rd ed.; pp. 4787–4795). Hershey, PA: IGI Global. doi:10.4018/978-1-4666-5888-2.ch470

Paulson, E. N. (2017). Adapting and Advocating for an Online EdD Program in Changing Times and "Sacred" Cultures. In I. Management Association (Ed.), Educational Leadership and Administration: Concepts, Methodologies, Tools, and Applications (pp. 1849-1876). Hershey, PA: IGI Global. doi:10.4018/978-1-5225-1624-8.ch085

Petersen, A. J., Elser, C. F., Al Nassir, M. N., Stakey, J., & Everson, K. (2017). The Year of Teaching Inclusively: Building an Elementary Classroom for All Students. In C. Curran & A. Petersen (Eds.), *Handbook of Research on Classroom Diversity and Inclusive Education Practice* (pp. 332–348). Hershey, PA: IGI Global. doi:10.4018/978-1-5225-2520-2.ch014

Pfannenstiel, K. H., & Sanders, J. (2017). Characteristics and Instructional Strategies for Students With Mathematical Difficulties: In the Inclusive Classroom. In C. Curran & A. Petersen (Eds.), *Handbook of Research on Classroom Diversity and Inclusive Education Practice* (pp. 250–281). Hershey, PA: IGI Global. doi:10.4018/978-1-5225-2520-2.ch011

Preast, J. L., Bowman, N., & Rose, C. A. (2017). Creating Inclusive Classroom Communities Through Social and Emotional Learning to Reduce Social Marginalization Among Students. In C. Curran & A. Petersen (Eds.), *Handbook of Research on Classroom Diversity and Inclusive Education Practice* (pp. 183–200). Hershey, PA: IGI Global. doi:10.4018/978-1-5225-2520-2.ch008

Randolph, K. M., & Brady, M. P. (2018). Evolution of Covert Coaching as an Evidence-Based Practice in Professional Development and Preparation of Teachers. In V. Bryan, A. Musgrove, & J. Powers (Eds.), *Handbook of Research on Human Development in the Digital Age* (pp. 281–299). Hershey, PA: IGI Global. doi:10.4018/978-1-5225-2838-8.ch013

Rawlins, P., & Kehrwald, B. (2010). Education Technology in Teacher Education: Overcoming Challenges, Realizing Opportunities. In R. Luppicini & A. Haghi (Eds.), *Cases on Digital Technologies in Higher Education: Issues and Challenges* (pp. 50–63). Hershey, PA: IGI Global. doi:10.4018/978-1-61520-869-2.ch004

Rell, A. B., Puig, R. A., Roll, F., Valles, V., Espinoza, M., & Duque, A. L. (2017). Addressing Cultural Diversity and Global Competence: The Dual Language Framework. In L. Leavitt, S. Wisdom, & K. Leavitt (Eds.), *Cultural Awareness and Competency Development in Higher Education* (pp. 111–131). Hershey, PA: IGI Global. doi:10.4018/978-1-5225-2145-7.ch007

Riel, J., Lawless, K. A., & Brown, S. W. (2017). Defining and Designing Responsive Online Professional Development (ROPD): A Framework to Support Curriculum Implementation. In T. Kidd & L. Morris Jr., (Eds.), *Handbook of Research on Instructional Systems and Educational Technology* (pp. 104–115). Hershey, PA: IGI Global. doi:10.4018/978-1-5225-2399-4.ch010

Roberts, C. (2017). Advancing Women Leaders in Academe: Creating a Culture of Inclusion. In S. Mukerji & P. Tripathi (Eds.), *Handbook of Research on Administration, Policy, and Leadership in Higher Education* (pp. 256–273). Hershey, PA: IGI Global. doi:10.4018/978-1-5225-0672-0.ch012

Rodgers, W. J., Kennedy, M. J., Alves, K. D., & Romig, J. E. (2017). A Multimedia Tool for Teacher Education and Professional Development. In C. Martin & D. Polly (Eds.), *Handbook of Research on Teacher Education and Professional Development* (pp. 285–296). Hershey, PA: IGI Global. doi:10.4018/978-1-5225-1067-3.ch015

Romanowski, M. H. (2017). Qatar's Educational Reform: Critical Issues Facing Principals. In I. Management Association (Ed.), Educational Leadership and Administration: Concepts, Methodologies, Tools, and Applications (pp. 1758-1773). Hershey, PA: IGI Global. doi:10.4018/978-1-5225-1624-8.ch080

Ruffin, T. R., Hawkins, D. P., & Lee, D. I. (2018). Increasing Student Engagement and Participation Through Course Methodology. In M. Khosrow-Pour, D.B.A. (Ed.), Encyclopedia of Information Science and Technology, Fourth Edition (pp. 1463-1473). Hershey, PA: IGI Global. doi:10.4018/978-1-5225-2255-3.ch126

Rutaisire, J. (2011). Innovations in Technology for Educational Marketing: Stakeholder Perceptions and Implications for Examinations System in Rwanda. In P. Tripathi & S. Mukerji (Eds.), *Cases on Innovations in Educational Marketing: Transnational and Technological Strategies* (pp. 214–233). Hershey, PA: IGI Global. doi:10.4018/978-1-60960-599-5.ch013

Sabina, L. L., Curry, K. A., Harris, E. L., Krumm, B. L., & Vencill, V. (2017). Assessing the Performance of a Cohort-Based Model Using Domestic and International Practices. In I. Management Association (Ed.), Educational Leadership and Administration: Concepts, Methodologies, Tools, and Applications(pp. 913-929). Hershey, PA: IGI Global. doi:10.4018/978-1-5225-1624-8.ch044

Santamaría, A. P., Webber, M., & Santamaría, L. J. (2017). Effective School Leadership for Māori Achievement: Building Capacity through Indigenous, National, and International Cross-Cultural Collaboration. In I. Management Association (Ed.), Educational Leadership and Administration: Concepts, Methodologies, Tools, and Applications (pp. 1547-1567). Hershey, PA: IGI Global. doi:10.4018/978-1-5225-1624-8.ch071

Santamaría, L. J. (2017). Culturally Responsive Educational Leadership in Cross-Cultural International Contexts. In I. Management Association (Ed.), Educational Leadership and Administration: Concepts, Methodologies, Tools, and Applications (pp. 1380-1400). Hershey, PA: IGI Global. doi:10.4018/978-1-5225-1624-8.ch064

Sarafidou, J., & Xafakos, E. (2015). Transformational Leadership and Principals' Innovativeness: Are They the "Keys" for the Research and Innovation Oriented School? In K. Beycioglu & P. Pashiardis (Eds.), *Multidimensional Perspectives on Principal Leadership Effectiveness* (pp. 324–348). Hershey, PA: IGI Global. doi:10.4018/978-1-4666-6591-0.ch015

Segredo, M. R., Cistone, P. J., & Reio, T. G. (2017). Relationships Between Emotional Intelligence, Leadership Style, and School Culture. *International Journal of Adult Vocational Education and Technology*, *8*(3), 25–43. doi:10.4018/IJAVET.2017070103

Shaik, N., & Ritter, S. (2012). Social Media Based Relationship Marketing. In I. Management Association (Ed.), E-Marketing: Concepts, Methodologies, Tools, and Applications (pp. 88-110). Hershey, PA: IGI Global. doi:10.4018/978-1-4666-1598-4.ch006

Shalev, N. (2017). Empathy and Leadership From the Organizational Perspective. In Z. Nedelko & M. Brzozowski (Eds.), *Exploring the Influence of Personal Values and Cultures in the Workplace* (pp. 348–363). Hershey, PA: IGI Global. doi:10.4018/978-1-5225-2480-9.ch018

Siamak, M., Fathi, S., & Isfandyari-Moghaddam, A. (2018). Assessment and Measurement of Education Programs of Information Literacy. In R. Bhardwaj (Ed.), *Digitizing the Modern Library and the Transition From Print to Electronic* (pp. 164–192). Hershey, PA: IGI Global. doi:10.4018/978-1-5225-2119-8.ch007

Siozos, P. D., & Palaigeorgiou, G. E. (2008). Educational Technologies and the Emergence of E-Learning 2.0. In D. Politis (Ed.), *E-Learning Methodologies and Computer Applications in Archaeology* (pp. 1–17). Hershey, PA: IGI Global. doi:10.4018/978-1-59904-759-1.ch001

Siu, K. W., & García, G. J. (2017). Disruptive Technologies and Education: Is There Any Disruption After All? In I. Management Association (Ed.), Educational Leadership and Administration: Concepts, Methodologies, Tools, and Applications (pp. 757-778). Hershey, PA: IGI Global. doi:10.4018/978-1-5225-1624-8.ch037

Skibba, K., Moore, D., & Herman, J. H. (2013). Pedagogical and Technological Considerations Designing Collaborative Learning Using Educational Technologies. In J. Keengwe (Ed.), *Research Perspectives and Best Practices in Educational Technology Integration* (pp. 1–27). Hershey, PA: IGI Global. doi:10.4018/978-1-4666-2988-2.ch001

Slagter van Tryon, P. J. (2017). The Nurse Educator's Role in Designing Instruction and Instructional Strategies for Academic and Clinical Settings. In J. Stefaniak (Ed.), *Advancing Medical Education Through Strategic Instructional Design* (pp. 133–149). Hershey, PA: IGI Global. doi:10.4018/978-1-5225-2098-6.ch006

Slattery, C. A. (2018). Literacy Intervention and the Differentiated Plan of Instruction. In *Developing Effective Literacy Intervention Strategies: Emerging Research and Opportunities* (pp. 41–62). Hershey, PA: IGI Global. doi:10.4018/978-1-5225-5007-5.ch003

Smith, A. R. (2017). Ensuring Quality: The Faculty Role in Online Higher Education. In K. Shelton & K. Pedersen (Eds.), *Handbook of Research on Building, Growing, and Sustaining Quality E-Learning Programs* (pp. 210–231). Hershey, PA: IGI Global. doi:10.4018/978-1-5225-0877-9.ch011

Souders, T. M. (2017). Understanding Your Learner: Conducting a Learner Analysis. In J. Stefaniak (Ed.), *Advancing Medical Education Through Strategic Instructional Design* (pp. 1–29). Hershey, PA: IGI Global. doi:10.4018/978-1-5225-2098-6.ch001

Spring, K. J., Graham, C. R., & Ikahihifo, T. B. (2018). Learner Engagement in Blended Learning. In M. Khosrow-Pour, D.B.A. (Ed.), Encyclopedia of Information Science and Technology, Fourth Edition (pp. 1487-1498). Hershey, PA: IGI Global. doi:10.4018/978-1-5225-2255-3.ch128

Stocklin, S. (2015). Building Capacity by Managing a Mission. In J. Feng, S. Stocklin, & W. Wang (Eds.), *Educational Strategies for the Next Generation Leaders in Hotel Management* (pp. 115–139). Hershey, PA: IGI Global. doi:10.4018/978-1-4666-8565-9.ch005

Storey, V. A., Anthony, A. K., & Wahid, P. (2017). Gender-Based Leadership Barriers: Advancement of Female Faculty to Leadership Positions in Higher Education. In V. Wang (Ed.), *Encyclopedia of Strategic Leadership and Management* (pp. 244–258). Hershey, PA: IGI Global. doi:10.4018/978-1-5225-1049-9.ch018

Stottlemyer, D. (2018). Develop a Teaching Model Plan for a Differentiated Learning Approach. In *Differentiated Instructional Design for Multicultural Environments: Emerging Research and Opportunities* (pp. 106–130). Hershey, PA: IGI Global. doi:10.4018/978-1-5225-5106-5.ch005

Stottlemyer, D. (2018). Developing a Multicultural Environment. In *Differentiated Instructional Design for Multicultural Environments: Emerging Research and Opportunities* (pp. 1–27). Hershey, PA: IGI Global. doi:10.4018/978-1-5225-5106-5.ch001

Swami, B. N., Gobona, T., & Tsimako, J. J. (2017). Academic Leadership: A Case Study of the University of Botswana. In N. Baporikar (Ed.), *Innovation and Shifting Perspectives in Management Education* (pp. 1–32). Hershey, PA: IGI Global. doi:10.4018/978-1-5225-1019-2.ch001

Swanson, K. W., & Collins, G. (2018). Designing Engaging Instruction for the Adult Learners. In M. Khosrow-Pour, D.B.A. (Ed.), Encyclopedia of Information Science and Technology, Fourth Edition (pp. 1432-1440). Hershey, PA: IGI Global. doi:10.4018/978-1-5225-2255-3.ch123

Swartz, B. A., Lynch, J. M., & Lynch, S. D. (2018). Embedding Elementary Teacher Education Coursework in Local Classrooms: Examples in Mathematics and Special Education. In D. Polly, M. Putman, T. Petty, & A. Good (Eds.), *Innovative Practices in Teacher Preparation and Graduate-Level Teacher Education Programs* (pp. 262–292). Hershey, PA: IGI Global. doi:10.4018/978-1-5225-3068-8.ch015

Taliadorou, N., & Pashiardis, P. (2015). Emotional Intelligence and Political Skill Really Matter in Educational Leadership. In K. Beycioglu & P. Pashiardis (Eds.), *Multidimensional Perspectives on Principal Leadership Effectiveness* (pp. 228–256). Hershey, PA: IGI Global. doi:10.4018/978-1-4666-6591-0.ch011

Taliadorou, N., & Pashiardis, P. (2017). Emotional Intelligence and Political Skill Really Matter in Educational Leadership. In I. Management Association (Ed.), Educational Leadership and Administration: Concepts, Methodologies, Tools, and Applications (pp. 1274-1303). Hershey, PA: IGI Global. doi:10.4018/978-1-5225-1624-8.ch060

Tam, F. W., & Kwan, P. Y. (2011). School Images, School Identity, and How Parents Select Schools for Their Children: The Case of Hong Kong. In P. Tripathi & S. Mukerji (Eds.), *Cases on Innovations in Educational Marketing: Transnational and Technological Strategies* (pp. 87–103). Hershey, PA: IGI Global. doi:10.4018/978-1-60960-599-5.ch005

Tandoh, K. A., & Ebe-Arthur, J. E. (2018). Effective Educational Leadership in the Digital Age: An Examination of Professional Qualities and Best Practices. In J. Keengwe (Ed.), *Handbook of Research on Digital Content, Mobile Learning, and Technology Integration Models in Teacher Education* (pp. 244–265). Hershey, PA: IGI Global. doi:10.4018/978-1-5225-2953-8.ch013

Tinoca, L., Pereira, A., & Oliveira, I. (2014). A Conceptual Framework for E-Assessment in Higher Education: Authenticity, Consistency, Transparency, and Practicability. In S. Mukerji & P. Tripathi (Eds.), *Handbook of Research on Transnational Higher Education* (pp. 652–673). Hershey, PA: IGI Global. doi:10.4018/978-1-4666-4458-8.ch033

Tobin, M. T. (2018). Multimodal Literacy. In M. Khosrow-Pour, D.B.A. (Ed.), Encyclopedia of Information Science and Technology, Fourth Edition (pp. 1508-1516). Hershey, PA: IGI Global. doi:10.4018/978-1-5225-2255-3.ch130

Torres, M. L., & Ramos, V. J. (2018). Music Therapy: A Pedagogical Alternative for ASD and ID Students in Regular Classrooms. In P. Epler (Ed.), *Instructional Strategies in General Education and Putting the Individuals With Disabilities Act (IDEA) Into Practice* (pp. 222–244). Hershey, PA: IGI Global. doi:10.4018/978-1-5225-3111-1.ch008

Toulassi, B. (2017). Educational Administration and Leadership in Francophone Africa: 5 Dynamics to Change Education. In S. Mukerji & P. Tripathi (Eds.), *Handbook of Research on Administration, Policy, and Leadership in Higher Education* (pp. 20–45). Hershey, PA: IGI Global. doi:10.4018/978-1-5225-0672-0.ch002

Umair, S., & Sharif, M. M. (2018). Predicting Students Grades Using Artificial Neural Networks and Support Vector Machine. In M. Khosrow-Pour, D.B.A. (Ed.), Encyclopedia of Information Science and Technology, Fourth Edition (pp. 5169-5182). Hershey, PA: IGI Global. doi:10.4018/978-1-5225-2255-3.ch449

Usman, L. M. (2011). Adult Education and Sustainable Learning Outcome of Rural Widows of Central Northern Nigeria. *International Journal of Adult Vocational Education and Technology*, *2*(2), 25–41. doi:10.4018/javet.2011040103

Vettraino, L., Castello, V., Guspini, M., & Guglielman, E. (2018). Self-Awareness and Motivation Contrasting ESL and NEET Using the SAVE System. In M. Khosrow-Pour, D.B.A. (Ed.), Encyclopedia of Information Science and Technology, Fourth Edition (pp. 1559-1568). Hershey, PA: IGI Global. doi:10.4018/978-1-5225-2255-3.ch135

Wang, V. C. (2013). Marketing Educational Programs through Technology and the Right Philosophies. In P. Tripathi & S. Mukerji (Eds.), *Marketing Strategies for Higher Education Institutions: Technological Considerations and Practices* (pp. 15–24). Hershey, PA: IGI Global. doi:10.4018/978-1-4666-4014-6.ch002

Wiemelt, J. (2017). Critical Bilingual Leadership for Emergent Bilingual Students. In I. Management Association (Ed.), Educational Leadership and Administration: Concepts, Methodologies, Tools, and Applications (pp. 1606-1631). Hershey, PA: IGI Global. doi:10.4018/978-1-5225-1624-8.ch074

Williams, D. D. (2006). Measurement and Assessment Supporting Evaluation in Online Settings. In D. Williams, M. Hricko, & S. Howell (Eds.), *Online Assessment, Measurement and Evaluation: Emerging Practices* (pp. 1–9). Hershey, PA: IGI Global. doi:10.4018/978-1-59140-747-8.ch001

Wolf, F., Seyfarth, F. C., & Pflaum, E. (2018). Scalable Capacity-Building for Geographically Dispersed Learners: Designing the MOOC "Sustainable Energy in Small Island Developing States (SIDS)". In U. Pandey & V. Indrakanti (Eds.), *Open and Distance Learning Initiatives for Sustainable Development* (pp. 58–83). Hershey, PA: IGI Global. doi:10.4018/978-1-5225-2621-6.ch003

Woodley, X. M., Mucundanyi, G., & Lockard, M. (2017). Designing Counter-Narratives: Constructing Culturally Responsive Curriculum Online. *International Journal of Online Pedagogy and Course Design*, *7*(1), 43–56. doi:10.4018/IJOPCD.2017010104

Woods, P. A., & Woods, G. J. (2011). Lighting the Fires of Entrepreneurialism?: Constructions of Meaning in an English Inner City Academy. *International Journal of Technology and Educational Marketing*, *1*(1), 1–24. doi:10.4018/ijtem.2011010101

Yell, M. L., & Christle, C. A. (2017). The Foundation of Inclusion in Federal Legislation and Litigation. In C. Curran & A. Petersen (Eds.), *Handbook of Research on Classroom Diversity and Inclusive Education Practice* (pp. 27–52). Hershey, PA: IGI Global. doi:10.4018/978-1-5225-2520-2.ch002

Zhao, J. (2011). China Special Education: The Perspective of Information Technologies. In P. Ordóñez de Pablos, J. Zhao, & R. Tennyson (Eds.), *Technology Enhanced Learning for People with Disabilities: Approaches and Applications* (pp. 34–43). Hershey, PA: IGI Global. doi:10.4018/978-1-61520-923-1.ch003

Zinger, D. (2016). Developing Instructional Leadership and Communication Skills through Online Professional Development: Focusing on Rural and Urban Principals. In A. Normore, L. Long, & M. Javidi (Eds.), *Handbook of Research on Effective Communication, Leadership, and Conflict Resolution* (pp. 354–370). Hershey, PA: IGI Global. doi:10.4018/978-1-4666-9970-0.ch019

Zutshi, A., Pogrebnaya, M., & Fermelis, J. (2014). Wellness Programs in Higher Education: An Australian Case. In N. Baporikar (Ed.), *Handbook of Research on Higher Education in the MENA Region: Policy and Practice* (pp. 391–419). Hershey, PA: IGI Global. doi:10.4018/978-1-4666-6198-1.ch017

About the Contributors

Heidi L. Schnackenberg, Ph.D., is a Professor and Department Chair in Teacher Education at SUNY Plattsburgh in Plattsburgh, NY. Specializing in educational technology, she currently teaches both undergraduate and graduate classes on the use of technology to enhance teaching and learning in the P-12 classroom. Her various research interests include the integration of technology into pedagogical practices, the complexities of women in leadership in higher education, and the challenges of being motherscholars in academia. She has also published numerous articles on educational technology, co-authored Challenges Facing Female Department Chairs in Contemporary Higher Education: Emerging Research and Opportunities, and co-edited Best Practices for Education Professionals, Best Practices for Education Professionals Volume 2, The Ethics of Cultural Competence in Higher Education, and Challenges and Opportunities for Women in Higher Education Leadership. Dr. Schnackenberg began her education career as an elementary music teacher.

* * *

Julia Bennett Grise is currently a mathematics instructor at the Beaver Area School District in Western Pennsylvania. She obtained her doctorate degree in Instructional Management and Leadership from Robert Morris University and is working towards her Supervision of Curriculum, Instruction, and Assessment certification. Julia has published multiple book chapters with IGI Global and her current research interests include technology integration and STEAM Education.

Claudia Bertolone-Smith has 25 years of classroom teaching experience and has instructed grades one through seven. In 2016, she completed her doctoral degree in curriculum, teaching, and learning with an emphasis in mathematics education at the University of Nevada Reno. She is currently an assistant professor at the State

University of New York at Plattsburgh. Her college students are pre-service teachers who are excited to join the education profession. Her research interests include mathematical discourse, fraction magnitude understanding, social positioning in mathematics, and the reflective practice of educators.

Brian Bourke is an Assistant Professor in the College of Education and Human Services at Murray State University, USA. Dr. Bourke teaches courses on student affairs practice and student characteristics and development for students preparing for professional roles in higher education administration. His primary research interests include: perspectives on student diversity and the characteristics and development of students in post-secondary education. His current research examines the role of social justice in student affairs practice in higher education institutions in the United States. Dr. Bourke has presented his research and led sessions on issues of professional practice at state, regional and national conference proceedings.

Anna CohenMiller is a qualitative research methodologist who focuses on issues of social justice and equity in education. She specializes in arts-based approaches to encourage participant voice, as a means for analysis, and also to present results to reach a broader audience. Dr. CohenMiller's research focuses on issues of gender in higher education and the workplace and on improving teaching and learning in preK – higher education contexts. Dr. CohenMiller is also Founder of The Motherscholar Project (www.motherscholar.org), Co-Founding Director of The Consortium of Gender Scholars (www.gen-con.org), and Editor-in-Chief of Dialogue: The Interdisciplinary Journal of Popular Culture and Pedagogy (www.journaldialogue.org).

Caoimhe Doran is a graduate student at SUNY Plattsburgh, studying in the B.S./M.S.Ed. program in Childhood Education and Special Education. With a background in theatre and acting, she developed a passion for teaching and working with students with disabilities through working with children in various preschools and public schools. An avid user of social media, Ms. Doran understands the opportunities and challenges it can present and feels passionately that students with disabilities have equitable access to such an integral part of present-day life. In the Spring of 2019, Ms. Doran will be student teaching and looks forward to a career as an educator in the New York City metro area.

Rachel E. Hugues is a graduate student in the Teacher Education Program at the State University of New York (SUNY) – Plattsburgh and is currently pursuing a degree in Special Education and Childhood Education (MSed/BS). Rachel's journey with research began after joining the Student Research Group at SUNY Plattsburgh. She previously presented research at the New York State Council for Exceptional Children Conference in 2017, after investigating co-teaching inclusion classrooms at the elementary level. This experience highly motivated her interests in organizing and implementing this method of teaching in her future classroom.

Rocci Luppicini is a Director of E-Business Technologies and an Associate Professor in the Department of Communication at the University of Ottawa, Canada. He is the Founder and Editor-in-Chief of the International Journal of Technoethics and a leading expert in technology studies (TS) and Technoethics. Main research areas include: Ethical Dilemmas with New Technology (media ethics, e-democracy, cybercrime, digital divide, hacking, information theft, cyber espionage, cyberbullying), E-Business and E-Society (virtual organizations, online communities, Social Networking, e-trust, social responsibility, e-health, e-government, socio-technical change), Identity and Technology (human-computer interaction, e-identity management, human enhancement, post-human, social robotics, cyberculture, technotherapy), Educational Technology (program planning and development, distance education, blended education, instructional design, technology integration, organizational studies (systems theory, organizational communications, organizational change, social movements).

Melissa S. Martin, Ph.D., is an Assistant Professor in the School of Education at the University of South Carolina Aiken. Currently, she teaches courses related to Special Education to preservice special educators. Previously, she was a self-contained special education teacher at an elementary school in South Carolina for several years. Her research interests include writing instruction and motivation for students with disabilities and collaboration and co-teaching in higher education.

Danielle McKain is a High School Mathematics Teacher at Beaver Area High School in western Pennsylvania. She has taught a variety of courses including Algebra I, Algebra II, Integrated Math, Probability and Statistics, Trigonometry, and Computer Assisted Algebra. Additionally, she has years of experience preparing students for the SAT. Dr. McKain earned her Ph.D. in Instructional Management and Leadership from Robert Morris University. She holds a Master of Science degree in Instructional Leadership with a concentration in Mathematics Education and a Bachelor of Science degree in Applied Mathematics. Her research interests include real-world math, test preparation, math anxiety, remedial math, and preparing future teachers.

Alison Puliatte, Ph.D, is an Assistant Professor of Teacher Education at the State University of New York at Plattsburgh. She earned a Ph.D. in Educational Psychology from the CUNY Graduate Center. She earned a C.A.S. in Educational Leadership, a M.S.Ed. in Special Education, and a B.A. in Psychology and Elementary Education from Queens College, CUNY. Previously, she was an elementary teacher and elementary school principal. Her research areas of interest include teacher knowledge, literacy instruction, and mental well-being of college students.

Victoria Reynolds is an Assistant Professor in Communication Sciences and Disorders at SUNY Plattsburgh. She teaches graduate courses in research design, voice and resonance and AAC. Dr Reynolds is also interested in the scholarship of learning and teaching and social issues in communication and swallowing disorders. She received a PhD in 2016 from the University of Western Australia, in Paedatrics and Child Health, on the topic of dysphonia in preterm children.

Ana Maria Spagna teaches creative writing in the MFA program at Antioch University, Los Angeles. She is the author of several award-winning nonfiction books including Reclaimers, stories of indigenous women reclaiming sacred land and water, 100 Skills You'll Need for the End of the World (as We Know It) a humor-infused exploration of how to live more lightly on the planet, the memoir/history Test Ride on the Sunnyland Bus: A Daughter's Civil Rights Journey, winner of the River Teeth literary nonfiction prize, and three essay collections, Potluck, Now Go Home, and most recently, Uplake: Restless Essays of Coming and Going. Her first novel for young people, The Luckiest Scar on Earth, appeared in 2017. Ana Maria's work has been recognized by the Society for Environmental Journalists, the Nautilus Book Awards, the Pacific Northwest Booksellers Awards, and as a three-time finalist for the Washington State Book Award.

Index

H

I

L

M

O

P

R

S

T

V

W

www.ingramcontent.com/pod-product-compliance
Lightning Source LLC
LaVergne TN
LVHW062121200926
848484LV00007B/1730